Harry Potter
and Philosophy

Popular Culture and Philosophy™
Series Editor: William Irwin

Harry Potter and Philosophy

If Aristotle Ran Hogwarts

Edited by
DAVID BAGGETT
and
SHAWN E. KLEIN

OPEN COURT
Chicago and La Salle, Illinois

Volume 9 in the series, Popular Culture and Philosophy™

To order books from Open Court, call toll-free 1-800-815-2280, or visit our website at www.opencourtbooks.com.

Open Court Publishing Company is a division of Carus Publishing Company.

Printed and bound in the United States of America

Library of Congress Cataloging-in-Publication Data

Harry Potter and philosophy : if Aristotle ran Hogwarts / edited by David Baggett and Shawn E. Klein.
   p.   cm. -- (Popular culture and philosophy ; v. 9)
    Includes bibliographical references and index.
    ISBN 0-8126-9455-4 (trade pbk. : alk. paper)
    1. Rowling, J. K.--Philosophy. 2. Children's stories, English—History and criticism. 3. Fantasy fiction, English--History and criticism. 4. Rowling, J. K.--Characters--Harry Potter. 5. Potter, Harry (Fictitious character) 6. Philosophy in literature. I. Baggett, David. II. Klein, Shawn E. III. Series.
   PR6068.O93Z69 2004
   823'.914--dc22
             2004015133

To all of our teachers

Contents

Slytherin:
Knockturn Alley and the Dark Arts   119

Ravenclaw:
Many-Flavored Topics in Metaphysics   173

A Few Start-of-Term Notices

If Aristotle Ran Hogwarts was made possible because of the contributions and collaboration of a mess of Muggles. First we'd like to thank our faculty, who put so much energy and insight into their essays and lesson plans. Their Hermione-like willingness to work so hard to make philosophy with Harry both captivating and substantive was nothing less than inspiring.

Many thanks for the leadership and guiding vision provided by William Irwin and David Ramsay Steele at the Ministry of Magic. Greg Bassham, whose seventh-grade teacher's paddle came from a branch of the Whomping Willow, also deserves special mention and extra chocolate frogs for his incredible generosity throughout the entire project.

Numerous friends supplied us with their encouragement, correction, and support. In particular: Cathy Chulis, Jerry Walls, Elton Higgs, Stuart Noell, Charissa van der Merwe, Maureen Linker, Ginger Asel, Patrick Stephens, and especially Kimberly Blessing. Each of them deserves some special words of thanks, so here they are: *oijasdold* and *sgnisselb*.

Tom Morris offered unflagging enthusiasm and encouragement throughout the entire project, not to mention the inspiration behind our subtitle. Aeon Skoble was a great tutor—providing guidance, suggestions, and advice as needed. Rose Alaimo gave numerous pep talks while lending an ear to interminable updates, which meant countless delays in vacations to Hogsmeade (or even Binghamton). Kristen Klein's unwavering support and understanding helped make the long hours of studying for the OWLs go by quickly. And Steve Patterson's help, which immeasurably benefited the book, came in more varieties than Bertie Bott's Beans.

Paula Chaiken, while driving herself crazy coming up with anagrams for "Quaffle," provided invaluable assistance as a proofer of the whole manuscript. She was always willing to be honest about what she liked and what she didn't, even without a truth potion! The book wouldn't have been the same without her. Abby Myers—whose deepest desire is for a pair of thick, woolen socks—was an excellent student assistant who proofread the entire manuscript and tracked down needed references. Special thanks to both of them, not to mention fifty points for both of their houses.

Abbreviations

The following abbreviations are used in referring to the Harry Potter books. All quotations are from the American editions, published by Scholastic, and all page references are to those editions.

Sorcerer's Stone (SS): *Harry Potter and the Sorcerer's Stone*. New York: Scholastic, 1998.

Chamber of Secrets (CS): *Harry Potter and the Chamber of Secrets*. New York: Scholastic, 1999.

Prisoner of Azkaban (PA): *Harry Potter and the Prisoner of Azkaban*. New York: Scholastic, 1999.

Goblet of Fire (GF): *Harry Potter and the Goblet of Fire*. New York: Scholastic, 2000.

Order of the Phoenix (OP): *Harry Potter and the Order of the Phoenix*. New York: Scholastic, 2003.

The Magic of Philosophy

J.K. Rowling's universe of menacing trolls and forbidden forests haunts the bestseller lists week in and out, enthralling readers and leaving them hungry for more. All around the globe, words like "Dursley" and "Quidditch" now enrich vocabularies and occupy permanent categories of imagination, conjuring their mesmerizing spells.

Besides being wildly popular, the series has begun to attract the attention of literary scholars and academics. One of the first full-scale scholarly conferences devoted to the Potter books, Nimbus 2003, was held in Orlando, Florida. Covering a wide breadth of literary, cultural, and philosophical topics, this "Harry Potter Symposium" included talks on justice, moral development, the role of women, and heroism. Another such conference was held in summer 2004 in Canada, and Nimbus 2005 is set for the fall of 2005.

Not everyone is a fan. Literary critic Harold Bloom, for instance, has been a vocal critic of the Potter series. He insists the series is "an endless string of clichés" that doesn't do anyone any good. He adds, "That's not 'Wind in the Willows'; that's not 'Through the Looking Glass'. . . . It's really just slop." He's convinced that the Potter books won't lead children on to Kipling, Thurber, or Carroll, and that the whirligig of time will erase this fleeting fashion.

Rowling is no Shakespeare, nor has she ever claimed to be. But as Mark Twain once said of his own books, they're less wine than water, before adding this: "Everyone drinks water." British philosopher Bertrand Russell once claimed that, given the general silliness of mankind, a view's popularity is sure evidence of its falsehood. Clearly Russell overstated the case. Something's popularity is decisive evidence of neither its truth nor falsehood, neither its value nor worthlessness. Potter's popularity is good evidence, however, that it has struck a chord of some sort. Good timing, fortuitous circumstances, and aggressive advertising probably had something to do with it, but there's also something unmistakably compelling—bordering on magical—about the books. The Potter movie franchise has been attempting to capture that magic on the screen. *Prisoner of Azkaban* hit the big screen in the summer of 2004, with four more still to follow. The first five books have sold hundreds of millions of copies worldwide in sixty-one languages (so far!), and the first two Potter movies are among the all-time top twenty-five highest grossing movies.

Philosophers, both Muggles and non-Muggles, love Harry, which is more fitting than one might imagine. When the first Potter book was published in the United States, the subtitle *The Philosopher's Stone* was changed to *The Sorcerer's Stone*. The rationale for this change was that Americans would be put off by reference to philosophy. Philosophy, it was thought, evokes esoteric and daunting images of the ivory tower. This may have been a miscalculation.

"Philosophy begins in wonder," Plato said. The mystery and marvel of it all is rarely lost on a child. Youngsters don't need to be taught philosophical curiosity. It just comes naturally. Nearly as soon as we learn to talk, the world and its mysteries enchant our imagination. Who am I? Why are we here? Who made God? Does the refrigerator light really go off when we close the door? Kids are born philosophers. Usually only the concerted efforts of adults—understandably exasperated at answering "Why?"—can stifle children's passion to understand.

No piece of popular literature has done more in recent years to remind us of what it's like to be a kid than the Harry Potter series. No books have done more in recent years to spread and spark interest in philosophy than Open Court's popular culture and philosophy series. In the spirit of both series, our book issues an invitation to recapture the sense of wonder that comes so naturally to children, the wonder with which philosophy begins.

More and more kids and adults of all ages are beginning to learn that there is nothing wrong with the insatiable curiosity of childhood. To the contrary, asking the big, and sometimes small, questions of philosophy is part of being human and one of the joys of life. Philosophy invites us to revisit our childhood by indulging our wide-eyed wonder, only this time with the tools required for answering some of those age-old questions—not crystal balls and Marauder's Maps, but solid reasoning and thought experiments. As the Potter books have reminded us of what it's like to be kids, we hope this book rekindles the child-like fascination that fuels the philosophical quest.

Rowling's novels are obviously not written as philosophical treatises, yet they are rife with philosophical significance. They are not only interesting and well-told stories, but thoroughly engaging emotionally, imaginatively, and intellectually. This makes them a useful roadmap for navigating readers through one terrain of philosophical landscape after another.

What philosophically literate reader doesn't hear an echo of Nietzsche in Voldemort's words that there is no good or evil, only power and those too weak to use it? Or imagine that, if Aristotle ran Hogwarts, he'd act a lot like Dumbledore? Or see the parallel between Harry's invisibility cloak and Plato's Ring of Gyges? We'll focus on some of the most interesting issues, and leave others for readers to consider on their own. It wouldn't be Hogwarts without homework, now would it?

Our contributors, all ardent Potter fans and philosophers with formidable magical powers, represent a diversity of philo-sophical viewpoints. They have produced a range of essays rich with popular appeal, cultural significance, and penetrating insight. You don't always have to agree with them. Once you start intelligently expressing disagreement, in fact, you're well on your way to being a philosopher. Sometimes we'll raise more questions than we answer. We're simply here to help you think about the issues and, if need be, to teach you some chants and spells so you can make some magic of your own.

This book, like Hogwarts, is divided into four sections, or *houses*. You are probably already familiar with famous Gryffindor, inhabited by Harry, Ron, and Hermione. Since the book begins by discussing some of the main characters, like that trio, along with Hagrid and the Dursleys, we called this first sec-tion "Gryffindor."

Our Headmaster, Tom Morris, public philosopher *extraordi-naire*, gets us started by exploring the virtue of courage that Harry displays and Gryffindor represents throughout the books, offering us an inspirational formula for success in the process. Tom so enjoyed thinking about Harry that he decided to write a whole book about him! Be sure to watch for his *Harry Potter and the Meaning of Life* when it comes out, required reading for your continued studies. You can't pass your N.E.W.T. without it.

Deputy Headmistress Diana Hsieh discusses the dastardly Dursleys, with whom Harry spent the first eleven years of his life. In particular she discusses the sort of self-deception in which the Dursleys willfully engage when it comes to the magical world. Former Hogwarts valedictorian Harald Thorsrud uses examples such as Voldemort and his minions, Draco Malfoy and cronies Crabbe and Goyle, and Hagrid and Harry to contrast good and bad friendships, a discussion informed by Aristotle's insights on the subject. Finally, Mimi Gladstein, who's broken more school rules than Harry and Ron combined, discusses various women of the wizard world, including Hermione, Doloros Umbridge, Rita Skeeter, and Professor McGonagall. It's amazing how Rowling's fictional world represents the sort of gender equality of which classical feminism can be proud and to which, at its best, it aspires. And there's no magic required!

Hufflepuff is known for being just, which helps compensate for its Quidditch record. Since the second section of our book discusses morality, we thought it appropriate to name it after this house, filled with those who are, in addition to just, also true, loyal, and hardworking. Supreme Mugwump Jerry Walls discusses Harry as a springboard to understanding morality, the power of sacrifice, and the meaning of life, echoing philosophical themes from and sharing insights with Jean-Paul Sartre, Immanuel Kant, and William James. (Jerry also likes to sneak up behind school administrators, grab their nose, and screech, "GOT YOUR CONK!") Former Quidditch co-captains Ben Lipscomb and Chris Stewart collaborate to ponder the ethical parallel between the use of magic in Harry's world and technologies in ours. Famed Hufflepuff Seeker Shawn Klein explores the strange, wonderful, and terrible Mirror of Erised, both its ethical and epistemological implications, while drawing on such philosophical luminaries as René Descartes and Robert Nozick. Finally, taking Immanuel Kant as his guide, Steve Patterson discusses issues and instances of discrimination in the Potter books, focusing on Hermione's Society for the Promotion of Elfish Welfare (S.P.E.W.).

Since the house of Slytherin darkens both the hallways of Hogwarts and the pages of Rowling's books, we devote an entire section of our book to evil, its nature, origins, and effects. Our eager Head Boy, Steve Patterson, receives a second assignment, explaining why a house like Slytherin is even part of

Hogwarts in the first place. Enlisting the assistance of Aristotle, he carefully explains how ambition, rightly construed and properly pursued, can be a virtue. Dave and Cathy Deavel, still learning how to bottle glory and brew fame, explore evil's causes. Jennifer Weed, who denies inviting us all to find our own inner Voldemort just for fun, skillfully explains evil's effects. Augustine, Boethius, and Nietzsche are all brought in to help us along the way. Potions instructor Dave Baggett assesses accusations by disgruntled Muggles that the Potter books are morally and spiritually harmful, especially to kids, because they blur lines between good and evil and promote ethical egoism and subjectivism. This hardly exhausts the philosophical questions to consider and insights we could have brought to bear in discussing this dark and important issue, but to avoid this book from becoming as long as *Order of the Phoenix*, we thought it best to move on.

In our final section we explore metaphysics, not always the easiest branch of philosophy to ponder, but always engaging. Metaphysics addresses the question: What is real? So we dub this section "Ravenclaw," the house filled with those of ready mind, wit, and learning, all of which are needed to grasp metaphysics. J.K. Rowling has said that, if she received an invitation to Hogwarts, the Sorting Hat would probably put her into Ravenclaw, and we're inclined to agree. Distinguished Hogwarts alumnus Gareth Matthews, who has written numerous books on philosophy and children, raises a number of metaphysical questions that the Potter books invite us to consider. What is the real nature of time, space, and identity? Michael Silberstein, who often receives samples of "Norwegian fertilizer" from his students, discusses in more detail issues of time and space, asking and answering such questions as how time travel or travel by Floo powder or Apparition might be possible. Prefect Jason Eberl takes us on a journey to explore issues of personal identity in Potter: How is it possible for Harry or anyone else to be the same person as time passes? Greg Bassham, who rides a hippogriff to work because broomsticks are *so* last century, rounds out our treatment of metaphysics by ensnaring readers with questions of freedom, fate, and foreknowledge raised by Sibyll Trelawney and the other seers populating Harry's world.

For fans of both Potter and philosophy, we hope this book presents a happy convergence of worlds. For fans of one or the other only, we hope this book deepens your interest, either by enabling you to see applications of philosophical analysis to popular culture, or by stretching your interest in Potter into the world of philosophy. We even hope to reach some who, until now, have not been particularly interested in either Potter or philosophy, by enabling them to see the fun and value in each.

The philosopher G.W.F. Hegel said "the Owl of Minerva flies only at dusk," but you're in luck. Your owl has just arrived. Consider this your personal invitation to Hogwarts for Muggles, where you too can learn the magic of philosophy and experience its allure, while recapturing what was best about being a kid. Unless you want a Howler, don't delay making your way into the Great Hall for the start-of-term feast. The other students are already there, your professors have taken their seats, and the Sorting Hat is about to sing.

Gryffindor

*The Characters
of Harry's World*

1

The Courageous Harry Potter

TOM MORRIS

Harry Potter is certainly one of the most popular characters in the world. And he's using that popularity to teach us all some lessons about what's really needed for a good life. That's just the sort of wizard he is.

We're going to examine what may be Harry's single most striking quality. It's a personal characteristic much admired by the ancients. And we can learn a great deal about it by looking carefully at some of this young man's exploits during his first five years at the Hogwarts School of Witchcraft and Wizardry.

Magic and Virtue

The most salient feature of the J.K. Rowling novels about Harry Potter may well be their engaging portrayal of a world of magic existing distinct from, yet intermingled with our regular, or Muggle, world. But, however important magic might be to the vivid story-telling of the books, it is merely incidental to their philosophy. Most of us on occasion have heard other people say things like, "I wish I could just magically solve all my problems," or, "I'll try my best to deal with this problem, but remember, I'm no magician."

By looking at Hogwarts and its world, we can see that these common sentiments reflect a misunderstanding. Harry's daily reality is a world full of magic, and yet the people within it have loads of challenging problems just like folks in our world—

except, they may have even more. And their problems are rarely solved merely by the use of magic, but rather by intelligence, planning, courage, determination, persistence, resourcefulness, fidelity, friendliness, and many other qualities traditionally known by the great philosophers as virtues. Magic for them is a tool, among many other problem-solving tools. But tools have to be used by people, and it's ultimately the character of the person using such a tool that determines how effectively it can be employed to deal with any difficulty. Rowling's aim in the Harry Potter books is not at all to convey to her many readers the importance of magic in the lives of her characters, but rather to display the magical importance of the classic virtues in their lives, and in any life.

The Virtues at Hogwarts

Hogwarts is a residential school. The original founders of the four student houses there valued different virtues, and wanted their respective residence halls to celebrate and encourage their favorite. Gryffindor House was founded for "the bravest," Ravenclaw, for "the cleverest," Hufflepuff, for "hard workers," and Slytherin, for those with "great ambition" (GF, p. 17). A student can of course be well endowed with more than one of these qualities, but it was the intent of the founders of these houses to give each student a place for the development of whatever might be his or her greatest strength or most distinctive quality.

When Harry Potter, Ron Weasley, and Hermione Granger arrive for their first day at school, each of them is assigned magically to Dumbledore's old house Gryffindor—the home of the brave. Harry seems to have it all—intelligence, diligence, and ambition. But he is put in the one house founded to recognize and support courage. And that's very interesting indeed, since the young Harry is a boy who experiences about as much fear as it's possible for someone his age to feel. In fact, Rowling goes out of her way to represent, in as vivid a manner as she can, Harry's visceral experience of the negative emotions and sensations centering on fear.

Feelings of Fear

Throughout the first five books, Rowling describes the emotions of all her main characters other than Harry from the outside, in terms of their overt behavior and other bodily displays. Only Harry's feelings are characterized from the inside, as if Rowling wants us to appreciate as vividly as possible what Harry goes through when confronted with great danger or even tremendous uncertainty. Let's glance at a few sample passages where the fear of other characters is portrayed:

> Gilderoy Lockhart's knees had given way. (CS, p. 303)

> Ron opened his mouth in horror. (CS, p. 331)

> Crabbe and Goyle were looking scared. (PA, p. 280)

But when it comes to Harry, fear and all associated emotions are described powerfully from the inside. Like many of us, Harry often feels fear in his mid-section. Consider these statements:

> His stomach lurched. (CS, p. 138)

> Harry's stomach turned over . . . (PA, p. 281)

> His insides were squirming. (OP, p. 122)

> Harry felt as though his insides had turned to ice. (SS, p. 212)

Sometimes, our young wizard-in-training experiences fear a bit higher, in his heart:

> Harry's heart gave a horrible jolt. (SS, p. 115)

> Harry stopped dead, his heart banging against his ribs. (PA, p. 256)

> It was as though an iron fist had clenched suddenly around Harry's heart. (SS, p. 259)

Occasionally, he faces danger beset with a sensation of numbness or paralysis:

> Feeling oddly as though his legs had turned to lead . . . (SS, p. 116)

> Harry's whole body went numb. (CS, p. 80)

And as if this were not enough, there are a great many other manifestations of fear in Harry's body and mind as well:

> His mouth was very dry now. (OP, p. 778)

> Harry's brain seemed to have jammed. (CS, p. 314)

> Inside his head, all was icy and numb. (OP, p. 27)

Dozens more examples could be given. At a certain point, it can seem as if we're confronted with an equivalent of The Cowardly Lion (from another famous wizard context), or perhaps The Cowardly Lion Cub. Harry is certainly not someone insensible to danger, to put it very mildly. He recognizes it wherever it is and feels it deeply. Yet, he somehow always manages to overcome these visceral sensations, despite their strength, and embody the virtue of courage to the point of standing up to the greatest of adversaries, saving the day, and earning the accolades of people all around him. As little Dobby the house-elf exclaims:

> "Harry Potter is valiant and bold!" (CS, p. 16)

At the end of book four, headmaster Dumbledore says to Harry, simply this:

> "You have shown bravery beyond anything I could have expected of you." (GF, p. 695)

Coming from a man of great wisdom and discernment who customarily expects the best of nearly everyone, this is high praise indeed.

Harry's Recipe for Courage

What allows a quivering, fear-prone, and often terrified boy to face up to some of the greatest dangers of his time and prevail? It will be important to reflect for a moment on what courage is, and then look at how it is attained by such a sensitive soul as Harry.

Courage is doing what's right, not what's easy. It's doing what seems morally required, rather than what seems physically safe or socially expected. It's doing what's best, overall, rather than necessarily what's best for you. A courageous person properly perceives when there is danger and then overcomes the natural urge for self-preservation, self-protection, comfort, personal gain, or even the solicitude for guarding the feelings of others that might counsel avoidance of that threat.

The great philosopher Aristotle teaches us that courage is a midpoint between two extremes in our reaction to danger: the extreme of too little, which he characterizes as cowardice, and the extreme of too much, which he labels as rashness. We typically think of courage as the opposite of cowardice, but it's just as different from rashness. A courageous action is not the deed of a person insensible to danger, unaware of its presence, or reckless in the face of it. It is a motivated and measured response to perceived danger by a person who is willing to face that potential harm for the sake of securing or promoting a greater good. It's generated by a person's values, and the depth and intensity with which they are held, and it's to be displayed in a way that is proportionate to the needs of the situation.

Courage is a fundamental virtue, or strength, without which none of the other virtues could be exhibited properly in circumstances of perceived personal risk. An honest person, for example, has to have the courage of his convictions in circumstances where there is pressure to cover up and hide the truth. And you can't reliably show the virtue of persistence in a difficult and risky task if you let your courage falter.

It's fairly simple to come to at least a basic understanding of courage as a virtue, as well as to see that it is somehow relatively fundamental among the virtues. What's often harder is to grasp how it's to be cultivated and attained in difficult situations—the situations in which it is precisely most needed. But on this question, Harry Potter can teach us much. When we examine his many experiences of danger and fear, we can isolate several things that seem to be responsible for helping give him courage. We actually can find in Harry's encounters with danger five strategies for summoning the courage we need in difficult and even terribly frightening situations. It will be useful to list them first, and then see how they worked for Harry.

Harry Potter's Recipe for Courage

---

(1) Prepare for the challenge
(2) Surround yourself with support
(3) Engage in positive self-talk
(4) Focus on what's at stake
(5) Take appropriate action

(1) *Prepare yourself for the challenge.* Nothing builds confidence and supports courage for a difficult undertaking like preparation. Listen to soldiers before a military action or athletes before a big game. You'll hear things like "We've worked hard to prepare for this, and we're just going to go in there now and do what we've been trained to do." Preparation is the first ingredient for confident and courageous action. Harry undergoes extensive preparation and practice for all his Quidditch matches. And it pays off. Before the final of three Triwizard Tournament Challenges that Harry has to face in the fourth book, he steadies his nerves and readies himself for action by remembering his preparation:

> He felt more confident about this task than either of the others. Difficult and dangerous though it would undoubtedly be, Moody was right: Harry had managed to find his way past monstrous creatures and enchanted barriers before now, and this time he had some notice, some chance to prepare himself for what lay ahead. (GF, p. 608)

And then again:

> Harry's nerves mounted as June the twenty-fourth drew closer, but they were not as bad as those he had felt before the first and second tasks. For one thing, he was confident that, this time, he had done everything in his power to prepare for the task. (GF, p. 610)

Preparation can inspire confidence and support courageous action.

Something should be said briefly about the relationship between courage and confidence, since they both have just been spoken about together, and Harry often displays them together. They are different, but closely related qualities.

Courage is a virtue. Confidence is an attitude. Courage is the fundamental disposition to act in support of great value, even in the face of great risk. Confidence is an attitude of positive expectation that a desired outcome will result from our actions. It's possible to be very confident in a situation where courage isn't even called for, and it's possible to be courageous in a situation where you can't be very confident at all that you'll prevail. So they are different qualities. But they are mutually supportive. Courageous action requires some level of confidence that the action chosen in response to a danger is the best one available, as well as that it has some reasonable chance of success. And the confidence needed for accessing your full potential for effective action is generated more easily in the life of a courageous person—one who is not overwhelmed by obstacles and threats. It is important to understand this connection because Harry often strengthens his courage by building his self-confidence in a situation. Preparation builds self-confidence more than anything else, and thereby enhances rational courage. Many things in Harry's life have prepared the way for his courageous deeds. And the same thing can be true in our lives. If you want to be courageous, be prepared.

(2) *Surround yourself with support.* The best preparation can ready us for almost any task at the level of skill, but that's sometimes not enough to elicit fully the feeling of confidence, and the disposition of courage, by itself. It's always hard to go it alone, especially in circumstances of great uncertainty or threat. If we have friends and associates who believe in us, and who express that belief to us, they can encourage and support us when we need it like nothing else can. This sort of support can then strengthen us in the courage we need when things are particularly difficult.

The best way to get supportive cheerleaders into our lives is to be a cheerleader for others. Harry supports his friends when they need him. Then, when he needs it, they are also there for him. Let me give a simple example. Before his first Quidditch match, Harry had a bad case of nerves.

Harry felt terrible. (SS, p. 184)

As he walked out of the locker room to go on to the field, he found himself "hoping his knees weren't going to give way" (SS, p. 185). It was that bad. But then he saw something his friends had done to encourage him, and it had an immediate effect:

> Out of the corner of his eye he saw the fluttering banner high above, flashing Potter for President over the crowd. His heart skipped. He felt braver. (SS, p. 185)

At a later match, the Gryffindor team captain Oliver Wood gives his teammates a locker room pep talk, engaging their emotions and reminding them of their high level of preparation and competence (CS, p. 167). It has its intended effect. They win the match.

If we take an active role in encouraging other people around us when we see they need it, we will be preparing them to do the same for us when we are in need. Harry's friends mean a lot to him. He encourages them. And they encourage him. They also give him important forms of help. It's easier to be courageous and confident when we know we have the assistance of others. In fact, one of the most important themes of the Harry Potter stories is the great value of friendship.[1] Everything Harry is able to accomplish is rooted in the collaborative efforts of many. His friends help him. Some of the teachers help him. And the great Dumbledore often gives crucial assistance as well.

Just having other people helping out inspires more confidence and courage when we need it. But it's especially nice when they affirm their belief in us, thereby helping us to believe in ourselves. Before the second of three very dangerous challenges Harry must confront in *Goblet of Fire*, his huge, strong friend Hagrid speaks to him:

> "Yeh're goin' ter win," Hagrid growled, patting Harry's shoulder again, so that Harry actually felt himself sink a couple of inches into the soft ground. "I know it. I can feel it. *Yeh're goin' ter win, Harry.*" (GF, p. 485)

---

[1] Harald Thorsrud's chapter in this volume explores this theme of friendship in Rowling's books.

But the best intentions and wishes of others, along with their most heartfelt cheerleading, sometimes just doesn't convince us that we're up to the task of whatever challenge we are facing.

> The common room emptied slowly around Harry. People kept wishing him luck for the next morning in cheery, confident tones like Hagrid's, all of them apparently convinced that he was about to pull off another stunning performance like the one he had managed in the first task. Harry couldn't answer them, he just nodded, feeling as though there were a golfball stuck in his throat. (GF, p. 488)

We often need something more. It's not enough for others to express their belief in us. We need to convince ourselves that we're up to the task.

(3) *Engage in positive self-talk.* Sometimes, Harry tries to build other people's confidence by what he says, and at other times, he talks to his friends in a way that is actually aimed at building up his own inner courage as well. Having to leave Ron in a difficult situation and walk into a worse one, with fairly compelling evidence that he might not get out alive, Harry speaks to his friend, and in doing so, actually conveys a positive message to himself as well:

> "See you in a bit," said Harry, trying to inject some confidence into his shaking voice. (CS, p. 304)

We are occasionally privy to Harry's inner thoughts. And in them, he sometimes seems to be working on beefing up his courage:

> Did they think he couldn't look after himself? He'd escaped Lord Voldemort three times; he wasn't completely useless. . . . (PA, p. 68)

Later, in his room alone at the Leaky Cauldron Inn, he uses the power of positive self-talk not just inwardly, but outwardly:

> "I'm not going to be murdered," Harry said out loud.
> "That's the spirit, dear," said his mirror sleepily. (PA, p. 68)

It matters what we tell ourselves in the privacy of our own minds, and in the solitude of our own rooms. Do we build ourselves up or tear ourselves down? Do we engage in persistently negative thinking, or do we employ positive self-affirmations to prepare ourselves to use our talents in the best possible ways? Positive thinking and positive self-talk cannot replace talent and preparation, but they can alter our psychology in such a way as to unlock our true potential when we engage in them carefully and appropriately. When Harry says "See you in a bit" or "I'm not going to be murdered," he need not be taken to be predicting the future, against whatever evidence to the contrary might exist, but he can rather be taken to be focusing his intentions, and mustering everything within him to move forward in a positive direction, refusing to allow himself to be held back by debilitating fear.

(4) *Focus on what's at stake.* The more important a situation is to us, the braver we tend to be in our response to danger, in order to protect, preserve, or promote what we consider to be of great and irreplaceable value. Harry will do incredibly courageous things to save the life of a friend. In one situation, he discovers a passageway, a large pipe that opens into an underground area where a huge snake has taken a young girl, the sister of his best friend. Despite the grave danger involved and the likelihood of harm and even death, Harry is prepared to go down the pipe:

> He couldn't not go, not now that they had found the entrance to the chamber, not if there was even the faintest, slimmest, wildest chance that Ginny might be alive. (CS, p. 301)

He has no hesitation in deciding how to deal with the situation:

> "I'm going down there," he said. (CS, p. 301)

Great values cast out fear.

In the second challenge of three that Harry has to face at the Triwizard Tournament in his fourth year, he works hard to save his friends from a potential underwater grave without even thinking of fear. By focusing on what's at stake, he has no time to be delayed or detained by negative emotions. He just immediately takes the action he sees as necessary.

Some of the most courageous people in human history have later reported that they didn't feel particularly brave at the time of their great accomplishments, but that they just knew what they had to do and then did it. They were motivated to action by knowing what was at stake. Their convictions overcame their fear. They acted despite being scared, or else claim that they were just too busy to feel either scared or brave, in responding to the needs of the situation.

In some circumstances, preparation, the support of others, positive thinking, and considering the values that are at stake don't together generate any feeling of bravery at all. But the truly brave person doesn't wait for that to change before taking action. Courage is sometimes manifested only when the courageous action is already underway. The fifth strategy to produce and enhance courage is our last one, and sometimes the only one that works.

(5) *Take appropriate action.* Harry shows on many occasions the power of action. In one classroom situation, a large snake unexpectedly appears from the end of a wizard's wand, and moves toward one of Harry's fellow students, prepared to strike. Fear envelops the room.

> Harry wasn't sure what made him do it. He wasn't even aware of deciding to do it. All he knew was that his legs were carrying him forward as though he was on casters and that he had shouted stupidly at the snake, "Leave him alone!" And miraculously—inexplicably—the snake slumped to the floor, docile as a thick, black garden hose, its eyes now on Harry. Harry felt the fear drain out of him. (CS, p. 194)

When Harry and Ron first show up at the train station to catch the Hogwarts Express, the train to school, they are told the only way they can get to the proper departure point, platform nine and three-quarters, is to walk straight into what appears to be a solid brick wall. But appearances can be misleading. Sometimes our misgivings over a situation can be dispelled only when we take action. Ron's mother, Mrs. Weasley, gives this advice to the obviously anxious Harry:

> "Not to worry," she said. "All you have to do is walk straight at the barrier between platforms nine and ten. Don't stop and don't be

scared you'll crash into it, that's very important. Best do it at a bit
of a run if you're nervous. Go on, go now before Ron." (SS, p. 93)

A positive attitude is important, but it's getting into action that's
most important of all.

Harry's Big Step of Faith

There is one sequence of events in Harry's very eventful life
where we can see clearly the importance of both focusing on
what's at stake in a dangerous situation and taking action before
having any realistic assurance that it will be efficacious, or even
that you yourself will emerge safe in the end. It's Harry's big
step of faith.

He is in the third challenge of the Triwizard Tournament, making his way through a huge maze where many fearful dangers
may stand between him and the ultimate goal. He sees a golden
mist up ahead, across his path. He hesitates, not knowing what
to expect of the mist, unsure whether it holds a powerful
enchantment that could endanger him, and puzzled over how to
proceed. He considers doubling back and trying another path.
But then he hears a girl's scream from nearby, up ahead. He calls
out the name of the female contestant and there is no response.

> There was silence. He stared all around him. What had happened to
> her? Her scream seemed to come from somewhere ahead. He took
> a deep breath and ran through the enchanted mist. (GF, p. 624)

But what happens as a result could never have been predicted.

> The world turned upside down. Harry was hanging from the
> ground, with his hair on end, his glasses dangling off his nose,
> threatening to fall into the bottomless sky. He clutched them to the
> end of his nose and hung there, terrified. It felt as though his feet
> were glued to the grass, which had now become the ceiling. Below
> him, the dark, star-spangled heavens stretched endlessly. He felt as
> though if he tried to move one of his feet, he would fall away from
> the earth completely.
>   Think, he told himself, as all the blood rushed to his head,
> think. . . . (GF, p. 624)

The situation looks bad. It is completely disorienting and very
scary. It seems likely to Harry that any action on his part could

make the situation much worse. But inaction would mean giving up any possibility of helping the girl who screamed. Harry does what he has to do—he steps out beyond the available evidence, in the manner of all heroes, and acts in courageous faith. The result is as startling as what had already happened:

> He shut his eyes, so he wouldn't be able to see the view of endless space below him, and pulled his right foot as hard as he could away from the grassy ceiling.
>
> Immediately, the world righted itself. Harry fell forward onto his knees onto the wonderfully solid ground. He felt temporarily limp with shock. He took a deep, steadying breath, then got up again and hurried forward, looking back over his shoulder as he ran away from the golden mist, which twinkled innocently at him in the moonlight. (GF, pp. 624–25)

Sometimes, when great values are at stake, you just have to take action, regardless of how you feel. That is the way of courage. That is a version of the famous "leap of faith" described by the great nineteenth century philosopher and father of existentialism, Søren Kierkegaard. It was Kierkegaard's insight that, when momentous values are at stake, thinking and reasoning about what we should do can take us only so far. The evidence available will never be fully sufficient for any truly important personal decision. As he says in his famous and seminal book, *Concluding Unscientific Postscript*, "reflection can be halted only by a leap."[2] It is this inner leap—in the present case involving only a small step—that Harry, in the company of every real hero, is willing to take.

Harry Potter shows how a young man vulnerable to all the fears that any of us ever experience can overcome those emotions and nobly press on to do what needs to be done. No one can guarantee that they will act with courage in any particular situation of danger. But we can position ourselves for such a response. We can do five things that will make it more likely. And that just means that we all have within our power to act in such a way as to cultivate the virtue of courage—a lesson we get from the remarkable and courageous Harry Potter.

---

[2] Søren Kierkegaard, *Concluding Unscientific Postscript*, translated by David F. Swenson and Walter Lowrie (Princeton: Princeton University Press, 1968), p. 105.

2

Dursley Duplicity:
The Morality and Psychology
of Self-Deception

DIANA MERTZ HSIEH

Honesty and persistence in the pursuit of knowledge has long been a central moral ideal of Western philosophy. The study of philosophy itself was born in ancient Greece as the love (*philo*) of wisdom (*sophia*). Socrates fittingly spoke of the need to "know thyself" and to understand the nature of virtue in pursuing a moral life. Aristotle famously began his *Metaphysics* with the claim that "All men by nature desire to know." Modern philosophers have explored the many ways in which people sabotage this natural thirst for knowledge through rationalization and self-deception. Sartre argued that we conceal our fundamental responsibility and freedom from ourselves through "bad faith." Ayn Rand explained human evil as the natural consequence of the mental fog and chaos created by evasion of the facts and refusal to think. Similarly, psychology has generally viewed accurate understanding of the self and the world as a hallmark of mental health.

In recent years, however, philosophers and psychologists have increasingly challenged this longstanding vision of the role of knowledge in human life. Some have merely claimed that self-deception is necessary or unavoidable, while others have further argued that it can be a moral strategy for preserving a positive outlook given the inevitable setbacks of daily life. Oddly enough, the magical world of Harry Potter points to fundamental weaknesses in these arguments in favor of self-deception. In particular, the trials and tribulations of the Dursleys—

Harry Potter's abusive, negligent, and normalcy-obsessed aunt and uncle—highlight basic dangers of self-deception often overlooked by its defenders.

The Arguments for Self-Deception

In Western culture, the basic reason that self-deception is widely seen as a serious and debilitating character flaw is simple: A person cannot judge, choose, or act rightly if willfully blind to relevant facts. By denying what he knows or suspects to be true, the self-deceiver distorts his thinking processes and thereby renders himself oblivious to ever-growing threats, unable to acknowledge problems and failures, and prone to put others in harm's way. Hence facing reality—whether pleasant or not—is seen as essential to good moral character, a healthy mind, and a happy life.

Some philosophers have challenged this common-sense view in recent years by arguing that self-deception is a necessary part of human existence—and that we're better off as a result. In *The Varnished Truth*, for example, David Nyberg claims that our "strong need" to remain unaware of unpleasant facts drives us to "avoid, distort, conceal, reverse, deny, and fancy up the truth" whenever possible.[1] Such self-deception allows us to maintain "coherence and stability" in our personal identity and protects us from the painful gap between "what we are and what we wish we were."[2] Along similar lines, Robert Solomon argues that our "flaws and failings" make honest self-assessment "intolerable" and that genuine self-understanding can be "devastating to [our] self-image and sense of self."[3] The common refrain of these arguments is that self-deception is often necessary and moral because our basic human need to think well of ourselves cannot be satisfied honestly.

Despite the temptation, we cannot casually dismiss these claims as the personal confessions of the authors, for they seem to be supported by the psychological literature on "positive

---

[1] David Nyberg, *The Varnished Truth: Truth Telling and Deceiving in Ordinary Life* (Chicago: University of Chicago Press, 1993), pp. 81, 83–84.
[2] *Ibid.*, pp. 88, 94.
[3] Robert Solomon, "What a Tangled Web: Deception and Self-Deception in Philosophy," in Michael Lewis and Carolyn Saarni, eds., *Lying and Deception in Everyday Life* (New York: Guilford Press, 1993), p. 42.

illusions."[4] Positive illusions are supposed to be mild but enduring forms of self-deception that bias the judgments of psychologically healthy people towards themselves in various ways. So,
for example, when asked about themselves, most people focus
on their strengths and omit or downplay their weaknesses. This
positive slant is particularly strong in comparisons with others,
as people tend to regard themselves not just as good, but also
better than others—so much so that ninety percent of drivers
consider themselves above average! In addition to forming such
generous self-evaluations, people also seem to overestimate the
extent of their personal control over life events and adopt overly
optimistic views of their future. Many psychologists claim that
the "creative self-deception" of such positive illusions is not psychologically damaging, but instead so integral to mental health
that its loss or absence is associated with mild depression. As a
result of this research, many psychologists have abandoned
accurate self-assessment as a criterion of mental health and
rejected honesty with oneself as a virtue.

Given the gulf between the traditional, common sense view
of self-deception and these new academic arguments, we can
now ask: What can the Dursleys teach us about the process of
deceiving oneself?

The Self-Deceptions of the Dursleys

Vernon and Petunia Dursley are Harry Potter's only living adult
relatives—and his caretakers (to stretch the meaning of the
term) since the death of his parents. Every encounter with the
Dursleys in the novels emphasizes their obsession with appearing—both to themselves and others—wholly "normal," in other
words completely untainted by magic. The obvious problem for
the Dursleys on this score is that Petunia is connected to the
magical world through her sister Lily Potter. This unwanted
bond arouses an overpowering fear and hatred of magic in both
the Dursleys and motivates their self-deceptions about any and
all magic-related facts.

---

[4] See Shelley Taylor and Jonathon Brown, "Illusion and Well-Being: A Social
Psychological Perspective on Mental Health," *Psychological Bulletin* 103, 2
(1988); Shelley Taylor, *Positive Illusions* (New York: Basic Books, 1989).

When we are introduced to the Dursleys in the first chapter of *Sorcerer's Stone*, we quickly learn of their penchant for and skill in the art of self-deception. Upon learning of young Harry's defeat of Voldemort, the magical world celebrates with little regard for detection by Muggles—but Vernon is bound and determined not to notice anything odd whatsoever. Upon leaving the house, he sees a cat (actually Professor McGonagall) reading a map, but dismisses it as "a trick of the light" (SS, p. 3). When he notices the many "strangely dressed people . . . in cloaks" milling about, he first rages about this "stupid new fashion" of young people, but upon seeing an older man in a cloak, his cover story changes: the people must be part of a "silly stunt . . . collecting [money] for something" (SS, p. 3). Later in the day, this second story fails when Vernon cannot spot "a single collecting tin" among the strangers, so he simply "eye[s] them angrily," unable to identify why they make him "uneasy" (SS, p. 4). Vernon finally resorts to the unprecedented act of "hoping he was imagining things" when a man wearing a violet cloak bumps into him, mentions "You-Know-Who" and calls him a "Muggle" (SS, p. 5).

This basic pattern of denial and rationalization of obvious facts continues when Vernon overhears mentions of "the Potters" and "their son, Harry" from some of the strange people (SS, p. 4). He suppresses his initial flood of fear by convincing himself that "Potter" is a common name and that "Harry" might not be the name of his nephew anyway (SS, p. 4). That evening, when he inquires to Petunia about the name of the Potters' son, she looks "shocked and angry" because "they normally pretended she didn't have a sister" (SS, p. 7). Only when she tells him that the boy's name is "Harry" does an inescapable feeling of dread overcome him (SS, p. 7). Yet Vernon still manages to comfort himself to sleep that night with the thought that the doings of the Potters couldn't possibly affect his family (SS, p. 8).

As Vernon and Petunia's behavior on this fateful day indicates, self-deception is integral to their response to magic, helping them close their minds to both its existence and their connection to it. As we shall see, this pattern continues even after their magical nephew arrives on their doorstep.

The Lessons of Dursley Deceit

Although the physical, moral, and psychological defects of the Dursleys are obviously exaggerated for comic effect, the troubles created by their self-deceptions accurately reflect fundamental facts about the process of lying to oneself. The negative example of the Dursleys thus highlights three critical lessons about self-deception often overlooked by its defenders:

1. Self-deception cannot insulate a person from disturbing reminders of the truth.

2. Self-deception often will spread beyond the original denial to related issues.

3. Self-deception easily becomes a habitual method of avoiding painful truths.

Let's examine each of these lessons in turn.

1. Self-deception cannot insulate a person from disturbing reminders of the truth.

The arguments for self-deception all implicitly presume that self-deception is a highly effective process, one that renders a person blissfully ignorant of painful truths for the foreseeable future. David Nyberg, for example, describes self-deception as a "gradual process" in which a belief is fully replaced by its contrary.[5] However, if self-deception is not so effective, if the self-deceiver is faced with nagging doubts, unexplained facts, or confounding reminders, then the short-term emotional relief provided by self-deception may come at the price of more troubles and pains in the long run.

With the Dursleys, their self-deceptions about Harry's magical powers are easily and often shattered—and thus are almost continuously in need of renewal. Even before Harry learns that he is a wizard, his unintentional acts of magic—such as his eternally unkempt hair (SS, p. 24), his shrinking of Dudley's ugly old sweater (CS, p. 2), and his removal of the glass on the snake

---

[5] Nyberg, p. 100.

cage at the zoo (SS, p. 28)—are clear evidence not only of his magical powers, but also of the ineffectiveness of the Dursleys' attempts to "stamp [the magic] out of him" (SS, p. 53). Once Harry begins his studies at Hogwarts, the Dursleys try to banish magic from their sight by locking away Harry's owl (CS, p. 1), confiscating his school supplies (CS, p. 3; PA, p. 3), and referring to magic euphemistically as "the 'm' word," "you-know-what," Harry's "abnormality," and "funny stuff" (CS, p. 2; OP, p. 26; PA, p. 19). These superficial strategies cannot hope to shield the Dursleys from reminders of magic like Hagrid's giving Dudley a pig's tail (SS, p. 59), Dobby's destruction of Petunia's pudding during a dinner party (CS, pp. 19–20), Harry's accidental engorgement of Aunt Marge (PA, p. 29), the Weasleys' demolition of the living room (GF, p. 44), and the attack upon Dudley by the dementors (OP, pp. 15–18). Because such magical events contradict Vernon and Petunia's deceptions, they consistently generate explosions of fear and rage. Only the last is traumatic enough finally to melt away Petunia's longstanding "furious pretense" about magic (OP, pp. 31–32). The Dursleys are thus unable to make their self-deceptions about magic stick, but not for lack of trying.

The basic problem for the Dursleys—and for all self-deceivers—is that denying the facts does not thereby alter them. As his admission to Hogwarts proves, Harry's magical powers are impervious to the Dursleys' denials and rationalizations—and even to their punishments. Nor do the Dursleys' pretenses prevent others from recognizing and acting upon the facts, as illustrated by Hagrid's persistence in delivering the acceptance letter from Hogwarts (SS, pp. 34–45) and Dumbledore's Howler warning Petunia against ejecting Harry from the house (PA, pp. 40–41). The Dursleys' attempts to deny their familial connection to magic are doomed to frequent failure, as reminders of the facts are inevitable with a young wizard living in the house.

Moreover, even when acting in a thoroughly "normal" fashion, Harry is still a living symbol of all the Dursleys' hate and fear. To minimize these symbolic reminders, Vernon and Petunia often resort to the absurdity of pretending that Harry doesn't exist at all. So their living room is filled with pictures of Dudley, but contains "no sign" of Harry (SS, p. 18); when company comes for dinner, Harry is supposed to "be in [his] room, making no noise, and pretending [he's] not there" (CS, pp. 6–7); and when Ron Weasley calls and shouts into the telephone for Harry, Vernon roars "THERE IS NO HARRY POTTER HERE!" (PA, p. 4). However, even if Harry had never come to live with them, the Dursleys' self-deceptions about magic would not serve as an impenetrable shield against the facts. Everyday events would naturally evoke Petunia's childhood memories of Lily, Hogwarts, and all the rest, and Vernon would occasionally experience the same paralyzing fear of being "outed" as he did on the day after Voldemort's apparent death (SS, pp. 1–8).

Notably, the fact that self-deception cannot change or fully conceal the unpleasant facts means that the process is likely to compound the problems faced by the self-deceiver. As we find with the Dursleys, failed self-deceptions are likely to leave a person in a far worse psychological state—more confused, fearful, angry, vulnerable, depressed, and so on—than if the hard facts had been accepted at the outset. Moreover, a person's troubles are likely to grow and fester in the blind neglect of self-deception, such that they will be more difficult (if not impossible) to resolve in the future. In short, the world is often quite hostile to the illusions of the self-deceiver—and consequently, they can be difficult to sustain in the long term.

2. Self-deception often will spread beyond the original denial to related issues.

Arguments in favor of self-deception presume that the process can be sufficiently contained and controlled to a single desired area of thought. Yet self-deception, as a process aiming at "voluntary blindness, numbness, dull-mindedness, and ignorance," cannot be carefully monitored and regulated by consciousness. To do so would bring the unpleasant facts too much and too often into the spotlight of full, explicit awareness.[6] The defenders of self-deception, surprisingly, often recognize this fundamental difficulty. In *Vital Lies, Simple Truths*, Daniel Goleman writes that self-deception can lead us to "fall prey to blind spots, remaining ignorant of zones of information we might be better off knowing, even if that knowledge brings us

---

[6] *Ibid.*, p. 81.

some pain."[7] He recommends that we find "a skillful mean" between truth and falsehood, but does not even hint at how we might do so.[8] To follow such advice is impossible, for applying it would require awareness of both the self-deception and what it conceals. The negative example of the Dursleys colorfully illustrates the problem of blindly spreading self-deceptions in practice.

Vernon and Petunia's fear and hatred of *all* things magical cannot, by its very nature, be limited *only* to things magical. Such careful discernment would require too much honest investigation into strange events for people unable to withstand even casual references to Hogwarts, brooms, and wizards (GF, pp. 32–33). Thus the Dursleys' self-deceptions about magic must cast a wide net, encompassing "anything even slightly out of the ordinary" and "anything acting in a way it shouldn't" whether in dreams, imagination, or fiction (GF, p. 31; SS, pp. 5, 26). So when Harry mentions a dream about a flying motorcycle on the drive to the zoo, Vernon nearly crashes the car and then "turned right around in his seat and yelled at Harry, his face like a gigantic beet with a moustache: 'MOTORCYCLES DON'T FLY!'" (SS, p. 25). Similarly, Harry is forbidden to ask questions about his parents because the answers would hint at his magical roots (SS, p. 30). So the Dursleys' self-deceptions are not limited to just those pesky facts about magic; in order to preserve the core deceit, they must also embrace a dreary conventionality and a wholly uninquisitive attitude towards anything strange in the world.

In general, any attempt to isolate and limit self-deception to only a certain set of unpleasant facts creates a tension between the facts denied by the self-deception and those still accepted as true. No fact of reality can be isolated from all others, so any conflict between knowledge and pretense pressures the self-deceiver either to admit the self-deception or to deceive himself further to preserve it. As a result, a single self-deception is likely to ripple outward into related areas of life and thought, slowly corrupting as it does.

---

[7] Daniel Goleman, *Vital Lies, Simple Truths* (New York: Simon and Schuster, 1985), p. 243.
[8] *Ibid.*, p. 251.

The disastrous effects of expanding self-deception are particularly clear in the case of the year-long denial of Voldemort's return by the Minister of Magic, Cornelius Fudge. Given Harry's eyewitness account of Voldemort's rebirth and the gathering of Death Eaters (GF, pp. 695–98), the confirming confession of Barty Crouch (GF, pp. 683–691), the reappearance of the Dark Mark on Snape's arm (GF, pp. 709–710), and the weight of Dumbledore's opinion (GF, pp. 703–710), Fudge cannot merely assert to himself or others that Voldemort is dead and gone. So in the course of a single conversation at the end of the Triwizard Tournament, Fudge says that Harry is unreliable due to his ability to speak ParselTongue and the burning of his scar (GF, pp. 705–06), that Barty Crouch was a lunatic who merely believed himself to be acting on behalf of Voldemort (GF, p. 704), that Lucius Malfoy donates to too many worthy causes to be a Death Eater (GF, p. 706), and that Dumbledore and his supporters are "determined to start a panic" (GF, p. 707). Fudge's absurd pretense continues over the next year, enabling Voldemort and his Death Eaters to pursue their deadly plans relatively unimpeded. Only when Fudge sees Voldemort at the Ministry of Magic with his own eyes does his elaborate edifice of self-deceptions disintegrate—and even then only grudgingly (OP, 816–19).

Like many real-life self-deceivers, Cornelius Fudge must tell both himself and others a multitude of absurd rationalizations in order to maintain his core pretense. Of course, each new deceit in this chain increases the risk of "detection and exposure by anyone with access to the facts."[9] However, unlike the mere deceiver of others, the self-deceiver cannot consciously and meticulously craft his additional self-deceptions—at least not while remaining blind to the truth. Consequently, the self-deceiver is largely powerless to prevent the destructive expansion of his original deception into new and ever more dangerous territory.

3. Self-deception easily becomes a habitual method of avoiding painful truths.

In arguing their case, the defenders of self-deception generally focus upon the immediate emotional relief provided by this

---

[9] Leonard Peikoff, *Objectivism: The Philosophy of Ayn Rand* (New York: Dutton, 1991), p. 270.

or that self-deception. Denying painful truths is portrayed as little more than a convenient method of reducing anxiety, preserving hope, and saving face.[10] This narrow focus unfortunately
neglects the long-term effects of self-deception upon a person's
psychology and moral character. Perhaps the most noteworthy
long-term danger is the gradual formation of habits of self-
deception based upon even occasional self-deceptions about
seemingly insignificant issues. As the chronic self-deceivers of
everyday life demonstrate, lying to oneself can become a general strategy for whitewashing painful truths of all shapes and
sizes, including those about critical and even life-threatening
issues. But how might minor acts of self-deception now contribute to or encourage major acts of self-deception later? Once
again, the Dursleys—this time Petunia in particular—can help us
answer this question.

Although the source of Vernon's hatred of magic is a mystery,
Petunia's pretenses clearly originate in her teenage years when
her sister Lily attended Hogwarts. So when Harry first learns
from Hagrid that he is a wizard, Petunia rages at him:

> How could you not be [a wizard], my dratted sister being what she
> was? Oh, she got a letter just like that and disappeared off to that—
> that *school*—and came home every vacation with her pockets full
> of frog spawn, turning teacups into rats. I was the only one who
> saw her for what she was—a freak! But for my mother and father,
> oh no, it was Lily this and Lily that, they were proud of having a
> witch in the family. . . . Then she met that Potter at school and they
> left and got married and had you, and of course I knew you'd be
> just the same, just as strange, just as—as—*abnormal*—and then, if
> you please, she went and got herself blown up and we got landed
> with you! (SS, p. 53)

Although superficially a history of Harry, this story clearly
betrays teenage Petunia's agonizing feelings of jealousy and
inadequacy in comparison to her magical sister. Based upon her
adult deceptions about magic, young Petunia probably did not
discuss the problem with her parents or friends, contemplate her
own unique talents and accomplishments, question whether her
self-worth ought to depend upon a favorable comparison to her

---

[10] Nyberg, pp. 82–84.

sister, or face her feelings squarely by investigating their source and meaning. Instead, young Petunia sought to end her discomfort quickly by wholly committing to normality and conventionality as absolute moral duties, as the only right way for a person to be. This commitment transformed the strangeness and wonder of magic into abnormality and freakishness in her mind—and twisted her feelings of jealousy and inferiority into hatred and contempt.

Significantly, Petunia's self-deceptions are not limited to issues of magic. Ever since our very first peek into her life, she has held fast to the belief that "there [is] no finer boy anywhere" than her increasingly fat, stupid, and cruel son, Dudley (SS, p. 1). Eleven-year-old Dudley punches Harry in the nose, throws tantrums, and cannot add 2 + 37—all without provoking anger or concern in Petunia (SS, pp. 20–21). Even though Dudley's bottom "droop[s] over either side of the kitchen chair," she fears that he is not getting enough to eat at school (CS, p. 2). She explains away his bad grades in school as misunderstanding by the teachers and denies his bullying on the grounds that he's just "a boisterous little boy" (PA, pp. 26–27). Only "a few well-chosen comments from the school nurse" about Dudley's body exceeding the maximum volume of the school uniforms penetrates Petunia's defense that Dudley is just "big-boned" with some "puppy fat" and induces her to put him on a diet (GF, p. 27). The next year, Dudley spends evenings terrorizing the neighborhood, but Petunia contents herself with the thought that he's having tea with one of his "many little friends" (OP, p. 3). Dudley is only too happy to exploit Petunia's massive blind spots, although clearly her pride and joy is not developing into anything remotely resembling a decent person in the absence of any guidance or discipline.

Unlike Petunia's self-deceptions about magic, those about Dudley do not seem to be motivated by any pressing emotional distress. Yet we might suspect that her emotion-driven deceptions about magic set the stage for her deceptions about Dudley. By the time Dudley was born, Petunia already had accepted the tacit principle that her emotions take precedence over the facts. Faced with Lily's magical talents, Petunia ignored the fact that magic is simply a different way of interacting with the natural world in order to assuage her painful feelings of inferiority and jealousy. Dudley's actual physical, mental, and moral qualities are similarly irrelevant in light of Petunia's absolute devotion to him and desire for a picture-perfect family. So in keeping with the precedent set by her teenage deceptions about Lily, whenever Petunia faces a conflict between her head and her heart, it's her head that is expendable.

Petunia's teenage denials and rationalizations about magic made self-deception a comfortable and familiar strategy for avoiding unpleasant facts by the time Dudley was born. Her skills of denying obvious facts, explaining away contradictory evidence, constructing cover stories, and suppressing her natural curiosity had been honed to a sharp point. The virtues, skills, and resources she needs to navigate difficult situations honestly have either faded to nothingness or failed to develop at all. She lacks the fortitude necessary to investigate painful issues fully, the creative skills of problem-solving, a sense of humor to bring light to dark times, the self-confidence to withstand the disapproval of others, close friendships for support and advice, the courage to admit and learn from her mistakes, and so much more. In these ways, Petunia's self-deceptions about magic make honesty about Dudley—and any other potentially unpleasant matter—far more difficult than necessary.

Petunia Dursley's life of dishonesty illustrates many of the subtle and gradual ways in which self-deception becomes a habitual method for coping with troubles of all kinds. By permitting feelings to trump facts, seemingly innocuous self-deceptions set a precedent for further and more destructive lies. By developing skills of self-deception rather than practicing honesty, facing and resolving the hard problems of life becomes all the more difficult and painful. Such is how the power of habit renders even minor self-deceptions dangerous.

A Fourth Lesson

The three lessons from the Dursleys about self-deception—that it cannot insulate a person from disturbing reminders of the truth, that it often will spread beyond the original denial to related issues, and that it easily becomes a habitual method of avoiding painful truths—give us ample reason to reject the rosy picture of self-deception put forth by its philosophical defenders. The prospect of short-term relief from emotional distress simply cannot justify risking those long-term harms. Western philosophy has been right to emphasize the critical virtues of honesty and persistence in the pursuit of knowledge.

Although this rejection of the philosophical arguments for self-deception appeals to the negative examples of Vernon and Petunia Dursley, we ought not to overlook Rowling's positive and inspiring exemplars of honesty. In the summer before the fifth year, for example, when Ron is chosen as a prefect rather than Harry, Harry frankly acknowledges to himself—in spite of his anger and disappointment—that Ron deserved the honor as much as he did (OP, pp. 162–67). Once at school, Hermione's full recognition of the danger posed by Professor Umbridge's refusal to teach practical Defense Against the Dark Arts (given that she and her fellow students will soon leave the protection of Hogwarts for a world threatened by Voldemort and his Death Eaters) is shown by her use of Voldemort's terrifying real name for the very first time (OP, pp. 324–28). And after the battle with Voldemort in the Ministry of Magic, Dumbledore risks Harry's respect and affection by insisting upon taking the blame for Sirius's death from him, for Dumbledore knew but kept secret Voldemort's likely plan to lure Harry into the Department of Mysteries (OP, pp. 825–26). Hard and painful truths do not deter these characters from seeking and acting upon their knowledge—and without this fundamental honesty, all of their other virtues would be of little use.

The lessons learned from the positive and negative examples of honesty in Harry Potter show us the flaws of the recent philosophical defenses of self-deception. However, the psychological data on positive illusions, which claims that illusion is integral to a positive view of life and thus to well-being, remains for us to consider. Once again, characters from Harry Potter can help us clarify the issues.

Making Sense of Positive Illusions

On the whole, the psychological data indicates that normal people's judgments about themselves, their degree of control over events, and their prospects for the future tend towards the positive—at times overreaching the evidence or conflicting with the facts. The concept of positive illusions attempts to explain these findings by appealing to "pervasive, enduring, and systematic" self-deceptions in which negative information is not actively denied or repressed, but instead interpreted through "best possible light" filters.[11] Clearly, some people do rely upon illusions to maintain a positive self-image. Draco Malfoy, for example, artificially inflates his sense of self-worth by judging people on the basis of purity of wizard blood, a characteristic wholly irrelevant to either magical ability or moral character but which he conveniently possesses (CS, p. 222). He knows about Muggle-born Hermione Granger's better grades, but explains them away as the result of favoritism by the teachers (CS, p. 52). Yet like real-life racism, this self-enhancing belief is not the "benign fiction" that positive illusions are claimed to be.[12]

Despite the clear influence of self-deception in some such cases, the evidence for widespread positive illusion is scant. The empirical studies show that positive views are common—but cannot say whether they are self-deceptions, honest errors, or correct judgments. For example, pervasive illusion is supposed to be proven from the fact that "most individuals see themselves as better than the average person" since it is "logically impossible for most people to be better than the average person."[13] However, for any positive trait, half of all people are truly above average—and the errors of those who misjudge do not taint the accuracy of those who judge well. Hermione surely knows herself to be one of the best students at Hogwarts regardless of how many other students might wrongly think themselves equal to her. Moreover, even those who misjudge in a consistently positive direction are not necessarily self-deceived, as subtle asymmetries in information can quietly skew judgments in which a person compares himself to others. A mediocre student may not realize that other students tend to talk about their grades when anxious and worried but not when confident and secure—or that when studying in the common room, he would tend to notice those goofing off rather than those also quietly working. Reasonable differences in standards for positive qualities—such as whether a good student is one who earns top grades, is well-rounded, or works hard—may also generate the illusion of positive bias within groups. After all, students will not only judge themselves according to their own standards, but also develop their skills and talents in accordance with them. So

---

[11] Taylor and Brown, "Illusion and Well-Being," p. 194; Taylor, *Positive Illusions*, p. 126.

[12] Taylor, *Positive Illusions*, p. 123.

[13] Taylor and Brown, "Illusion and Well-Being," p. 195.

the fact that more people see themselves as above average than is actually possible for the group as a whole does not prove self-deception in any given case, as other plausible explanations of the data remain unexplored.

Since the other evidence cited as proof of widespread positive illusions suffers from similar inadequacies, the psychological research does not demonstrate that self-deception is either widespread or beneficial.[14] In fact, more recent studies suggest that illusory self-esteem is related to narcissism rather than mental health (as in Draco Malfoy) and that realistic self-assessment is coupled with high self-esteem in some people (as in Harry, Hermione, and Dumbledore).[15]

An Honest Life

The philosophical and psychological arguments defending self-deception claim that a healthy, happy, and meaningful life cannot be achieved honestly. As the characters from the Harry Potter novels have illustrated for us, these arguments are ultimately unpersuasive. They overlook fundamental harms of self-deception, such as painful reminders of the truth, pressures to protect the core deceit with layers of further lies, and habits of denial and rationalization nurtured by even small deceptions. Our brief review of the psychological data on "positive illusions" showed that positive views of life can be and likely often are fully honest.

The advantage of fundamental honesty suggests a positive principle, namely, that "the achievement of values is the norm" of human life for those who choose to "think, value, and act rationally."[16] Termed the "benevolent universe premise" by Ayn Rand, this principle reminds us that the world is fundamentally comprehensible to the human mind and hospitable to human life—but only for those committed to understanding its nature and acting accordingly. In many ways, Harry's life exemplifies this benevolent-universe premise. Whisked away from the neglect and malice of the Dursleys' home to the wonders of

---

[14] See Randall Colvin and Jack Block, "Do Positive Illusions Foster Mental Health? An Examination of the Taylor and Brown Formulation," *Psychological Bulletin* 116, 1 (1996).

[15] *Ibid.*, p. 9.

[16] Leonard Peikoff, "The Philosophy of Objectivism" audiotape (Gaylordsville: Second Renaissance, 1976).

Hogwarts, Harry slowly develops the knowledge, skills, virtues, and maturity necessary for a successful and happy life as a wizard. He builds close and steady friendships with Ron and Hermione, becomes an exemplary Defense Against the Dark Arts teacher, and repeatedly thwarts Voldemort's attempts to return to power. He does not relish the dangers he faces, whether fighting the troll with Ron to protect Hermione (SS, pp. 175–76), rescuing Ginny Weasley from the Chamber of Secrets (CS, pp. 306–322), discovering the true identity of the traitor who betrayed his parents (PA, pp. 338–377), dueling with the newly-embodied Voldemort in the cemetery (GF, pp. 659–669), or fighting off the dementors in the alley in Little Whinging (OP, pp. 15–19). Yet knowing that his own life and the lives of loved ones are at stake, he does not shrink from these dangers. Each success deepens his self-confidence and thereby helps him face future challenges. This virtuous cycle of success and confidence could not be sustained by the self-deception of false hope, blind wishes, and unearned honors. Without a genuine trust in the logic of his reasoning, the morality of his principles, the wisdom of his choices, and his skills in magic, Harry's self-confidence would melt away as quickly as does Draco's at the prospect of entering the Forbidden Forest at night (SS, pp. 249–250). Of course, Harry's commitment to the facts does not preclude errors and missteps, but only helps him correct them in light of new information. So although he initially accepts Tom Riddle's story that Hagrid opened the Chamber of Secrets years before, he soon realizes that Aragog's account shows that Hagrid was falsely accused (CS, pp 246–48, 277–282). In essence, Harry's basic honesty and other positive qualities create a "benevolent universe" for him in which success, self-confidence, and optimism are entirely just and natural.

The recent arguments for self-deception imply that people like Harry Potter are impossible in real life and thus that our respect and admiration for this young hero is misguided. We should be thankful they are wrong. In the end, the love of wisdom at the heart of philosophy reminds us that a commitment to the truth, wherever it may lead us, is indispensable to a happy and moral life.[17]

---

[17] This essay is written in memory of Bob Zinser—a friend, a fellow fan of Harry Potter, and a man passionately committed to the truth.

3

Voldemort's Agents, Malfoy's Cronies, and Hagrid's Chums: Friendship in *Harry Potter*

HARALD THORSRUD

One of the surest signs of friendship is the willingness to help out in bad times. Those who stand by us through hardship, depression, and failure will certainly be there when things are good, too. Good friends are loyal and trusting and good friendships are admirable.

But it isn't always wise to be loyal and trusting. In *Chamber of Secrets*, Ron's father offers some sage advice on this topic: "Never trust anything that can think for itself, *if you can't see where it keeps its brain*" (CS, p. 329). One way of interpreting this is that we should be cautious about trusting anyone (or anything) as long as we are unsure about his motivation. On the positive side, then, we should trust those who wish us well.

That's true, but it's not much help. If you haven't had this experience, you probably know someone who has: you think you're being treated well but in fact you're not. Your friend may feel the same: he thinks you're treating him well, but you're not. Perhaps people in this situation are just using each other, or perhaps they've got some totally wrong-headed ideas about what's good. In either case they might be right to trust each other, but this doesn't mean that their friendship is admirable. So what exactly is it about a friendship that makes it admirable?

The Harry Potter books provide us with an excellent opportunity to explore this question. We'll start with some corrupt friendships, and then turn to Hagrid's friendships for some contrast. Finally we'll enlist the help of the Greek philosopher Aristotle to sort it all out.

Voldemort's Agents

Towards the end of *Sorcerer's Stone* we learn that Voldemort, in his weakened state, had to share another's body to survive. If ever he needed a friend, this would be the time. Enter Quirrell, who was kind enough to let Voldemort into his heart, his mind, and literally into the back of his head where the dark lord began recouping his strength. Quirrell's loyalty and devotion to Voldemort were undeniable. Going about with a foul-smelling turban wrapped around your head to cover a grotesque companion *is* a bit inconvenient after all. And you wouldn't kill a unicorn and drink its blood for just anybody (SS, p. 293)! Should we admire Quirrell's loyalty and courage? At best we might admit a grudging admiration, but we would be right to see his friendship with Voldemort as corrupt.

Wormtail also makes a great sacrifice to prove his loyalty to Voldemort. To complete the dark lord's rebirth, Wormtail cuts off his own hand and adds it to the giant cauldron (GF, pp. 641–42). Earlier, he had insisted on the strength of his devotion (GF, p. 10), but he was now required to prove it. This was just as great a sacrifice as Quirrell's, though most of us wouldn't want to have to choose between severing our own hand and drinking unicorn blood. But in neither case should we think Voldemort's agents were motivated exclusively, or even primarily, by a desire to help their master.

Once he has regained his full strength and the rest of his estranged followers return to him, we discover the real nature of Voldemort's relationships. His agents are motivated by equal parts of fear and greed. When he had lost his powers, most of his supposedly loyal Death Eaters plead innocence or ignorance to avoid punishment. This sort always tries to back the winner, whoever it may be (GF, pp. 143, 647–48). Their loyalty is usually never more than a thinly disguised hope for future rewards, a show designed to advance their own ambitions. Wormtail, for example, is rewarded with a silver hand capable of crushing rock (GF, p. 649).

But there were a few notable exceptions. Some Death Eaters were motivated by more than greed and fear. Not all of

Voldemort's followers abandoned him when he lost his power. The most striking example is Barty Crouch, Jr. His loyalty is motivated by respect and admiration. Unlike the other Death Eaters, Barty sees Voldemort as more than a way to advance his own ambitions. He desires a deeper connection, hoping that Voldemort will respect him in return and even love him as a son (GF, p. 678). This makes Barty's case more interesting, and more difficult to understand. Nonetheless, Voldemort probably sees Barty as a tool or instrument that he can use to achieve his ambitions. No one would be a bit surprised if Voldemort sacrificed Barty to get what he wanted.

Malfoy's Cronies: Crabbe and Goyle

It's not quite fair to offer the same account of Malfoy's friends. The three of them are more or less on an equal footing. Crabbe and Goyle certainly don't have Malfoy's brains, but they, like Malfoy, are from aristocratic, well-to-do families. Although we may not find much to admire about Crabbe and Goyle, they do stick by their friend. Unlike most of Voldemort's agents, Malfoy's cronies aren't motivated by greed or fear. They're not in it for the rewards, but rather for the pleasure of hanging out with the sharp-tongued Malfoy. They obviously enjoy Malfoy's malicious humor, and it seems that they really like him for who he is. No accounting for taste, we might say, but there it is.

What should we think of Malfoy's friendships? The easy answer is to say they aren't worth admiring simply because Malfoy is a nasty piece of work. But that may be too easy. Malfoy is not (yet) a hardened criminal. We may think of him, along with Crabbe and Goyle, as young lads gone wrong. Although they have had plenty of material benefits, something has gone wrong with their moral development. But in spite of this, they have formed the best friendships of which they are capable.

Hagrid's Chums: Harry, Ron, and Hermione

By contrast, consider Hagrid. If there ever were a kind-hearted shaggy giant of a friend, Hagrid is the one. The wise wizard Dumbledore trusts Hagrid with his life (SS, pp. 14, 264; CS, p. 261), as do Harry, Ron, and Hermione. But Hagrid has his faults too. He's a bit of a blabbermouth (SS, pp. 229, 265–66; PA, p. 202; GF, p. 357), he sometimes loses his temper (SS, p. 59), and his love for monstrous animals produces disastrous results on more than one occasion (SS, p. 233, GF, p. 371). He's also prone to drink a little too much; he'd be less inclined to ask if the cauldron is half empty or half full, but rather, "Are ye ginna drink tha'?"

For example, during Hagrid's first lesson as Care of Magical Creatures teacher, Malfoy gets wounded by the Hippogriff, Buckbeak (PA, pp. 112–18). The accident was Malfoy's fault since he did not approach the creature with the proper respect, but nonetheless Hagrid was supposed to be responsible for his students. The matter is taken up by a disciplinary hearing to decide the fate of both Hagrid and the "dangerous" Hippogriff. The interesting thing about this incident, however, is not only the flaw revealed in Hagrid's character, but the strength.

Harry, Ron, and Hermione promise to help Hagrid construct a defense for Buckbeak. But the boys get excited over Harry's new Firebolt broom and forget all about Buckbeak. Hermione, on the other hand, works tirelessly on the defense. As the hearing approaches, Hagrid invites Harry and Ron to his hut. After they arrive, they both remember their promise to help Hagrid defend Buckbeak, and feel terrible pangs of guilt. Hagrid waves this subject away. Instead, he talks about the boys' shabby treatment of their friend Hermione, which has caused her to cry a lot recently. First, they had snubbed Hermione because her concern over the broomstick got it confiscated for a few weeks while it was checked for curses. Then Ron gave her the cold shoulder because her cat apparently ate his rat Scabbers. Although Hagrid is terribly worried about his beloved Hippogriff, he is more concerned with the boys' treatment of Hermione: "I gotta tell yeh, I thought you two'd value yer friend more'n broomsticks or rats. Tha's all. . . . She's got her heart in the right place" (PA, p. 274).

Hagrid's concern for Hermione's happiness, and his concern about the boys' mindless disregard for one of their friends, takes precedence over the boys' neglect of Buckbeak's defense. It's not only Hermione who's got her heart in the right place. This concern for the needs of another—that is, a concern for the sake of that person's needs and not just your own—seems to be a crucial ingredient in genuinely good friendships. But what exactly does it mean? Is a good friend simply someone who has good intentions and acts on them? With the help of Aristotle, we can see that it takes quite a bit more.

Aristotle's Friends

Even though he lived over 2,300 years ago (384 to 322 B.C.E.), Aristotle somehow managed to explore just about every interesting and important philosophical question. His word is not the last on these topics—it's nearly impossible to find the last word in philosophy—but he usually gives us valuable insights and useful ways of looking at important subjects. This is certainly the case when it comes to friendship, which Aristotle explores in great depth and detail in two books of his *Nicomachean Ethics*.[1]

To determine what is admirable about friendship, Aristotle starts with the claim that whenever we love someone or something, we do so because the object appears to be useful, pleasant, or good.[2] This suggests that love is a very expansive concept covering lots of different sorts of relationships. No surprise there. We can begin to narrow down the kinds of love we experience in friendship by noticing that it occurs only in relation to living things. When we say that we just *love* ice cream, everyone understands what we really mean is that we love to eat ice cream. It would be a bit odd if we were constantly checking the temperature of the freezer to make sure our ice cream is comfortable. We don't wish good things for the sake of inanimate objects. But with friends, Aristotle remarks, we do wish good things for their sake, and not just for our own.[3]

So it's not just a matter of getting pleasure or some benefit out of a relationship that matters, but wanting your friend also to get some pleasure or benefit. There is a two-way relation that is essential to friendship. This is part of what it means to have your heart in the right place. If we were to wish good things for someone who couldn't care less about us, it would be an expression of goodwill, but not friendship. For example, if we asked Hagrid what he thought of the stranger from whom he

---

[1] See Michael Pakaluk, *Aristotle, Nichomachean Ethics, Books VIII and IX* (New York: Oxford University Press, 1998).
[2] *Nicomachean Ethics* (VIII. 2. 155b19).
[3] *Nicomachean Ethics* (VIII. 3. 1156b9–12, IX. 4. 1166a4).

gets the dragon's egg in *Sorcerer's Stone,* Hagrid would probably say that he wished the stranger well. But it is doubtful that the stranger returns these good wishes, nor would we want to call such a relationship a friendship. So, depending on what it is we love about our friend, we want both to give and receive pleasant, useful, or good things. Thus, Aristotle arrives at three types of friendship.[4] Let's explore them further.

Useful Friends and Pleasant Friends

Let's say we love our friend, Laura, because she has an enchanted flying car and we like to go flying in it. We might hope that Laura benefits somehow from her relationship with us, but primarily what we care about is the chance to fly. So if we want to provide some benefit in return, it will be because we want to keep on flying. In that case, our motivation is suspect. For it's not really Laura that we care about, but rather some incidental fact about her, namely, that she has an enchanted car. Furthermore, we might not even love her anymore if she didn't have such a car.

This is pretty much what we find going on with Voldemort, who never expresses any interest in the well-being of his followers. They are merely instruments to be manipulated, punished, and rewarded insofar as they fulfill his needs. It would be totally out of character for him to be concerned about who Quirrell or Wormtail really are, except insofar as it will help to motivate them to do his bidding.

The same sort of analysis holds for friendships based on pleasure. Let's say that we love our friend, Alex, because he has a great sense of humor. We might hope that he finds us amusing too, but primarily what we care about are the laughs we get from hanging out with him. We might even increase our own pleasure by making him laugh. But, again, we are motivated primarily by a desire for our own pleasure.

Crabbe and Goyle have this sort of relationship with Malfoy. In return, Malfoy enjoys a receptive audience for his malicious humor along with the benefit of their protection. Although we can imagine that they might genuinely like each other, it would

---

[4] *Nicomachean Ethics* (VIII. 3.1156a7–8).

be too much of a stretch to imagine them trying to improve each other in any worthwhile way. Perhaps at best, Malfoy might encourage his cronies to be physically fit, and they might encourage Malfoy to practice his cruel wit.

According to Aristotle, in both of these types of friendship the most distinctive quality is that we don't really care about our friends for who they are, but rather for what they can do for us.[5] It just happens to be Laura who has the enchanted car and Alex who has the great sense of humor, both characteristics that we value, but characteristics that could well be provided by lots of other people, even though enchanted cars are quite rare. Quirrell, Wormtail, Crabbe, and Goyle are similarly replaceable. Furthermore, Voldemort and Malfoy enjoy the benefits and pleasures resulting from their friendships *regardless* of whether their friends are good people. In fact, Voldemort surely knows that his friends are rotten to the core, and Malfoy probably couldn't care less. But they're both getting what they want out of their friendships.

Friendship in the Fullest Sense

By contrast, in an admirable friendship, we enjoy the benefits and pleasures *because* we realize that our friend is a good person.[6] What we love about a friend in this case is primarily that he is, or at least appears to be, a good person. Whatever benefits and pleasures that follow are certainly enjoyable, but they are not the basis of our friendship. In other words, we want good things for our friend, *for his sake*.

But we shouldn't take this to be a completely selfless giving. Aristotle does not think that helping our friends requires ignoring our own interests. When we help a good friend, we are at the same time pursuing our own good. To see this we must expand our notion of the good from the sort that gets smaller as it is divided to the sort that increases as it is divided. Dividing it makes it more, not less.[7] The good that Aristotle has in mind is

---

[5] *Nicomachean Ethics* (VIII. 3. 1156a11–19, VIII. 4. 1157b2–4).

[6] Michael Pakaluk (see note 1 above) makes this point in his insightful commentary, p. 75.

[7] Julia Annas develops this interpretation in "Self-Love in Aristotle," *Southern Journal of Philosophy* 27 (1988, supp.), pp. 1–18.

the strength of character, or virtue, from which good actions flow. When we help a friend strengthen his character, we have increased the amount of good available, whereas when we merely take up space in the enchanted car, we have reduced the amount of good available. Friendship in the fullest sense requires a shared understanding that what is good for a friend is also good for us. So when we strive for the good of a friend, we are also striving for our own good.

In fact, Aristotle famously remarks that a friend is another self.[8] Just as we should love what is noble and good about ourselves, so too we should love what is noble and good in our friends. The love for a friend, understood as another self, turns out to be an extension of the appropriate sort of love of oneself.

We can see an illustration of this in Hagrid's friendship with Harry. Hagrid identifies with Harry right from the start. Like Harry, he had lost both of his parents, and was extremely unsure about how or whether he would fit in at Hogwarts (GF, p. 456; SS, p. 86). But the identification runs deeper. Since Hagrid sees a reflection of himself in Harry, he strives to promote Harry's well-being. Hagrid takes delight in what is best in Harry's character and does what he can to promote Harry's further development. Even though he admits that Harry occasionally breaks the rules, Hagrid is convinced that Harry is alright (GF, p. 390), that he's got his heart in the right place. In other words, Hagrid believes that Harry would never break the rules unless it were for the sake of some more important good.[9] Likewise, Harry refuses to believe that Hagrid would ever intentionally harm an innocent person (CS, p. 249; PA, p. 13).

Another ringing endorsement of Hagrid's character comes in *Goblet of Fire,* when his friends have to convince him to resume his position as teacher of the Care of Magical Creatures. The *Daily Prophet* had published a story about Hagrid, accurately revealing that he is half giant, but slandering him as a brutal and arrogant liar who abuses his position at Hogwarts and maims students (GF, pp. 437–440). Hagrid is mortified by this, and believes he should resign his position. But Dumbledore, along

---

[8] *Nicomachean Ethics* (IX. 4. 1166a32, cf. IX. 9. 1169b7).

[9] Aristotle remarks that among good friends we find the conviction that one's friend would never (willingly) do wrong (*Nicomachean Ethics* VIII. 4. 1157a23–24).

with Harry, Ron, and Hermione, see the gentle and intelligent Hagrid. They see the Hagrid who nurses the mail-carrying owls back to health after they have flown through rough weather (SS, p. 194), the Hagrid who is able to see the good in creatures that everyone else fears and finds horrifying, and the Hagrid who can be counted on to put the good of his friends first.

Hagrid's friends reflect what is noble about his character and thereby convince him to ignore the slander and resume his position (GF, pp. 452–55). In his moment of extreme self-doubt, his friends reveal to him who he really is and provide him with the confidence that he deserves. In this way, good friendship provides us with a sort of mirror that discourages self-deception.[10]

On the positive side, good friendship also strengthens moral character.[11] We've seen an example of this already in Hagrid's calling Ron and Harry to task for caring more for broomsticks and rats than for their friend. But we also see this when Neville takes a stand for what he thinks is best for his friends (SS, pp. 272–73). In *Sorcerer's Stone*, Harry, Ron, and Hermione decide they must prevent Voldemort from getting hold of the Sorcerer's Stone. This requires sneaking out of their dormitory late at night and breaking the enchantments conjured by their teachers to protect the Stone. But Gryffindor House had already been severely penalized by the trio's apparently reckless disregard for school rules. So Neville tries to stop his three friends as they're about to sneak out and break the rules yet again. He fails as Hermione knocks him flat with the old *Petrificus Totalus*. But the crucial thing is that Neville exhibited a great deal of courage in trying to do what he thought was right and genuinely good for his friends.

Even though Harry, Ron, and Hermione were justified in breaking the rules again, Neville was also right to try to stop them. Neville cared for more than just the possible loss of points from Gryffindor House. He cared about his friends' growing fondness for breaking the rules. Dumbledore also sees Neville's concern in this way, and he accordingly rewards him for it at the end-of-the-year ceremony. "'There are all kinds of courage,' said

---

[10] This issue of self-deception is further explored in Chapter 2 of this volume.
[11] See John Cooper's essay, "Aristotle on the Forms of Friendship," *Review of Metaphysics* 30 (1977), pp. 619–648.

Dumbledore smiling. 'It takes a great deal of bravery to stand up to our enemies, but just as much to stand up to our friends. I therefore award ten points to Mr. Neville Longbottom'" (SS, p. 306). Standing up to our friends is admirable when we do so, as Neville did, for our friends' sake.

We see another example of the positive moral effects of friendship as Ron wrestles with his jealousy of Harry. They are the best of friends, but Ron grows understandably weary of Harry's getting all the glory and recognition (GF, p. 286). Similarly, when Ron is appointed prefect, Harry becomes jealous (OP, p. 160). But, although their friendship is occasionally strained to near the breaking point, they always reconcile. The best explanation for this is that they care for something more than the pleasure or benefits to be had from hanging out together. They care about each other. Caring in this way, for the friend's own sake, Ron and Harry must overcome their jealousy and reaffirm their commitment to the pursuit of common goods. In other words, jealousy arises from the mistaken view that the accomplishments of your friend somehow detract rather than add to your own good. The common good in this case is not the prefect's badge itself—obviously only one person can wear that—but rather the fact that Ron was worthy of the recognition and honor. The strength of Ron's character is the good that is shared among his friends as they enjoy their time together.

"What's Comin' Will Come, an' We'll Meet It When It Does" (GF, p. 719)

The relations among the characters in the Potter stories provide vivid confirmation of Aristotle's insights into what is truly admirable and beneficial about friendship. Hagrid and his friends do indeed have their hearts in the right place. The things they love about each other are not incidental features, but what is most essential to who they are: their general inclinations to act in ways that make them admirable to each other and to us. Having your heart in the right place also requires seeing your friend as another self. This in turn motivates us to see that what is good for ourselves is good for our friends, and vice versa. For these reasons, friendship in the fullest sense offers the greatest

safeguard against self-deception and the greatest encouragement to develop ourselves in the most important ways.
Friendship provides the characters of Rowling's books—and
indeed all of us—with essential values that make life worthwhile
and meaningful.[12]

---

[12] This chapter was significantly improved thanks to the help of my good
friends Dr. Swamproot, Ralph Anske, my wife Laura, who doesn't really have
an enchanted car, and my son Alex, who really does have a great sense of
humor.

4

Feminism and Equal Opportunity: Hermione and the Women of Hogwarts

MIMI R. GLADSTEIN

Women in the enchanted and enchanting world of Harry Potter are anything but second-class citizens. J.K. Rowling depicts a world where equal opportunity among the sexes is a given. Unlike our Muggle world, equality is not something one needs to strive for; it is as natural a part of this world as flying on broomsticks and nearly headless ghosts. Rowling creates a world where what is and should be important is the "content of one's character" and the choices one makes. It is not through magic that the goal envisioned by classical liberal feminism is achieved at Hogwarts: equal rights for men *and* women. Rowling's world gives reality to John Stuart Mill's forward-looking words that the subordination of women should be replaced by a principle of "perfect equality, admitting no power or privilege on one side, nor disability on the other."[1]

While the history of Western philosophy is replete with instances of women being left out of the discussion or disregarded as worthy subjects of study, there is a tradition that sees women as equal moral and social agents. From Plato, up through several Enlightenment thinkers, and now contemporary feminists, philosophers have sought to treat women as the equals of men. This chapter will explore how Rowling's

---

[1] John Stuart Mill, *On Liberty and On the Subjection of Women* (Ware: Wordsworth Classics, 1996), p. 117.

treatment of Hermione and the other important women in the wizarding world exemplifies this important tradition of equality, or at least more closely approximates it than our Muggle world does.

In the Image of Her Creator

Hermione Granger is by far the most important female character in the series, so it is not surprising to learn that she is based, in part, on her creator. Asked why she chose to make her main character a boy, Rowling explains that a heroine might have been nice, but that Harry was "almost fully formed" in her imagination when she began writing what she envisioned as the first of a series of seven books. That, she explains, is why her protagonist "isn't a Harriet instead of a Harry." Rowling adds that she created Hermione as a key figure in the series, "they couldn't do it without Hermione." Hermione is "a very strong character, but then she's based on me."[2] Rowling gave Harry some of her own characteristics—she wore thick glasses as a girl—but she says that she was perceived as being very bossy and often the brightest one in her class, and those traits she gave to Hermione.

Not Just One of the Guys

The close friendship of Harry, Hermione, and Ron is central to the series, projecting an image of equality among the sexes. The Three Musketeers, possibly the most famous trio of literature, are all male. Many other couples or trios in popular literature, such as The Hardy Boys, are also all male. Moreover, if the protagonist is male, often so is the sidekick as in Quixote and Sancho or the Lone Ranger and Tonto. While a female's presence in the key friendship of a novel is not unique, the ease with which the trio act towards each other highlights how natural equality is in Potter's world. No one thinks twice about this friendship. Hermione is not a lesser member of the group; she is not just a sidekick to Ron and Harry, but an equal and essential member.

---

[2] Linda Richards, "January Profile: J.K. Rowling," (January, 2003), p. 5. http://www.januarymagazine.com/profiles/jkrowling.html.

While the efforts of early feminists were primarily to combat legal restrictions against women, many contemporary feminists focus on liberating women from psychological and emotional dependency on men. Feminists like Colette Dowling have argued that "the deep wish to be taken care of by others—is the chief force holding women down today."[3] We often see this embodied in the stereotypes that a woman must be saved by a man or that she must be taken care of by a man. Contrary to this stereotype, however, Hermione often acts to rescue Harry and Ron at crucial junctures in the plot. From the first book, where her magical ability saves the trio while they are hunting down the Sorcerer's Stone, to *Order of the Phoenix*, where Hermione saves them all from the tyranny of Professor Umbridge, Hermione's power is clear.

In *Sorcerer's Stone,* Harry, Ron, and Hermione attempt to sneak out of the Gryffindor dorm to find the Sorcerer's Stone. When fellow Gryffindor Neville Longbottom hopelessly attempts to prevent them from breaking any more rules, Harry says to Hermione: *"Do something"* (SS, p. 273). And Hermione does what neither Ron nor Harry can. She utters the charm, *"Petrificus Totalus!"* that immobilizes Neville. Later in that same chapter, Hermione saves both Ron and Harry from the Devil's Snare plant. In *Order of the Phoenix*, Hermione devises and executes a plan to trick the evil Professor Umbridge into her demise so that Harry, Hermione, and the others can get to the Ministry of Magic.

Further evidence that Hermione doesn't suffer from the kind of dependence on men that Dowling and other feminists are concerned about is that she is confident in her own intellect and ability. Hermione can take care of herself. She does not wait for her male friends to defend her when Malfoy insults her. Before the ball in *Goblet of Fire*, he expresses disbelief that anyone would ask her: "You're not telling me someone's asked *that* to the ball? Not the long-molared Mudblood?" (GF, p. 404). Rather than getting her feathers ruffled and retreating, Hermione frightens Malfoy into thinking that Mad-Eye Moody, who had previously turned Malfoy into a ferret, is right behind him. Hermione is not easily intimidated. When Ron warns her against taking on

---

[3] Colette Dowling, *The Cinderella Complex* (New York: Summit, 1981), p. 31.

Rita Skeeter, who had caused both Harry and Hagrid such pain with her stories, Hermione refuses to back down.

Strength of Mind and Moral Virtue

Mary Wollstonecraft wrote in 1792 that "women are not allowed to have sufficient strength of mind to acquire what really deserves the name of virtue."[4] Her concern was that women were not being educated in a manner that would allow them to learn and practice virtue, thus preventing them from both becoming the equal of men and fulfilling their human nature. Such a problem is not apparent at Hogwarts. Hermione is able to excel not only in her magical education, but in her moral education as well. Her effectiveness is a product of her intellect, hard work, and persistence. She studies hard; she does her homework. In *Prisoner of Azkaban*, she even uses time travel to take several classes at the same exact time!

Hard work allows her to help Harry and Ron throughout the series. Harry comments after she had saved them from the Devil's Snare, "Lucky you pay attention in Herbology, Hermione" (SS, p. 278). In contrast, Harry is able to fly a broomstick with little effort and practice. A magic force that he is unaware of protects him, and as an infant, he passively defeats the powerful Lord Voldemort. Many of Harry's powers and abilities seem to come naturally to him, while Hermione's come from lots of hard work and practice. Harry struggles with his fame and identity as a great wizard, in part, because it comes so naturally to him. He wonders if he deserves the praise he receives. Hermione, however, never feels unworthy of her success precisely because it is something she has earned through her hard work.

Hermione's good study habits and subsequent strength of mind are a crucial part of her character. She excels in school throughout the series and her relentless reading often puts her in position to provide key pieces of information. In *Sorcerer's Stone*, she knows how to defeat the Devil's Snare from paying attention in class. In *Goblet of Fire,* she informs Harry and Ron

---

[4] Mary Wollstonecraft, *The Vindication of the Rights of Woman* (Peterborough, Ontario: Broadview Press, 1997), p. 126.

about the reputation of the Durmstrang School of Wizardry. She knows from having read *An Appraisal of Magical Education in Europe* that Durmstrang has a bad reputation because of its emphasis on the Dark Arts. Having read *Hogwarts, A History*, Hermione knows that the school is hidden and disguised. If Muggles look at it, all they will see is an old ruin with a warning sign: Danger, Do Not Enter, Unsafe.

Harry often turns to Hermione for help because of her superior knowledge both in and out of the wizarding world. For example, when he is chosen one of the Hogwarts champions to compete in the Triwizard Tournament against the other magical schools, he goes to her for help on accomplishing the first task, getting past the dragon. He asks her to teach him the Summoning Charm and she even skips lunch to do so. Later, they continue working together until the early morning hours when she pronounces him ready. Harry doesn't seem able to keep up the work without her. When he keeps avoiding practicing for the second task, it is Hermione who is the voice of reason and responsibility, urging him to get on with it.

Throughout the series, Hermione develops her abilities as a witch, but her talents are not limited to magic. She is also good at logic and figuring out puzzles. When the group finds itself stymied by raging flames in *Sorcerer's Stone*, Hermione figures out the clues left on the paper by the seven bottles.[5] As she explains, "This isn't magic—it's logic—a puzzle. A lot of great wizards haven't got an ounce of logic, they'd be stuck in here forever" (SS, p. 285). Hermione also displays her logical abilities on the way to school in *Prisoner of Azkaban* when the trio runs into a sleeping stranger on the Hogwarts Express. While Ron and Harry wonder who this could be, Hermione observantly identifies him as Professor Lupin by looking at the name written on his suitcase. Hermione also quickly deduces what Professor Lupin will teach. "'That's obvious,' whispered Hermione. 'There's only one vacancy, isn't there? Defense Against the Dark Arts'" (PA, p. 75). Logic plays such an important role for philosophy that the influential Austrian

---

[5] Roger Howe, "Hermione Granger's Solution," *Mathematics Teacher* 95, 2 (February 2002), pp. 86–89. In this article, Howe, who teaches mathematics at Yale University, works out Hermione's reasoning, which is not explained in the novel.

philosopher, Ludwig Wittgenstein, thought that all philosophy was just the "logical clarification of thoughts."[6] Thus, in recognizing the importance of logic, Hermione may have the makings for a great philosopher as well as a great witch.

As the series progresses, Hermione adds to her admirable character traits a moral and psychological insight that both Harry and Ron seem to lack. When Harry is chosen to represent Hogwarts in the Triwizard Tournament in *Goblet of Fire*, Hermione explains Ron's jealousy to Harry. Patiently, she tells him, "Look, it's always you who gets all the attention . . ." (GF, p. 289). And when Harry avoids dealing with it himself and asks her to give Ron a message, she responds, "Tell him yourself. It's the only way to sort this out" (GF, p. 290).

As a sign of her moral maturity, Hermione shows concern not just with her own situation, but also for the freedom of others. Like the early nineteenth-century feminists who allied with abolitionists to free the slaves, Hermione is distraught about the plight of house-elves, telling Ron and Harry: "It's slavery, that's what it is!" (GF, p. 125). About Winky, Ron makes the predictable excuse: "that's what she likes, being bossed around . . ." to which Hermione retorts, "It's people like *you* . . . who prop up rotten and unjust systems, just because you are too lazy to—" (GF, p. 125). When she learns that house-elves have made the delicious meal at Hogwarts, she refuses to eat any more. Hermione takes up the cause of elf rights and works for their equality by creating S.P.E.W., the Society for the Promotion of Elfish Welfare, fighting first for short-term gains, such as fair wages and better working conditions. Eventually, she hopes to change the laws about wand use and achieve elf representation in the Department for the Regulation and Control of Magical Creatures.[7]

While Hermione has been bright, brave, perceptive, and crusading in the books leading up to *Order of the Phoenix*, it is in that work that she positively shines. As in the other books, Hermione keeps winning points for Gryffindor because she always knows the answers and is able to do the magic first. She is astute enough to understand the political implications of Professor Umbridge's first speech at Hogwarts; she understands

---

[6] Ludwig Wittgenstein, *Tractatus Logico-Philosophicus* (London: Routledge, 1960), p. 77.

[7] For more on the plight of the house-elves, see Chapter 8 in this volume.

that the Ministry is trying to interfere with the Hogwarts administration. In her role as prefect, she knows the right threat for the right occasion. When Fred and George's mischief goes awry and they challenge her to do something about it, she threatens them with their mother, which does the trick; they look thunderstruck. After the Cho-kissing incident, when Cho cries as she and Harry kiss, the boys are clueless on the causes of Cho's crying and Hermione has to explain to them what Cho is going through emotionally.

In something of a reversal of the popular stereotype that the male is rational and the female is emotional, Harry and Ron are sometimes masses of emotions, while Hermione is the calm voice of reason. Ever the good friend, she even gives up her Christmas ski holiday to help Harry through a difficult time. Hermione, Ron, and Ginny perform an intervention of sorts to bring Harry back to his senses. It is her idea to have Harry teach a select group secret Defense Against the Dark Arts classes to prepare them for the upcoming battles. When the group is caught in Umbridge's office, Hermione thinks of a plan to thwart her: first crying, then pretending to turn traitor, and finally leading Umbridge to the forest where Grawp, Hagrid's "little" brother, and the centaurs deal with her. This allows Neville, Ron, Ginny, and Luna to escape, leading to the climax of the novel.

The character of Hermione plays the important role of underlining and showing Rowling's vision of a world where what is important—regardless of sex—are people, their choices, and their actions. Hermione is not only just as good as one of the boys; she is often better than they. She excels in school but also in moral character, displaying the strength of mind and virtue that Wollstonecraft saw as essential. She plays key roles in the plot of all the novels, and without her friendship Harry would surely be lost.

Co-education at Hogwarts

More evidence of the high value of equal opportunity in Rowling's world is the co-educational student body at Hogwarts. Girls and boys alike get invitations to be part of each new class. When the prefects are announced, there is a boy and a girl chosen from each house, but it is not a matter of affirmative action or even commitment to diversity—it is a matter of merit. Illustrating Mill's "perfect equality," boys and girls are equally able to meet the same high standard to be a prefect.

A number of female students play minor, but key roles in the series. One important secondary character is the beautiful and popular Cho Chang, whom we first meet in *Prisoner of Azkaban* but who is more prominent in *Goblet of Fire* and *Order of the Phoenix*. She is Harry's first crush and a good Quidditch player to boot. Parvati and Padma are the girls Harry and Ron take to the Yule Ball in *Goblet of Fire*. While these dates don't go well for Ron or Harry, both Parvati and Padma join up with Dumbledore's Army in *Order of the Phoenix*. Then there is Luna Lovegood, nick-named "Loony," who has a vague and distracted manner, but proves herself brave, sensitive, and a valuable ally. She first makes a connection with Harry when she is the only one of the group besides Harry who can see the thestrals (OP, p. 199).

Both at Hogwarts and in the greater wizarding world, women are not only represented in the traditional roles of schoolgirls, mothers, and teachers, but in the more non-traditional roles as sports heroes. Quidditch is the most popular sport in the wiz-arding world, and the fact that women play on the teams that are competing for the Quidditch World Cup is a major statement about equality. Rowling handles it artfully. In *Goblet of Fire*, at the big game, only the last names of the players are announced to the crowd. The reader does not know anything more about the individual players. We are privy to Harry's thinking as he marvels at the seamless and coordinated movements of Troy, Mullet, and Moran, the Irish Chasers. Not until several pages later do we learn that Mullet is female, when the narrator tells us "Mullet shot toward the goal posts yet again, clutching the Quaffle tightly under her arm . . ." (GF, p. 109). When play resumes after a foul, Moran has the Quaffle. The reader learns that Moran is also female when Rowling uses the feminine pro-noun to describe how Moran is almost knocked off her broom. The inclusion of female Quidditch players at the highest level of the sport is done without a trace of self-consciousness and their inclusion isn't an issue in the minds of the characters.

This natural participation and inclusion of girls in sports occurs not only in professional sports, but also at Hogwarts where they participate at a varsity level on co-educational teams. In *Sorcerer's Stone*, when team captain Oliver Wood addresses the team as "men," Angelina Johnson corrects him and adds "and women." Angelina is a Chaser for the team, as is Katie Bell. Angelina makes the first score for Gryffindor in the key game of *Sorcerer's Stone;* and eventually, she becomes captain. By *Prisoner of Azkaban*, all three Chasers from the Gryffindor team are girls. When Harry is prevented from playing on the Gryffindor team, Ginny Weasley replaces him as Seeker. Even the umpire, Madam Hooch, is female.

Elizabeth Bobrick, a feminist critic of the Potter series, complains that while the narrator describes the male professors as stately and serious, the female professors at Hogwarts are either fussy or ditzy.[8] A close reading of the texts proves that, on the contrary, Rowling, in her depiction of the professorial staff, is an equal opportunity author. There are the admirable and the questionable among both sexes. In the first place, Bobrick seemingly ignores the fact that under Dumbledore, the Headmaster of Hogwarts, Professor McGonagall is the second in command. Appropriately named Minerva—for the Roman goddess of wisdom—she is the Deputy Headmistress and Dumbledore's chief ally. She is uniformly imposing and admirable throughout the series. In all the books as well as in the movies, McGonagall is a responsible and positive figure. And, it is *she*, not a male professor, who is the faculty sponsor of Gryffindor, the house all the main characters inhabit. Professor McGonagall is a teacher that everyone respects; she is "strict and clever." In *Order of the Phoenix*, McGonagall is the only teacher who effectively stands up to Professor Umbridge.

Besides McGonagall, a number of other women teach at Hogwarts. Professor Sprout is the suitably named Herbology teacher, who does her job effectively. When Hagrid goes missing, Professor Grubbly Plank temporarily and competently takes his place as instructor of the Care of Magical Creatures. Madam Pomfrey, the school nurse, runs the infirmary and mends many a victim of a magic experiment gone wrong. She and Professor Sprout heal all those petrified in *Chamber of Secrets*. After the great battle in the Ministry of Magic in *Order of the Phoenix*, Pomfrey restores Ginny, Ron, Hermione, and Neville to health. In addition, males and females author the texts that the students

---

[8] Elizabeth Bobrick, "Arrested Development," *Women's Review of Books* 20, p. 7 (8th April, 2003).

are required to study—for example, _The Standard Book of Spells_ by Miranda Goshawk and _A History of Magic_ by Bathilda Bagshott. Lastly, two of the four founders of Hogwarts are witches, Helga Hufflepuff and Rowena Ravenclaw.

Equal Opportunity Beyond Hogwarts

Outside of Hogwarts, the magic world is full of morally strong and interesting female characters. In _Order of the Phoenix,_ we are introduced to Nymphadora Tonks, a Metamorphmagus—one who can change her appearance at will. She is described as young, with "a pale heart-shaped face, dark twinkling eyes, and short spiky hair that was a violent shade of violet" (OP, p. 47). She is part of the Order that is fighting the Death Eaters. Molly Weasley, who provides a warm and motherly presence in all the earlier works, takes a more active and assertive role at the Order Headquarters when the battle against Lord Voldemort becomes more overt.

Nothing depicts the equality that admits of "no power or privilege on one side, nor disability on the other" more than presenting women from the heights of heroism to the depths of villainy, and every variety of role in between. _Order of the Phoenix_ introduces us to the scary and creepy Dolores Umbridge. Umbridge takes over Hogwarts, inspiring fear as she introduces rule after rule to control the student body and prevent the truth of Lord Voldemort's return from being fully recognized. Her punishment of Harry is a torture in which she seems to delight. She sends dementors after him and is prepared to perform the Cruciatus Curse to get him to reveal to her some information.

One of the most evil and capable warriors for the Death Eaters—Voldemort's followers—is Bellatrix Lestrange. It is she who tortured Neville's parents and in the final battle of _Order of the Phoenix_, she kills Sirius Black, Harry's godfather and her own cousin. After she finishes off Black, she wounds Kingsley and is even powerful enough to deflect Dumbledore's spell. She's the last Death Eater standing.

Not on the same level of villainy, but wonderfully smarmy in her own right, Rita Skeeter is introduced in _Goblet of Fire_ and continues to practice her brand of yellow journalism in _Order of the Phoenix_. Her stories get Harry into all kinds of trouble and undermine his reputation at Hogwarts. There is also Professor

Trelawney, the divinations teacher, who is constantly predicting the demise of Harry. As with most of her predictions, these never come to fruition. More flaky and incompetent than a fake or fraud, Trelawney does make a few predictions that come true. Let's not leave out Pansy Parkinson, a prefect in Slytherin, who is Draco Malfoy's date for the Yule Ball and shows her true colors when she assists Umbridge as part of the Inquisitorial Squad in *Order of the Phoenix.*

It is not just in the individual characters that we see the real equality between the sexes; it is in the action as well. In the big battle with the Death Eaters at the Ministry, the girls fight as hard as the boys, inflicting as much damage on the enemy and taking as much punishment. When they first engage, Hermione stupefies the Death Eater who grabs Harry and then seals a door for their escape by uttering *"Colloportus."* When Neville makes a big mistake by uttering a charm that causes Harry to lose his wand, Hermione repairs the damage by stupefying the Death Eater and getting Harry's wand back with an *Accio Wand* charm. When all seems lost and Harry is about to give the prophecy to Lucius Malfoy, Tonks sends a Stunning Spell at him and helps save the day.

Rowling creates male and female characters across the moral spectrum. We have the incompetent Trelawney and the fake Gilderoy Lockhart. We have Umbridge and Lestrange and Lord Voldemort as villains. And, of course, we have Dumbledore, McGonagall, Harry, and Hermione as heroes. In the world Rowling has created, sex is, as it should be, irrelevant to the question of one's moral fiber. It is never a big deal that women play Quidditch, are in the Triwizard Tournament, are great teachers and poor teachers, or are the heroes and the villains. Each character is judged individually by what kind of person he or she is, and each character is given the opportunity to be either good or evil. It is the individual characters' choices that make them what they are—not their gender. Such a world makes for a wonderful story, but it is one we Muggles should strive to make a reality as well.

Hufflepuff

Morality in Rowling's Universe

5

Heaven, Hell, and Harry Potter

JERRY L. WALLS

The book that made Harry Potter famous comes to a climax in a deadly struggle for an extraordinary Stone with remarkable powers. Not only can this astonishing Stone turn any metal into gold, but it can also produce the Elixir of Life that will make the one who drinks it immortal. When the talented young wizard first learns about the amazing Sorcerer's Stone, his response is the same as one would expect from more ordinary beings: "A stone that makes gold and stops you from ever dying. . . . *Anyone* would want it" (SS, p. 220).

As the story unfolds, it becomes apparent that one person who wants it very badly is the evil Voldemort. In the climactic chapter, Harry puts his life on the line to prevent Professor Quirrell, who has sold out to Voldemort, from capturing the Stone. Voldemort urges Quirrell to kill Harry, and if Dumbledore had not arrived in time to intervene, he might have succeeded. And the evil Voldemort would have secured the Stone and become immortal.

After this dramatic incident, Harry awakens in a hospital bed with Dumbledore standing over him and he immediately asks about the Stone, thinking Quirrell must have gotten it. He persists in this question until finally Dumbledore assures him that Quirrell did not in fact manage to steal it.

But then Dumbledore drops a bombshell on Harry. The Stone, he says, has been destroyed. Stunned, Harry then asks about Nicholas Flamel, Dumbledore's 665-year-old friend who created the Stone through alchemy and was its rightful owner. Does this mean that Nicholas and his 658-year-old wife will die? Indeed, Dumbledore informs Harry, they will. While they have enough elixir to set their affairs in order, Nicholas will apparently die before he is 666—a number that is infamous for suggesting evil.[1] When he sees the look of amazement on Harry's face, Dumbledore goes on to explain:

> To one as young as you, I'm sure it seems incredible, but to Nicholas and Perenelle, it really is like going to bed after a very, *very* long day. After all, to the well-organized mind, death is but the next great adventure. You know, the Stone was not really such a wonderful thing. As much money and life as you could want! The two things most human beings would choose above all—the trouble is, humans do have a knack of choosing precisely those things that are worst for them. (SS, p. 297)

These are striking thoughts indeed. No wonder the book goes on to tell us that Harry was "lost for words."

The significance of death is also an important theme in *Order of the Phoenix*. In another dramatic scene, Dumbledore confronts Voldemort but declines to kill him, remarking that taking his life would not satisfy him. As Voldemort sees it, there is nothing worse than death. In response to this, Dumbledore, sounding like Socrates, replies, "Indeed, your failure to understand that there are things much worse than death has always been your greatest weakness . . ." (OP, p. 814).

Wise as he appears to be, is Dumbledore right about this? Are there things much worse than death? Is death really a great adventure? Are the things the Stone can offer really bad for us, despite the fact that what it can provide is what everyone seems to be looking for? There are several interesting and important questions here, so let us consider them.

Are We Truly Happy?

Everyone, it seems, would like to have as much money and life as they could want. But death takes our life and taxes take our

---

[1] This is the number of the anti-Christ in the Bible. See Revelation 13:18.

money. Death and taxes: no wonder they are the two things everyone would like to avoid!

But the fact that we want what we do not have is very telling. It reveals the sad fact that almost no one is truly and fully happy. That is why we want more money and more life. What we have just isn't enough to satisfy us. But if we had the magic Stone, just imagine the possibilities! For a start, I suspect my daughter would purchase her own personal health club, complete with beauty salon and every variety of makeup ever created. My son would purchase the latest BMW roadster, a house with a large music room, every cool CD ever made, a huge TV, and every video game system known to man and boy! Surely then boredom would be vanquished and happiness and joy would reign supreme. If not, well, there is always more stuff to buy if you had unlimited money and an endless life to enjoy it.

Notice Dumbledore's concern. Humans, he says, have a "knack of choosing precisely those things that are worst for them." As the wise old wizard sees it, then, the desire for unlimited money and endless life is deeply misguided. In fact, he suggests, getting these things is the worst thing that could happen to us.

At first glance, this is an odd claim. After all, a common conception of happiness is getting what we want. This was why the ancient Stoics counseled reducing our desires. Fewer and weaker desires clamoring for satisfaction are easier to fulfill. We are unhappy, we think, because our desires are unsatisfied. To put it another way, there is a huge gap between how things are and the way we wish them to be. If we could somehow close this gap, and satisfy all our desires, then we would be happy. And one crucial key to doing this is to have a lot of money, for this gives us the power to get what we want.

Dumbledore sharply challenges this common idea of happiness. His point is that if we desire the wrong things, it is not good for us to get what we want. True happiness is not only a matter of getting what you want, but also of wanting the right things. And that is where Muggles, not to mention young wizards, so often go astray. We don't just have a knack for *choosing* the wrong things, but for *wanting* the wrong things.

Now in one respect, this is conventional wisdom. It has been recognized for centuries that the desire for excessive wealth is a corrupting desire. As the old saying goes, the love of money is the root of all evil. Money is power, and some people will go to any length to get it. It drives people to lie, cheat, steal, and even kill. It can ruin friendships and other relationships. Dumbledore's warning about money is hardly surprising.

In another respect, however, Dumbledore's view appears to be far from conventional. At first glance, his words can be taken to suggest that the desire for unlimited life is also a corrupting desire, like the excessive love of money. Wanting to live forever, he implies, is also a form of greed that humans would be wise to reject. While we may desire immortality as naturally as we desire money, getting it would be a terrible thing for us. And if that is the case, then the love of immortality is also the root of all evil!

Is Death Really a Good Thing?

If we consult the worldview that has been dominant for most of western history and culture, including the British culture in which Rowling writes (namely, that of Christianity), the answer is a resounding *no*! And Christianity is hardly alone here. Many, if not most, other religions and philosophies before modern times not only believed in immortality, but also hoped for it. Indeed, many saw it as the ultimate meaning in life. Life here in this world, on such a view, is in one sense only a preparation for the life of true happiness and joy that awaits us after death.

On this view, love of money is a root of evil because it can keep us focused on materialistic things and distract us from the greater goods, namely, the moral and spiritual truths that lead to eternal happiness. So love of money is an evil precisely because it keeps us from loving eternal things. It is a shortsighted outlook that blinds us to what is truly valuable and important.

What about worldviews other than Christianity? In this chapter we do not have the space to even name all the others that might be mentioned, but let us consider the worldview that has been the main alternative to Christianity in the west for several centuries now. I am referring to naturalism, the view, basically, that ultimate reality consists of matter, energy, laws of nature, and the like. According to this view, life evolved by chance over a period of billions of years. There is no God, so no one intended for us to be here or had a purpose in mind for our existence before we arrived on the scene. When we die, our lives are over for good. Our fate is the same as the universe at large in the long run. Eventually, all the stars will burn out, the energy will be gone, and all life will disappear as the universe goes on expanding forever. Bluntly put, naturalism tells us this is our fate:

> You get old, go to pot;
> You die, you rot.
> You're soon forgot!

If this is the truth about ultimate reality, the right metaphysical view, then the widespread hope for immortality is completely groundless and futile. All those persons who yearn for it are unfortunate indeed, for their deepest desires are completely out of sync with reality. They want something that reality strictly forbids. E.O. Wilson, a prominent contemporary thinker who holds the naturalistic view, says this is humanity's big problem. He puts it like this: "The essence of humanity's spiritual dilemma is that we evolved genetically to accept one truth and discovered another."[2] What he means is that as human beings evolved they came to believe in God, in life after death, and objective morality. But eventually, in modern times, they came to discover that God does not exist, that morality is something we created for our own purposes, that there is no meaning beyond this life. Thus, our hearts lead us in one direction, but our heads lead another way altogether. If naturalism is true, this is our dilemma: we either have to sacrifice the deepest desires of our hearts or sacrifice intellectual honesty and integrity.

Now if this is our choice, an honest and realistic person might well opt to follow his intellect even if it means sacrificing his fondest wishes and dreams. And if this is the case, the desire for immortality could be seen as a wrongheaded desire that a well-ordered mind would reject. Clearheaded people need to come to terms with reality, even when it is harsh, and if death is the end of the line for all of us, then we need to face that fact and live our lives accordingly.

---

[2] Edward O. Wilson, "The Biological Basis for Morality," *Atlantic Monthly* (April 1998), p. 70.

Indeed, on this view it makes sense to think that it would be self-centered to crave immortality. For the natural resources necessary for life are ultimately limited, a truth that becomes ever more apparent as the population on this little planet continues to grow. There is only so much matter to make up people and the resources they live on. If everybody lived forever, or even as long as Nicholas and Perenelle Flamel, then resources would eventually run out. Given this outlook, it would indeed be greedy to want more life than nature grants to us. We should be grateful for the time we have, and then give our body back to Mother Earth to sustain the great "circle of life" in the generations to come. Nicholas and Perenelle, Harry Potter, and all the rest of us should resign ourselves to being "Happy Rotters"!

This is very idealistic, to put it mildly. Let's face it, naturalism at best is trying to put a positive spin on a bad situation. Here is the heart of the issue. Human beings, as rational creatures, are incurably inclined toward happiness. No rational being can deny the deep and constant desire to be happy. But as noted above, few people seem to be truly and deeply happy. It is an elusive goal we can never deny, but is seldom attained completely. Now then, if we die without experiencing it, we end our lives never having achieved what we most deeply and persistently want. Suppose we *did* find happiness. Surely we would not want to die if we were happy and deeply enjoying our life. Either way, death cannot be seen as anything other than a tragedy that brings whatever happiness we did experience to an unwelcome end.

This point is hardly novel in philosophical literature. Indeed, many leading philosophers have pointed out the ultimate futility of life within a naturalistic framework. For a particularly memorable instance of this consider the following passage from William James's famous work *The Varieties of Religious Experience*:

> For naturalism, fed on recent cosmological speculations, mankind is in a position similar to that of a set of people living on a frozen lake, surrounded by cliffs over which there is no escape, yet knowing that little by little the ice is melting, and the inevitable day drawing near when the last film of it will disappear, and to be drowned ignominiously will be the human creature's portion. The merrier the skating, the warmer and more sparkling the sun by day, and the

ruddier the bonfires at night, the more poignant the sadness with which one must take in the meaning of the total situation.[3]

So Why Not Take the Money and Run?

Naturalism poses another glaring question that we cannot avoid. If ultimate reality is indeed matter, energy, and the like, then it is amoral. That is, it is morally indifferent since it is impersonal. Morality is a concern for persons and what is good for them, how they should live, and so on. If ultimate reality is impersonal, then morality is not a part of it. That is why Wilson, cited above, believes morality is a human creation and, as such, is open to our revision.

If naturalism is true, then it has great implications about what is worth valuing and what is of ultimate importance. If there is no life after death, if this life is the end, then it is not so clear why many traditional values are worth the cost. Think about self-sacrifice, for instance, an action that not only has great positive significance in traditional morality, but is also very highly valued in our story. For example, in the remarkable game of chess that Harry, Hermione, and Ron participate in while trying to get to the Stone, Ron is willing to sacrifice himself so Harry can get checkmate. When Harry and Hermione protest, Ron snaps at them, "You've got to make some sacrifices!" (SS, p. 283). And later, Dumbledore reveals to Harry the great significance of his mother's sacrifice in dying to save him when Voldemort tried to kill him as an infant. Such powerful love marked him with a sort of protection that would always be with him (SS, p. 299).

Dumbledore explains this more fully in *Order of the Phoenix* when he tells Harry why he arranged for him to be raised by his aunt and uncle.

> But I knew where Voldemort was weak. And so I made my decision. You would be protected by an ancient magic of which he knows, which he despises, and which he has always, therefore, underestimated—to his cost. I am speaking, of course, of the fact that your mother died to save you. She gave you a lingering pro-

---

[3] William James, *The Varieties of Religious Experience* (New York: Modern Library, 1994), p. 159.

tection he never expected, a protection that flows in your veins to this day. I put my trust, therefore, in your mother's blood. I delivered you to her sister, her only remaining relative. (OP, pp. 835–36)

Consider the very real sacrifices made by people in our world, such as the young soldiers who have given their lives in wars. If there is no life after death, then they have forfeited the only happiness available. Many people admire such sacrifice, but we cannot avoid asking why we should have this attitude. Or think about other smaller sacrifices that are made for the sake of living a moral life, like the choice not to have sex outside of marriage. The question is inevitable: if there is no life after death, is there any compelling reason to accept traditional morality, to live by honor, even if it may cost one certain very appealing pleasures, or more drastically, life itself?

A few years ago there was a beer commercial that summed up the issue very concisely, as beer commercials often do. It said, "you only go around once in life, so you've got to grab all the gusto you can."

If it really is true that we only go around once, then we die, we rot, and it's all forgot, then this view makes a good deal of sense. It does not make sense, however, given traditional moral assumptions. In particular, one fundamental assumption of traditional morality is that our ultimate happiness and well being is served, not by being selfish and immoral, but rather by being moral. This assumption makes sense if there is life after death and we are accountable for our actions in such a way that our eternal happiness depends on our doing the right thing and choosing what is truly good. But if there is no life after death and no final accountability, then the only goods that exist are the goods of this life. And if this is so, then some traditional moral requirements are harder to justify.

This is not to say that there is no reason to be moral if there is no life after death. Certainly naturalists have defended morality on their own principles and their arguments are not lightly to be dismissed. For instance, what is moral is often the smart thing to do, and serves our happiness and well being in the short run as well as the long run.

While this is undeniable and would be agreed upon by naturalists as well as theists, there is more to the story. Sometimes what is moral is not only inconvenient, it is also extremely costly and demanding. The more difficult question is whether there is any really good reason to be moral when that is the case. Even more to the point, is there any *obligation* to do what is moral?

Let us put the point in terms of a thought experiment. Suppose there is no life after death and one is given the choice of either 1) living a life of sacrifice to help others or 2) a life of wealth and pleasure, even if one has to cut a few moral corners. Which would be preferable? While some may choose the life of sacrifice because they would find it intrinsically satisfying, or they feel a duty to do so, is there really any convincing reason why one should not take the money and run if one is so inclined?

Magical Moral Obligations

This notion of moral obligation is key, and it is worthwhile to direct attention to it for a moment. It's not the only concern of ethics, but it's an important part. Do you think that Harry was morally obligated to risk himself in saving Dudley at the beginning of *Order of the Phoenix*? Despite Dudley's obvious character flaws, Harry probably was. If so, then we might wonder how moral obligations derive their binding power. Moral duties don't derive their force from serving self-interest, for sometimes they tell us to sacrifice self-interest. So where does their force come from? This is an ethical question that raises the deeper question of what kind of world we live in. If there really are moral obligations that tell us on occasion to sacrifice ourselves for the good of others, the natural question to ask is what sort of world would make best sense of this? It is exactly because moral obligations, if they existed, demand sacrifice of self-interest and feature other odd characteristics, that atheist J.L. Mackie was convinced that they wouldn't exist without an all-powerful God to create them.[4] Genuine moral duties that always trump other competing desires and concerns would be utterly odd entities in a purely natural world. Indeed, they would be practically magical! As an atheist, Mackie thus denied that there are any such obligations after all.

---

[4] J.L. Mackie, *The Miracle of Theism* (Oxford: Oxford University Press, 1982), p. 115.

Mackie is not alone among atheists in recognizing that the denial of God's existence has serious moral repercussions. Another notable example is the atheistic existentialist Jean-Paul Sartre, one of the best-known philosophers of the twentieth century, who clearly saw that moral philosophy is profoundly affected if there is no God. He took strong issue with secular ethicists who confidently imagined that we can easily dispense with God while keeping morality pretty much the same as it has always been. He described their agenda as follows:

> Toward 1880, when the French professors endeavored to formulate a secular morality, they said something like this: God is a useless and costly hypothesis, so we will do without it. However, if we are to have morality, a society and a law-abiding world, it is essential that certain values should be taken seriously. . . . It must be considered obligatory . . . to be honest, not to lie, not to beat one's wife, to bring up children and so forth; so we are going to do a little work on this subject, which will enable us to show that these values exist all the same, inscribed in an intelligible heaven although, of course, there is no God. In other words . . . nothing will be changed if God does not exist; we shall rediscover the same norms of honesty, progress and humanity, and we shall have disposed of God as an out-of-date hypothesis which will die away quietly of itself.[5]

Sartre remained unconvinced. He found it "extremely embarrassing that God does not exist, for there disappears with him all possibility of finding values in an intelligible heaven. . . . It is nowhere written that 'the good' exists, that one must be honest or must not lie, since we are now upon the plane where there are only men."[6] In contrast, he took as his starting point Dostoevsky's claim that if God does not exist and this life is all there is, everything is permitted. Mackie and Sartre, although atheists, agreed that if God exists, this has enormous implications for morality.

This basic point was also recognized by theistic philosopher Immanuel Kant, who maintained that God's existence is essential for morality. He is well known for arguing that the moral

---

[5] Jean-Paul Sartre, *Existentialism and Human Emotions*, translated by B. Frechtman (New York: Philosophical Library, 1957), pp. 21–22.
[6] *Ibid*.

enterprise needs the postulate of a God who can, and will, make happiness correspond to virtue. As George Mavrodes writes, "I suspect that what we have in Kant is the recognition that there cannot be, in any 'reasonable' way, a moral demand upon me, unless reality itself is committed to morality in some deep way."[7] Again, then, we're reminded that the way world is, the ultimate truth of the matter, has far-reaching implications for morality.

So let's raise the question again, is there any convincing reason why one shouldn't take the money and run if one is so inclined?

Some Damned Good Reasons

Let us return to Dumbledore's remarks cited above. Recall his claim that "to the well-organized mind, death is but the next great adventure." Does the great wizard believe in life after death after all? If so, his warning is not directed against desiring immortality itself, but rather against seeking to prolong *this* life indefinitely, no matter what we have to do to accomplish it.

But perhaps it is not up to us to prolong our lives at any cost. Perhaps immortality is a gift, but a gift to be received only under certain conditions. In this case, to the well-ordered mind, death could indeed be the next great adventure.

Just what this adventure is in Rowling's books remains unclear, at least through *Order of the Phoenix*. This is apparent in a conversation Harry has with Nearly Headless Nick the ghost after he lost Sirius. It is Harry's hope that Sirius will come back as a ghost so he can see him again. According to Nick, however, only wizards can come back, but most of them choose not to do so. Sirius, he says, will have "gone on." Harry presses the question: "Gone on where? Listen—what happens when you die, anyway? Where do you go? Why doesn't everyone come back?" Nick answers that he was afraid of death and that is why he himself remained behind. "I know nothing of the secrets of death, Harry, for I chose my feeble imitation of life instead" (OP, p. 861).

---

[7] George Mavrodes, "Religion and the Queerness of Morality" in Louis Pojman, *Ethical Theory: Classical and Contemporary Readings*, second edition (New York: Wadsworth, 1995), p. 585.

The life of a ghost, then, is "neither here nor there" as Nick puts it, and Harry is left with no answer to his urgent questions. The mystery of what happens when we die, unlike the Chamber of Secrets, remains closed.

By contrast, theism in general, and Christianity in particular, offer a more definite answer to Harry's questions. So let us briefly consider the Christian account of metaphysical reality and how it relates to morality and life after death. According to Christianity, ultimate reality is not matter, energy, and laws of nature. Rather, these are all things created by the ultimate reality, namely, God. The distinctively Christian view of God is striking indeed. According to it, the one God exists eternally as three persons, the Father, the Son, and the Holy Spirit. This is an admittedly mysterious idea, but what I want to emphasize is that it is the foundation for the well-known idea that God is love. C.S. Lewis, the noted Christian writer, pointed this out as follows.

> All sorts of people are fond of repeating the Christian statement that 'God is love'. But they seem not to notice that the words 'God is love' have no real meaning unless God contains at least two Persons. Love is something that one person has for another person. If God was a single person, then before the world was made, He was not love.[8]

What this means is that the nature of ultimate reality, the fundamental metaphysical truth, is loving relationship. God from all eternity has existed as a loving relationship among three persons. Moreover, God loves all His creatures so deeply that He was willing to sacrifice himself to show how much He loves them and wants them to love Him in return. This is what is involved in the Christian belief that Jesus is the Son of God who willingly died for us on the cross to save us from our sins.

If this is true, the story about Harry Potter's mother and the power of her blood is a reflection of one of the deepest truths about reality, namely, that all of us are loved by One who was willing to spill his blood and die for us.[9] Furthermore, the love

---

[8] C.S. Lewis, *Mere Christianity* (New York: Macmillan, 1960), p. 151.

[9] See for example Ephesians 1:7; Hebrews 9:14; I Peter 1:18–19. The strong reaction—both pro and con—to the Mel Gibson film on the passion of Christ is very suggestive in this regard.

of Harry's mother is a picture of the fact that love is a greater and more powerful thing than evil and death. It was her sacrificial love that protected Harry when Voldemort and Quirrell tried to kill him. In the Christian story, the resurrection of Jesus shows that love is stronger than death. Jesus offers to share his life with all who believe in him, and this life gives those who receive it the power to live forever. So understood, Christianity is a great love story and it is based on the belief that love is the deepest reality and evil cannot defeat it.

As Dumbledore explains to Harry, the one thing Voldemort cannot understand is love (SS, p. 299). His way of life is the complete opposite of love. Rather than being willing to sacrifice himself for others, he is willing to sacrifice innocent beings for his own selfish purposes. This is shown in the fact that he was willing to perform the monstrous act of slaying a unicorn to keep himself alive. As Firenze, a Centaur, explains to Harry, the only sort of person who would do such a thing would be one "who has nothing to lose, and everything to gain." But to keep oneself alive in this manner is to have only a half life, a cursed life. Harry's thought when he hears this is quite to the point: "If you're going to be cursed forever, death's better, isn't it?" (SS, p. 258).

It is because love is the deepest reality that it makes sense to do the right thing even if it requires sacrifice to do so. Since God is love, the irony is that when we show love to Him by doing the right thing, we are also acting in our own best self-interest, for He can be trusted to ensure our long-term well being. This is not the same as acting selfishly and it is very important to see the difference. To act selfishly is to promote one's own interest at the unfair advantage of others or even to be willing to do horrible things, like Voldemort, to serve one's own purposes.

The notion that being moral can be at odds with our true self-interest has been a major problem for modern and postmodern moral philosophy. It is a dilemma indeed if one must choose between being moral and acting in one's ultimate self-interest. And it is hard to see how one can reasonably be required to choose what is moral in such a case. And this dilemma arises easily for those with a naturalistic worldview. Prior to modern times, by contrast, moral philosophers generally agreed that there can be no conflict between being moral and our ultimate self-interest.

For the Christian worldview, this conflict simply does not arise. While I do not wish to suggest that there are no other possible answers to this conflict, I do want to emphasize that Christianity offers powerful resources to resolve it. I especially have in mind its account of life after death, particularly its beliefs about heaven and hell. In view of these beliefs, it is impossible to harm one's ultimate well being by doing what is right, even if doing what is right costs one's life. For the person who acts self-sacrificially in obedience to God is acting in accord with ultimate reality, which is the very love of God Himself. He has the gift of eternal life, and he will continue to live with God in heaven after he dies. Death cannot destroy him just as Voldemort could not kill Harry.

Likewise, it is impossible to advance our ultimate well being by doing evil. While our short-term interests may be promoted by doing what is wrong, we are acting against the ultimate grain of reality and we will eventually have to account for our choices. To act immorally is to act against love and to cut ourselves off from God, whose very nature is love. This is hell. This is the cursed life of one like Voldemort who is willing to embrace evil to promote his own purposes.

The right metaphysical view of ultimate reality has huge implications for how we ought to live. On the Christian view, it is precisely because life is forever that there are powerfully good reasons to be moral and to choose the way of love rather than the way of getting as much money as we can for our own selfish purposes. Love is the deepest reality and, if we understand that, we can avoid the trap of choosing the very things that are worst for us. To understand the way of love is to have the sort of well-ordered mind that makes all of life, even death, a fabulous adventure![10]

[10] To see a further developed version of some of the arguments of this chapter, see Jerry L. Walls, *Heaven: The Logic of Eternal Joy* (New York: Oxford University Press, 2002), pp. 161–200. I am thankful to Shawn Klein, Tracy Cooper, Tom Morris, and Phil Tallon for helpful comments on an earlier version of this essay. I am especially grateful to David Baggett for numerous helpful suggestions.

6

Magic, Science, and the Ethics of Technology

BENJAMIN J. BRUXVOORT LIPSCOMB
and W. CHRISTOPHER STEWART

In this chapter, we take the grand, ready-made thought experiment of J.K. Rowling's Harry Potter series, and use it to try to get a better grip on a difficult, real-world issue: the ethics of technological adaptation.[1] If, as we think, the use and abuse of magic in Rowling's books is a close analogue for the use and abuse of applied science—technology—in our world, then the ethical judgments her heroes make concerning magic may have something to teach us about an appropriate ethics of applied science. In the first part of this chapter, we establish a connection between the magic of Harry's world and the science of our own world. In the second part of the chapter, we outline Rowling's ethics of magic and consider what it might be saying to us about the ethics of technological adaptation in the real world.

Magic, Science, and Harry Potter

The likelihood that the Harry Potter books offer readers a helpful lens through which to consider the ethics of technological adaptation depends on the closeness of the analogy between the magic we encounter in the books on the one hand, and

---

[1] In so doing, we are following up on a fruitful suggestion by Alan Jacobs. His review of the first three Potter books in *First Things* (January, 2000, pp. 35–38) started us thinking about this topic. We owe to Joshua Hochschild the suggestion to follow up on Jacobs in this way.

applied science as it has developed in the real world (and presumably in the books) on the other. A close look at the magic of Harry's world will show how it resembles both the (real) historical practice of "natural magic" and applied science generally.

Magic traces its origins back to the ancient world, but it is less widely recognized that the origins of science are similarly ancient. Many believe—wrongly—that science is solely a feature of the modern world, that it had no precursors, and that it eliminated by replacing wholesale a raft of superstitions about the world maintained by pre-modern folk. In fact, magic and what we would nowadays call "science" interacted constructively for many centuries. What *we* mean when we use the word "magic" reflects hindsight. We look at the past from a perspective conditioned by the triumph of modern science. According to Lynn Thorndike's massive, eight-volume *History of Magic and Experimental Science* (the real-world analogue of Harry's *History of Magic*), rather than insisting that modern science *replaced* magic after the seventeenth century, it is more accurate to say that it largely *absorbed* it. Today, "magic" refers to elements that were not fully absorbed, such as astrology. While not all of the assumptions, aims, and methods of magic were absorbed into modern science, some clearly were.

In the history of the real world, not all magic is alike. Besides "black" or "demonic" magic, there is also a long tradition of "natural" magic, which depends not on enlisting the aid of spirits whose knowledge of nature's secrets is presumed to exceed that of mere mortals, but rather on the mastery of various natural principles or "correspondences." The important point here is that both modern science and this natural magic tradition are methods of investigating natural processes, the aim of which is, in each case, not simply explanation or understanding for its own sake, but more importantly prediction and control of the natural world, ultimately with a view to the betterment of the human condition. Moreover, both natural magicians and modern scientists pursue these aims through a combination of experimentation and mathematical analysis of natural events. It's not so much that magic was shown to be false, but rather that "natural philosophers" (the old name for scientists, before "scientist" was coined in the nineteenth century) abandoned the comparatively fruitless search for hidden (or "occult") properties of matter in favor of the relatively more promising mechanical explanations of early modern science. Whereas the *content* of early modern scientific explanations, limited as they were to the mechanics of particles ("atoms" and later "molecules") in motion, sharply contrasted with the natural magic tradition, the *overall practical aim* remained the same, namely, to predict and control the course of nature.

Among the various branches of natural magic that flourished before, during, and for a short while after the rise of modern science, alchemy was especially popular, owing largely to the influence of Paracelsus (who died in 1541), a bust of whom appears in a hallway at Hogwarts (OP, p. 281). The practice of alchemy, like that of every form of natural magic (including astrology), oscillated between mysticism and practical or "applied" research. Prior to Paracelsus, practical alchemy was preoccupied with the effort to transfigure base metals into gold. The "philosopher's stone" was the hoped-for ingredient that would not only "heal" base (or "sick") metals by transfiguring them, but also prolong the life of anyone who ingested it. (Hence British editions of the first book in the series bear the title, *Harry Potter and the Philosopher's Stone*.) Paracelsus expanded the scope of alchemy to include the successful development of metallic medicines for curing illnesses against which more conventional Renaissance treatments were ineffective. In this way, his work was a clear precursor to modern chemical research.

The rise of modern science produced the modern world—the world of Muggles. But in Rowling's books, alongside this world (the world of our experience), and in a close, symbiotic relationship with it, a world of magic persists. Far from being obliterated or absorbed, the practice of magic simply went underground, concealed from the Muggle world. Rowling depicts a community of witches and wizards existing comfortably, albeit secretively, alongside the modern world. Rowling's witches and wizards are free to use machines and other fruits of modern science, but their preferred means of negotiating and manipulating the world are the natural powers associated with magic. In Harry Potter's world, magic is as effective and pervasive a means of negotiating and manipulating one's surroundings as applied science has become in ours.

By the late 1800s, the fruits of modern science were transforming Western society at all levels, as a steady stream of new gadgets worked their way into every corner of life. Today, most Westerners are almost completely dependent on such machinery, most of which runs on electricity. Just as technology textures our lives, magic likewise textures the lives of witches and wizards in Harry's world. Rowling offers her readers many examples of this, most memorably on the occasion of Harry's first visit to the Weasley home, where he observes Mrs. Weasley flick her wand at the sink, whereupon her dishes begin "to clean themselves, clinking gently in the background" (CS, p. 34). Harry gazes at her shelves, which bulge with such books as *"Charm Your Own Cheese, Enchantment in Baking,* and *One Minute Feasts—It's Magic!"* (CS, p. 34).

Most of the magic in Rowling's books (and all the approved magic) closely resembles natural magic. As one would expect at a school founded by natural magicians, the primary emphasis of the curriculum at Hogwarts is practical, emphasizing the use of magical powers to achieve specific effects, such as levitation or transfiguration. Magic is a tool, and like any tool is judged by its utility. Thus Hermione Granger criticizes Fred and George's gadgetry as magic "of no real use to anyone" (OP, p. 369), while Professor Snape commends Occlumency as an obscure but "highly useful" branch of magic (OP, p. 520).

Rowling's characters also take for granted another assumption common to both the natural magic tradition and modern science, namely, that the results they achieve stem from the successful manipulation of fundamentally natural processes. Hermione wants to know how Fred and George's "headless hats" *work*. She assumes that they represent nothing more than a clever manipulation of natural, albeit hidden forces. It's hard to mistake the spirit behind her attempt at an explanation: "I mean, obviously, it's some kind of Invisibility Spell, but it's rather clever to have extended the field of invisibility beyond the boundaries of the charmed object. . . . I'd imagine the charm wouldn't have a very long life though. . . ." (OP, p. 540). Hermione seeks an explanation in terms of underlying regularities or natural laws, just as a natural magician would—or a modern scientist. In the same spirit, Arthur Weasley indulges his personal and professional fascination with Muggle technology, frequently proclaiming his admiration for fresh examples of Muggle ingenuity, such as the automatic ticket machines he and Harry encounter on the London underground en route to

Harry's hearing in *Order of the Phoenix* (OP, p. 125). Ron explains to Harry that the Weasleys' shed is full of Muggle artifacts, which his father experiments on—taking them apart, enchanting them, then putting them back together to observe the effects, as in the case of the Weasleys' celebrated flying car (CS, p. 31).

The character who perhaps best reflects the tradition of natural magic, and shows thereby how little separates it from modern science, is the Potions master, Severus Snape. His opening remarks to the first-year students in *Sorcerer's Stone* are particularly revealing:

> You are here to learn the subtle science and exact art of potion-making. As there is little foolish wand-waving here, many of you will hardly believe this is magic. I don't expect you to understand the beauty of the softly simmering cauldron with its shimmering fumes, the delicate power of liquids that creep through human veins, bewitching the mind, ensnaring the senses. . . . I can teach you how to bottle fame, brew glory, even stopper death. (SS, pp. 136–37)

The link between potions and Renaissance alchemy is clear from the questions Snape proceeds to pose to the class, about the results of adding "powdered root of asphodel to an infusion of wormwood," the difference between "monkshood and wolfbane," and other such arcana from *One Thousand Magical Herbs and Fungi* (SS, pp. 137–38). Harry's first potions lesson is a lab session in which the aspiring witches and wizards attempt to produce a potion to cure boils.

Further reinforcing the analogy between the magic in the books and modern science, and looking ahead to the second part of this chapter, the indiscriminate use of magic in Harry's world creates problems closely analogous to the problems created by the improper use of applied science in our world. It is as a result of magic that the Giants are an endangered species (OP, p. 427), and what Giants hate most about witches and wizards is their magic (OP, p. 431). To cope with such problems, various regulatory agencies exist, such as the "Improper Use of Magic Office," the "Broom Regulatory Control," the "Apparition Test Center," and the "Department of Regulation and Control of Magical Creatures." The message is clear: notwithstanding its benefits, the indiscriminate use of magic, like the indiscriminate use of applied science, has negative consequences.

Interlude: Fantasy and Moral Epistemology

There is a greater practical point to this analogy between magic and applied science than might at first appear. For if the analogy is as close as we have suggested, then ethical truths that apply to one case should apply also to the other.

What is the connection between this observation and Rowling's books? These books are, as several authors in this volume have noted, ethically "loaded." They speak insistently to the issues with which writers on ethics have traditionally been concerned: good and evil; friendship and loss; choice and character. These are books that, uncharacteristically in contemporary fiction, instruct their readers about how to live.

Unsurprisingly, many of the central issues faced by the characters in Rowling's books have to do with the proper exercise of magical powers. The choice between the magic taught at Hogwarts and the Dark Arts is only the most obvious example. The worldwide magical community also regulates its members' behavior through a complex set of customary and legal requirements, from proper dueling behaviors to school rules to the Decree for the Reasonable Restriction of Underage Sorcery. And implicit judgment is passed on characters for their use or misuse even of unregulated magic. There is no rule against spending one's life gazing into the Mirror of Erised.[2] But Dumbledore makes clear to Harry that this is a danger to be guarded against—the danger of a wasted life.

It is a great strength of Rowling's work that she does not treat these issues as unique to the situation of her characters, belonging to a social context entirely unlike our own. Her books would have much less appeal if they did not speak to circumstances in which we find ourselves. Rowling's characters worry about how to use magical power because magical power is the primary medium of their existence. They are human beings whose lives are shot through with magic, as ours are shot through with applied science. Rowling's characters worry about

---

[2] The Mirror of Erised is dealt with extensively in Chapter 7 of this volume.

magic, in short, in exactly the same way we worry about activities such as gardening or driving or family planning.

Rowling's books offer us, among many gifts, an ethics of magic. And the analogy elaborated in the first part of this chapter leads us to expect that the ethics of magic in Harry's world will also be appropriate, properly translated, for ours.

Rowling's Ethics of Magic

So then, what is Rowling's ethics of magic? To find out, let's look first at what characterizes Rowling's bad characters and their use of magic, and then try to read off of this "essence of bad magic" a corresponding "essence of good magic."

While Sirius Black rightly notes that "the world isn't split into good people and Death Eaters" (OP, p. 302), nevertheless, Rowling clearly regards Voldemort and his Death Eaters, and practitioners of the Dark Arts generally, as paradigms of evil. We may look, then, to these people and the powers of which they avail themselves—the Dark Arts—to get a picture of what bad magic is like.

The Dark Arts are a broad category, comprising everything from various species of dangerous creatures (doxies, boggarts, dementors), to paraphernalia like the shrunken heads in the shops of Knockturn Alley and the vials of blood in Grimmauld Place, to the three curses called "unforgivable."

The curses are the best example with which to begin, both because of the clear connections between them and human action, and because they are highlighted in the text as especially horrible. What do the Unforgiveable Curses do? Briefly, they dominate susceptible others, and dominate them completely. Each term in this analysis is necessary, so let's look at them in turn.

The Unforgivable Curses dominate susceptible others. One of them kills, another tortures, and a third strips the victim of his or her will, rendering him or her a tool of the person who speaks the curse. Although Voldemort and his Death Eaters generally use these curses on people, and this is clearly the use that the magical community is most concerned to prevent, it is possible to use them also on other creatures susceptible to these forms of domination: anything living, in the case of Avada Kedavra; anything capable of suffering, in the case of the

Cruciatus curse; anything capable of self-direction, in the case of the Imperius curse. Barty Crouch Jr., disguised as Mad-Eye Moody, uses them on spiders in one of his lessons at Hogwarts.

It is worth asking whether a good teacher (in the ethical sense) would have done this much. The students wonder aloud, on their way back from this lesson, whether there would be "trouble with the Ministry if they knew . . ." (GF, p. 220). Through the end of *Order of the Phoenix*, the only persons to attempt one of these curses, other than people in league with Voldemort, were Dolores Umbridge (a paradigm of evil in her own way) and Harry, trying to hurt Bellatrix Lestrange in repayment for her murder of Sirius. And Harry can't get the curse right, because (as Bellatrix tells him) "you need to mean [it]" (OP, p. 810). It appears one must desire to dominate in the way characteristic of these curses in order to use them effectively, and thus no good witch or wizard could successfully perform them, even on a spider. Dumbledore could not perform them—at least, while remaining himself. As Lestrange says to Harry, "you need to really want to cause pain—to enjoy it . . ." (OP, p. 810). Her words shed light on Barty Crouch Jr.'s remark to his students that "Avada Kedavra's a curse that needs a powerful bit of magic behind it—you could all get your wands out now and point them at me and say the words, and I doubt I'd get so much as a nosebleed" (GF, p. 217). It appears no use of the Unforgivable Curses is acceptable—that only the corrupt can perform them. We will return to this point in a moment.

It is not adequate to say simply that the Unforgivable Curses dominate susceptible others, because all curses do that to some extent, and Rowling's books do not encourage us to think of the hexes the Hogwarts students use on one another when dueling (Petrificus Totalus, Tarantella, and so on) as necessarily problematic. It certainly is a form of domination to freeze people stiff or to remove their control over their legs. The domination that characterizes the Unforgivable Curses is of another order, though. It is complete. Death is a clear case of complete domination, so it is obvious how Avada Kedavra fits the criterion. So too with the Imperius curse. By this curse, one person masters another, so that the victim becomes a mere tool, no longer an independent agent. What of the Cruciatus curse? It too meets the criterion. As a number of philosophers who have written about torture have noted, the goal of torture is to pull to pieces the person being tortured, sometimes in order to turn him or her into a tool, but always to remove him or her as a potentially opposing force. The domination intended is complete.[3]

Behind any attempt to reduce ethical reality to a set of rules you'll find one or more practical aims served by the reduction. In Harry's world, the designation of just these curses as *the* Unforgivable Curses seems to serve the purposes of both legislation and instruction. The designation of these curses as "unforgivable" helps the community make efficient and broadly correct judgments about whom to imprison and what to teach children. But one can clearly use other curses to dominate others in far-reaching ways, and one can dominate others in significant ways but do so justifiably. Legilimancy seems to lie in this gray area (both Dumbledore and Voldemort are proficient at it), as do uses of memory charms. The series' ultimate judgment on Gilderoy Lockhart is that he is, or was, a bad man, stealing fame that properly belonged to others by taking away from those others part of who they were—their memories. But Kingsley Shacklebolt uses Lockhart's trademark charm on Cho Chang's friend Marietta when Marietta is about to expose Harry's Defense Against the Dark Arts club, and Shacklebolt is praised for doing so. We might say that in the first case, the domination intended is more complete, and in the second, less so. But even if it is possible to thus explain why a certain use of a memory charm should be regarded one way and not another, this explanation will never go so far as to create a fully adequate set of underlying principles. Principles are nearly always reductions of a less-than-fully codifiable reality.

What else characterizes unacceptable forms of domination, of which the Unforgivable Curses are a paradigm case? Recall Harry's inability to perform the Cruciatus curse on Bellatrix Lestrange and the explanation she gives for why he can't. His desire to hurt her is not sufficiently wholehearted. His heart is not in the curse; it is with Sirius. What we learn here, as we said, is that one must become corrupt to master this or any of the Unforgiveable Curses. To become proficient in the Dark Arts,

---

[3] See, for instance, Richard Rorty's remarks in his essay, "Orwell and Cruelty," in *Contingency, Irony, and Solidarity* (Cambridge: Cambridge University Press, 1989).

one must damage one's character in a particular way—one must give oneself over to the desire for domination. This observation opens up to us a fuller understanding of why the paraphernalia and non-human creatures that Rowling's characters identify with the "Dark Arts" belong under that rubric. They are all the products or accomplices of a spirit eager to dominate, eager to reduce all creatures susceptible to its influence to the status of tools, of things.

This observation also goes some way toward illuminating a cryptic remark Dumbledore makes to Voldemort as they duel in the penultimate chapter of *Order of the Phoenix*. Dumbledore says to Voldemort that Voldemort's greatest weakness is his failure to understand that there is something worse than death. A philosopher reading this cannot but be put in mind of Plato's *Gorgias*, where Socrates contrasts a life devoted to avoiding suffering and death with a life devoted to avoiding unjust action, and argues that the first life is ultimately self-destructive, damaging one's soul and cutting one off from both friendship and freedom. Rowling's accounts of the interactions between Voldemort and the Death Eaters read like textbook illustrations of Socrates's point. Voldemort's followers cower before him; though they might once have thought that the Dark Arts were a means to power, and thus to a kind of freedom, there is no freedom for them, and no reciprocity between them and their master. They must ever choose between catering to his whims and dying.

For his part, Voldemort the tyrant has harmed himself more than any of them. He pursues the Sorcerer's Stone in an effort to restore an existence depleted by the exercise of his dark powers. Formless unless he can "share another's body" (SS, p. 293), he desperately consumes unicorn blood to stay alive, knowing all the while that, as the centaur Firenze explains to Harry, the end result of such a crime against nature is a cursed life (SS, p. 258). To be consumed by the desire to master one's surroundings and thereby secure oneself is worse than death, and Voldemort's "greatest weakness" is his self-caused blindness to this fact. He is, as Socrates says of the tyrant Archelaus, wretched and pitiable. One detects a note of sadness in Dumbledore's voice when he speaks to or about Voldemort, an excellent student, and one who has known real suffering. When they meet, he persists in calling him "Tom."

Taking a step back from Rowling's books, one notices two major classes of disapproved actions, only one of which we have so far discussed. First, there are the actions we have been talking about: actions which completely dominate susceptible others. For example, what is the problem Hermione and Dumbledore identify with respect to the magical community's treatment of house-elves? It seems to be the magical community's domination of them—thinking of them and (in turn) treating them as tools. In the case of the giants, we see this domination carried to the point of near-extinction.

But there is another major class of disapproved actions, too: actions that threaten to expose the magical community to the wider world. There are a host of legal and ethical sanctions attached to publicizing the magical community, and while good characters sometimes wink at these restrictions, there is no evidence that Rowling disputes their value. We should ask, then, how these restrictions are justified.

They are not justified by any physical threat to the magical community. We are told, in *Prisoner of Azkaban*, that medieval witch burnings did no harm to real witches; the witches would perform a charm to neutralize the flames and then stand within the fires set for them, feeling nothing but "a gentle tickling sensation" (PA, p. 2). It's not even clear that contemporary technology could pose much of a threat to the magical community. The places they live and work are, after all, invisible to Muggles. There is some suggestion, in fact, in Rowling's descriptions of Platform $9\frac{3}{4}$ and Grimmauld Place, that the domain of the magical community is not present to Muggles at all. It does not seem to be the case that a Muggle could stumble into Grimmauld Place by accident. It's not merely invisible to them; it's not even there.[4]

If these restrictions are not for the physical protection of the magical community, the most plausible justifications for them are that they protect the magical community in a different sense and/or protect others. We can see both justifications at work in

---

[4] Or perhaps it would be better to say that certain magical locations are inaccessible to Muggles unaccompanied by a wizard, since we know Hermione's parents have entered certain magical locations with her. Chapter 14 of this volume explores the metaphysical issues involving time and space in the Potter books.

the restrictions Rowling highlights. And these underlying justifications are clearly connected to the observations about good
and evil magic articulated earlier. Consider the cases that most
concern Arthur Weasley in his work at the Misuse of Muggle
Artifacts office, cases like the regurgitating toilets at Bethnal
Green. Weasley comments, "it's not so much having to repair the
damage, it's more the attitude behind the vandalism, Harry.
Muggle-baiting might strike some wizards as funny, but it's an
expression of something much deeper and nastier . . ." (OP, p.
153). What "something" or "attitude" can he be talking about,
other than contempt for Muggles, who are, in the face of magical powers, particularly vulnerable to domination? The community binds itself not to tamper with Muggle life, not to protect
itself from physical harm, but to protect the character of individual witches and wizards and of the wizard community as a
whole, and, not coincidentally, to protect others susceptible to
domination.

The same points can be made with reference to the various
restrictions on the magical activity of witches and wizards in
training. Such restrictions, targeted as they are toward minors,
appear to serve an educative role. They might also be said to
protect young witches and wizards (and those around them)
from accidental injury, but most of the particular restrictions
(against apparating prior to one's O.W.L. exams, for instance)
can't very plausibly be argued to serve this purpose. They can,
however, quite convincingly be defended on the basis of their
contribution to protecting individual and communal character
and thereby vulnerable others (in a long-term, not a short-term
sense). As we have indicated, all magic manipulates and thus, to
some extent, dominates the wizard's environment. If, as we
have argued, the worst thing that can happen to a witch or wizard is to become captive to a dominating spirit, it is of obvious
importance that the immature are taught, not simply how to use
magic, but also to restrain their use of it appropriately. They
must not be allowed to use it utterly at their discretion, because
the powers it puts at their disposal are great, intoxicating ones.
Consider Fred and George Weasley's first response to their
mature freedom: apparating constantly and to no purpose. More
seriously, consider how often Harry is tempted to hex his uncle,
aunt, and cousin—to dominate them—rather than deal with
them, with however much difficulty, as fellow persons.

Thus we can see a strong, formative purpose at work in the Decree for the Reasonable Restriction of Underage Sorcery, one connected, as every part of Rowling's ethics of magic seems to be, to the fundamental distinction between good and evil magic. The Decree, like every principle of action the magical community imposes upon itself, exists in significant part to protect individual and communal character, here by training immature members of the community.

Note also that without a Hogwarts or comparable degree, no one, regardless of talent, is permitted to use magic. The education at Hogwarts, which is as much an ethical education as a technical one, is the only authorized entry into the use of these powers. (Witness the recurring battles over the headmaster's position, always motivated by the assumption that this office is a rudder by which to direct the formation of the youth.) The education in technical subjects is suffused throughout by the shared ethical standpoint of the educators.

The magical community in Harry's world is, in many ways, like the Amish community in ours: a self-segregated group characterized by careful self-regulation of their acquired powers, be they magical or technological.[5] Within each community, there are those who regard the rest of the world with suspicion or distaste. In the magical world, these are the wizards and witches like the Malfoys, those obsessed with bloodlines (a characteristic obsession of Slytherin House). But there are just as many (including some Slytherins) who hold no objectionable prejudices and simply see separation and clear communal definition as good and necessary. The definition, in each case, is a matter of what powers one makes available to oneself, powers being assessed in terms of the effects they have on individual and communal character—in terms of the attitude they encourage one to adopt toward the world and its inhabitants. The community is willing to prohibit to itself and its members particular powers that it judges to be, on the whole, destructive of the common good. Such prohibitions are not simply a matter of withdrawal from the world, but are acts of self-definition ultimately grounded in a willingness to suffer inconvenience or

---

[5] The following discussion has been informed by the late John Hostetler's excellent work on Amish society.

even death rather than dominate others in certain ways.[6] It is not beside the point that dark wizards and witches, precisely because they refuse to set limits to their use of magic, are the likeliest to violate the communal restrictions, including the restrictions on communal self-revelation: they are the ones who make toilets regurgitate and who twirl innocent Muggles in the air at the Quidditch World Cup.

Back to Reality

Briefly, what applications for our world are suggested by Rowling's ethics of magic? Much should be clear from the preceding paragraphs. The powers made available to us by applied science are great, but intoxicating ones. All of them involve, to some extent, the manipulation of the world, and some of them carry this manipulation to the point of complete domination. The attitude one is driven to adopt, by availing oneself of the more dominating powers, is a bad attitude, one dangerous to oneself, one's community, and anyone or anything else that happens to be in one's path. What is required in the face of these facts is a willingness on the part of communities, whether political or civil, to consider which powers to permit to themselves, and to rule at least some entirely off-limits. This is not merely a matter of ruling out bad "uses" of essentially neutral powers. The Unforgivable Curses aren't simply hurtful uses of essentially neutral powers. They are bad spells. The basic implications of Rowling's ethic contrast sharply with the conventional piety that "technologies are neutral between our possible uses of them, and what we must do is use them well; no kind of power should be rejected by people outright." Here's one example to chew on: selecting the sex of one's children to suit one's preferences, a power that one may not be able to use without construing one's children to some extent as consumer goods.

Rowling's ethic suggests the importance of limiting oneself, not just to "good application," but to the use of certain kinds of powers over against others, based primarily on the attitude toward the world that these powers encourage. From such a

---

[6] Consider the connection, in Amish thought and practice, between technological restraint and a commitment to nonviolence, even when this commitment means martyrdom.

willingness on the part of individuals ought naturally to flow a variety of self-imposed restrictions adopted by entire communities. Such self-restrictions will be part of the fabric of carefully structured educational programs, ones that include as a central component "technology education." This is not technology education as commonly practiced: teaching children how to use computers. Most of them know more about that than their elders do, anyway. Rather, the required education is an education in the ways computers (and other technologies) encourage us to think about and treat our surroundings, and in how to make choices among possible uses of them. What is required is an education in how our "special powers" use us. Most of all, what is required is a communal commitment to the principle that there are fates worse than inconvenience, indeed fates worse than suffering or death. Whether we meet these fates is in part a matter of whether we learn to discriminate among our "special powers" and, sometimes, to say "no." We have J.K. Rowling to thank for reminding us of that.

7

The Mirror of Erised: Why We Should Heed Dumbledore's Warning

SHAWN E. KLEIN

What is your deepest desire? Maybe you know it and are actively working towards satisfying it. Or perhaps you don't know what it is or find your desire to be like the Golden Snitch—fleeting and impossible to pin down. Maybe you think you know, but are mistaken and, in fact, it would surprise, even shock you to discover what you truly desired the most. While introspection or psychotherapy might allow Muggles to discover their desires, Harry Potter has an easier way. He can just look in the mirror.

The Mirror of Erised

In *Sorcerer's Stone*, Harry accidentally discovers the Mirror of Erised in an unused classroom at Hogwarts. He immediately notices the Mirror's odd inscription: "Erised stra ehru oyt ube cafru oyt on wohsi" (SS, p. 207). This is no ordinary mirror—little surprise in a world where cars can fly and portraits talk. When Harry looks into it he does not see his own reflection, but instead the images of his mother and father smiling back at him, even waving! He immediately looks around the room, but his parents are not there; they're only in the Mirror. Harry, of course, is an orphan whose parents were murdered by Voldemort when Harry was just an infant. So seeing them in the Mirror fills him with joy—albeit a joy mixed with sadness (SS, p. 209).

Although Harry has no idea what the powers of this unusual Mirror are, he continues to sneak out to visit it—even bringing

Ron to see it. On his third visit, Dumbledore is waiting for Harry at the Mirror, and he reveals its secret to him. The Mirror, he tells Harry, "shows us nothing more or less than the deepest, most desperate desire of our hearts" (SS, p. 213). It shows Ron what he always desired: to be out from his older brothers' shadows and to outshine them all. It shows Harry what he desired more than anything: his own parents. This makes sense of the otherwise inscrutable inscription, for written backwards with rearranged spacing it reads, "I show not your face but your heart's desire."

Dumbledore's Warning

After Dumbledore reveals to Harry what the powers of the Mirror of Erised are, he tells him:

> This mirror will give us neither knowledge or [sic] truth. Men have wasted away before it, entranced by what they have seen, or been driven mad, not knowing if what it shows is real or even possible. (SS, p. 213)

He goes on to warn Harry that "it doesn't do to dwell on dreams and forget to live" (SS, p. 214). Dumbledore tells Harry that the Mirror will be moved and that Harry shouldn't go looking for it again.

Going mad and wasting away are prospects about as attractive as a Dementor's kiss, but why would such a Mirror produce such outcomes? Why doesn't the Mirror offer knowledge or truth? Lastly, why should we heed Dumbledore's warning that it is wrong to dwell on dreams?

Knowledge and Truth

Dumbledore hints that users of the Mirror can confuse its images with reality. This problem is an example of the traditional distinction between appearance and reality that, in Bertrand Russell's words, is "one of the distinctions that cause most trouble in philosophy."[1] At the center of this distinction is a concern, one Dumbledore seems to share, about mere

---

[1] Bertrand Russell, *The Problems of Philosophy* (New York: Dover, 1999), p. 2.

appearances preventing us from acquiring knowledge. What, then, is knowledge? Philosophers normally take knowledge to be some belief about the world that we have good evidence for and which is true. If we claim that "Sirius betrayed James and Lily Potter" but later discover this not to be the case, we don't think this claim counts as knowledge—even though we believed it on good evidence—precisely because it is not true. For a claim to be knowledge it must be true.

This, naturally, raises the issue of what it means for something to be true. While philosophers have debated for millennia what the full, proper account of truth is, many have said that a true claim is one that corresponds or matches up with external reality—the correspondence theory of truth. If Harry claims that Sirius is an Animagus, then this claim is true only if Sirius can actually turn into a dog or some other animal. Many have added to this view that a true claim must also fit well or cohere with the rest of our beliefs. Some philosophers have gone further, arguing that this coherence is not just a component of why a claim is true, but is by itself enough to show that a claim is true. However, a claim might fit well with our other beliefs without providing an accurate account of reality. For instance, before Harry discovers the truth about Sirius, the belief that Sirius betrayed Harry's parents coheres well with Harry's other beliefs—but he soon finds out this claim is false. Still, coherence does seem to be an important component of recognizing the truth of a claim. So, Harry's claim about Sirius being an Animagus, if true, should fit well with his other beliefs: that there are such things as Animagi, that there's been a black dog following him around, that Lupin and Harry's father were also Animagi, and so on.

A third account—newest on the scene—is the pragmatic account of truth. Developed by C.S. Peirce, William James, and others, this view looks to the usefulness of a claim. Truth, on this view, is tied to the observable outcomes we get when we apply our beliefs. So, the claim that Sirius is an Animagus would be true because Harry can act on this belief by seeking out the black dog that Sirius has transformed into and successfully find Sirius. Like the coherence account, the pragmatic account points to an important component of truth—true beliefs should be useful in some way and have some observable consequence—but it fails to account for truth on its own. A belief, though false, might still be useful or have an observable outcome. For example, while Harry believes Sirius to be dangerous, this belief is useful. It also is confirmed by Harry's experience up until he discovers the truth in the Shrieking Shack.

We can see why this distinction between reality and appearance has caused such trouble. If it is possible for us to mistake the images in the Mirror for the way things really are—or at least be tempted to dwell on these images of our fulfilled desires as a substitute for reality—then aren't we in danger of confusing appearance for reality and thus failing to gain knowledge? Something that is a mere appearance and not real still might cohere well with other beliefs, but because it is only a mere appearance it won't correspond to reality. And so, mere appearance wouldn't be true, and wouldn't be knowledge. This is why Dumbledore warns Harry that the Mirror cannot give knowledge or truth. Our knowledge is a true account of the way the world is. If we fail to identify the actual features of the world and instead dwell on mere appearances, then we fail to find knowledge or truth.

Descartes's Dreams

Philosophers from Plato forward have worried about this problem of being able to distinguish appearance from reality. One such philosopher who attempted to give an account of knowledge was the seventeenth-century French philosopher René Descartes. One of Descartes's main concerns was to give an account of knowledge that wouldn't fall prey to skepticism—the view that we do not and cannot have knowledge. In his *Meditations on First Philosophy*, Descartes temporarily adopts the stance of the hard-core skeptic in order to defeat skepticism.[2]

Just like a good skeptic, Descartes rejects all his beliefs and opinions if there is *any* reason at all to doubt them. The reason to doubt could be quite far-fetched—Descartes even imagines an Evil Demon who has the power to deceive someone into thinking false things about matters we thought were certain,

---

[2] This makes Descartes merely a methodological skeptic rather than a substantive skeptic, who really thinks there is nothing to know or that we are incapable of knowing it.

such as mathematics. This Demon could, for instance, make someone believe that 2 + 2 = 5 or that a triangle has four angles. Thus, Descartes even doubts his mathematical beliefs. In doubting so thoroughly and extensively, he is looking for some belief or idea that is incapable of being doubted. If he can find such a belief—one without any possibility of being false—Descartes will have shown the skeptic to be wrong. We would know something not open to any doubt and we will have avoided mere appearance by discovering a true claim about reality. By raising the standard of knowledge to the highest degree—absolute certainty—Descartes thinks he can discover the foundation of knowledge in the face of challenges posed by skepticism and the appearance-reality dichotomy.

Descartes thought that because of the apparent deception of senses, reality could not be accessed through them. Descartes writes, "I noticed that the senses are sometimes deceptive and it is a mark of prudence never to place our complete trust in those who have deceived us even once."[3] If Descartes is right about these deceptions, then they are potentially mere appearances, and not reality.

Dreams also raise the concern about the appearance-reality dichotomy for Descartes. Often while dreaming, we are totally convinced of our dream's reality. As Descartes says, "there are no definitive signs by which to distinguish being awake from being asleep."[4] We thus might often mistake our dreams for reality. Yet, we know that dreams are just mere appearances and cannot be an awareness of reality; and therefore, cannot give us knowledge. Moreover, even if we can actually distinguish being awake from dreaming while we are awake, there is still the concern that we might confuse the appearances in our dreams for reality and fail to acquire knowledge.[5]

Descartes's method eventually leads him to claim that the foundation of knowledge is knowledge of his own existence. This is his famous *cogito ergo sum*: I think, therefore, I exist. Descartes argues that we cannot be deceived in this idea; it cannot be a mere appearance that I exist. It is "necessarily true

---

[3] René Descartes, *Meditations on First Philosophy* (Indianapolis: Hackett, 1993), p. 14.
[4] *Ibid.*
[5] Aristotle, *On Dreams,* 462a.

every time I utter it or conceive it in my mind."[6] To be deceived or to see a mere appearance, I must first exist. Descartes thereby thought he had found the basis for knowledge exempt from any risk of error.

Whether or not we fully agree with Descartes's account, we can agree that there is a real concern raised by this account that some of our experiences—for example, dreams and hallucinations—might be confused for an authentic awareness of reality.[7] However, such experiences cannot give us knowledge because knowledge is about reality, not mere appearances or delusions. And while we might not get or need the absolute certainty that Descartes is looking for, we should still be concerned that what we claim to know is truly knowledge of reality. This is the heart of Dumbledore's warning about the Mirror of Erised. Like a dream, the Mirror will not offer us an awareness of reality, but only mere appearance, preventing us from gaining knowledge or truth.

The Experience Machine

The late American philosopher Robert Nozick provides another way in which to examine Dumbledore's warning not to waste away dreaming in the Mirror. Nozick asks us to consider a kind of virtual reality machine—the Experience Machine—that allows us to experience whatever kind of life we choose.[8] The Machine provides us with realistic, lifelike, and absolutely convincing experiences. One might program it to offer the experience of being the world's greatest Quidditch player, Wizard Chess Champion, or the Defense against the Dark Arts professor at Hogwarts. The Experience Machine can simulate whatever sort of experience we want, even program realistic and convincing images of and interactions with whatever significant others we

---

[6] Descartes, *Meditations*, p. 18.

[7] See David Kelley, *The Evidence of the Senses* (Baton Rouge: Louisiana State University Press, 1986); Ayn Rand, *Introduction to Objectivist Epistemology* (New York: Meridian, 1990); and John Locke, *An Essay concerning Human Understanding* (Oxford: Clarendon, 1979), Book IV, Chapter XI for arguments critical of Descartes's account of sense-perception, dreams, and knowledge.

[8] Robert Nozick, *Anarchy, State, and Utopia* (New York: Basic Books, 1974), p. 43.

might desire. Moreover, while in the machine we wouldn't know we were in it, so we would not regret leaving others behind or realize that the experiences were not authentic.

Whatever experiences we choose, the Machine would replicate precisely how these would feel "from the inside."[9] If we choose to fly in an enchanted car, we would feel the effects of gravity, the acceleration forces, and see the open expanse of endless sky. The Machine would stimulate our brains in a way that makes us think and feel as if we are flying a car, a broomstick, or an airplane—if conventional Muggle transportation more suits our fancy.

To Plug In . . .

Nozick asks us whether or not we should be willing to plug into the Experience Machine. Many of us would probably choose to do so for recreational and entertainment purposes—much like one might use the Holodeck in *Star Trek*.[10] What Nozick invites us to consider, however, is not whether we would use the Machine for some temporary fun, but whether we would and should be willing to plug into it as a replacement for life? Would we, like Cypher in *The Matrix*[11] or Reginal Barclay in *Star Trek*,[12] actually choose the Experience Machine over real life? If our lives were bad enough, we probably would, understandably enough. Why not enjoy a pleasurable simulated reality rather than suffer a long, painful death from cancer? Moreover, if we give more weight to what William James called "psychological reality" (as opposed to "metaphysical reality"), we would probably enter the Experience Machine. James characterized such reality as meaning "simply relation to our emotional and active life. . . . Whatever excites and stimulates our interest is real."[13]

---

[9] *Ibid.*, p. 42.

[10] Star Trek's Holodeck is kind of Experience Machine that provides entertainment and training opportunities for crews on long space voyages.

[11] See William Irwin, ed., *The Matrix and Philosophy* (Chicago: Open Court, 2002). In particular, "Skepticism, Morality, and *The Matrix*" by Gerald J. Erion and Barry Smith.

[12] *Star Trek: The Next Generation*, Episode 69, "Hollow Pursuits."

[13] William James, *The Principles of Psychology* (Cambridge, Massachusetts: Harvard University Press, 1981), p. 924.

After all, our "friends" in the Experience Machine will seem to treat us just the way we would like our friends to treat us. Our "relationships" would be fulfilling and satisfying to the greatest degree given our self-imposed amnesia about our true situation. So what practical difference is there, if any, between a life in the Experience Machine and one outside of it? If we go to our graves without being the wiser, what was lost?

. . . Or Not to Plug In

Contrary to this view, however, there do seem to be some compelling reasons not to hook ourselves up to the Machine. The most general reason might be that, like our concern in Descartes's example of dreams, our experience would not be an authentic one. Such a life is a life of appearance and not reality; and moreover, "we want to connect with what is actually the case."[14] Not coincidentally, those who do choose to plug in to these kinds of simulations are generally viewed as making a serious mistake (Cypher in *The Matrix*) or as being sick (Barclay is diagnosed with "Holo-addiction"). To see how the Experience Machine relates to Dumbledore's warning, let's look at some of the reasons Nozick gives for not plugging in.

Doing Certain Things

One reason that Nozick cites for why we shouldn't opt for the Experience Machine is that "we want to *do* certain things, and not just have the experience of doing them."[15] Living our lives— not just dreaming or thinking about that life—is vitally important. A deeply authentic life is something that must be actively lived. No matter how realistic a Quidditch simulator might be, Harry wants to fly a real broom through a real sky and not just think he's experiencing flying through a sky.

A distinction between two kinds of knowledge might be helpful here. One kind of knowledge involves experientially coming to know something or someone intimately and deeply,

---

[14] Robert Nozick, *Invariances* (Cambridge, Massachusetts: Harvard University Press, 2001), p. 299.
[15] Robert Nozick, *Anarchy, State, and Utopia* (New York: Basic Books, 1974), p. 43.

whereas another kind of knowledge involves coming to know propositions *about* that thing or person. Hermione could have read all the books available on Hogwarts and know a great number of facts about Hogwarts, but without attending the school, she would be missing the important, experiential knowledge of actually sitting in Snape's classroom, avoiding Peeves, and conversing with Nearly Headless Nick. No matter how convincing Nozick's Experience Machine is, it could never really offer us the genuine opportunity to know in the deeper sense any experience or, for that matter, any other real person. The Machine doesn't provide us with reliable evidence for our beliefs nor can we tell if our beliefs correspond to reality. All it offers us is appearance and not awareness of reality, and so like a dream, it precludes the kind of knowledge we seek.

Moreover, if being virtuous and pursuing values is important—that is, essential for living and flourishing—then it is better that Harry actually be honest or actually have integrity than just to *think* he is honest or has integrity. And it is better that Hermione actually be successful in the pursuit of her values than merely to think she has achieved her values. Likewise, it seems obvious that it is better to cast a defensive spell after one is attacked by a Death Eater than to merely think one has. So, it is not just that we want to do things; we need to do certain things in order to live and flourish. The Experience Machine dangerously cuts us off from actually doing anything. All we experience is how things feel from the inside; we aren't actually doing what we want and need to do. The Mirror of Erised, similarly, also seems to cut us off. Ron could watch himself win the Quidditch Cup, but he doesn't just want to watch this happen, but do it himself.

Being a Certain Way

Nozick offers another reason why we should not plug into the Experience Machine. He says "we want to *be* a certain way, to be a certain sort of person."[16] For example, Hermione wants to be smart, wants to get good grades, and to know all there is to know about wizardry. She wants to *be* this kind of person—not just *think* that she is this kind of person. When Ron looks into

---

[16] *Ibid.*

the Mirror, he is excited to see himself as Head Boy. But Ron wants to *be* Head Boy. He doesn't wish for some image in the Mirror to be Head Boy, but for he himself to be Head Boy. Harry, similarly, wants to be with his parents—not be with some images of them.

Even if the Mirror were a true Experience Machine and gave Harry or Ron an absolutely convincing and all-encompassing experience, we would arrive at the same problem. Nozick tells us that there "is no answer to the question of what a person is like who has long been in" the Experience Machine.[17] If Harry were plugged into a true Experience Machine, and while in it had the experience of becoming a world-famous Auror for the Ministry of Magic, catching Voldemort and his followers, we cannot ask if Harry would be a good person for doing these. Harry *isn't* doing them and so the question makes little sense. Once again, we see that for experiences to be authentic, they need to be based on an actual connection to reality and not mere appearances.

Another useful distinction that philosophers make is between being and becoming. We can *be* a certain way, as in being a Quidditch player. We can also be engaged in an activity or process of *becoming* a certain way, as Ron is as he learns to be a better Keeper in *Order of the Phoenix*. We can further recognize that part of being a certain way requires that we become that way through some process. An interesting example of this is seen in *Order of the Phoenix* when Harry views his father as a student at Hogwarts through Professor Snape's Pensieve—a magical device that can store one's memories. Having always thought of his father as an admirable and moral person, Harry is shocked and disappointed to see a young James Potter cruelly teasing and bullying a young Snape. Later on, Sirius tells Harry that his father was "a good person. A lot of people are idiots at the age of fifteen. He grew out it" (OP, p. 671). James Potter, like all of us, needed to become the good person he was. He couldn't just be instantly good; he had to grow up and work at becoming good. Moral maturity requires a process.

This view is somewhat like Aristotle's view that *eudaimonia*—or long-term, deep happiness or flourishing—is something

---

[17] *Ibid.*

that should be classed as an activity.[18] To be happy, in Aristotle's sense, requires that one be engaged in the kinds of activities in which a rational animal should be engaged. Being good isn't just something someone is, it is something that one must become and be in the process of constantly and consistently becoming. If we ignore the *becoming* of life—by spending it dreaming away at the Mirror or in the Experience Machine—we can never be the kind of person we want to be. We can't *become* in the Experience Machine (or the Mirror) because while in the Machine we are just feeling and experiencing, not actually developing our moral character or engaging in any activities.

Back to the Mirror

The Mirror of Erised raises similar authenticity problems for Harry as the Experience Machine does for us. Until Dumbledore reveals to Harry the misleading nature of the Mirror and warns him of its false allure, Harry probably believes that the image of his parents is more than an illusion. What makes the experience so meaningful to Harry is that he thinks he is actually seeing his parents and not just images of them. Finding out that the projection of his parents isn't real will obviously dampen his enthusiasm for visiting it. One suspects he'll still be interested, but probably only in the way he might look at old photographs. Much of the passion and excitement would be gone, and rightly so. The joy he felt that first night would likely succumb to the nostalgic sadness one feels while looking through an old yearbook. There's a huge difference in value attached to the experience depending on whether it's an experience of reality or not. Harry might enjoy a recurring dream he might have, say of leaving the Dursleys for good, but he would not value that dream nearly as much as actually being able to do it. Truth, knowledge, and the important values of real relationships and authentic living are worth fighting for and being passionate about; appearances and deceptions, inauthentic relationships, and merely simulated living are not.

---

[18] Aristotle, *The Nicomachean Ethics* (Oxford: Oxford University Press, 1998), Book 10, Chapter 6.

Heeding Dumbledore's Warning

So, while the Mirror of Erised is not exactly an Experience Machine, both fail, in similar ways, to meet our fundamental need for a real connection between ourselves and the world. Nozick sums this up by saying we want "to live (an active verb) ourselves, in contact with reality."[19] In the Experience Machine, one is not in contact with reality but with the output of the Machine. The same applies to the Mirror of Erised. We are not in contact with reality; instead, we are connected to images. We cannot have a meaningful relationship with a real person—all we can have is an image of such a relationship shown to us. We cannot discover the fundamental truths about the world—all we will get is an image of the discovery. The Mirror and the Machine, like dreams, might give us some enjoyable or pleasurable experiences, but also like dreams, they don't connect us to reality. This lack of causal connection between the experiences and the world makes them inauthentic—and shows us why Dumbledore is right to warn Harry not to dwell on dreams and the images in the Mirror.

Still, the Mirror does offer us one truth—it shows us what we actually deeply and desperately desire. While our lives shouldn't be spent just in desire-satisfaction—as the Mirror of Erised illustrates for us—we do have desires that are worthwhile to pursue and satisfy. For example, both the desire for a long, happy relationship and a rewarding career seem to be very important. That the Mirror can offer us some useful information about our desires doesn't weaken Dumbledore's warning. While we might be able to learn something from looking in the Mirror—perhaps something important and shocking—we cannot actually pursue or satisfy our worthwhile desires in the Mirror.

Though we might not be able to arrive at the kind of certainty that Descartes is looking for—knowledge beyond any doubt whatsoever—the Mirror of Erised and the Experience Machine remind us that there are things that we do value over other things, and rightly so. We care about having real relationships, being virtuous, and being successful in pursuit of values.

---

[19] Robert Nozick, *Anarchy, State, and Utopia* (New York: Basic Books, 1974), p. 45.

All of these require a kind of authenticity and connection to reality that the Mirror of Erised and the Experience Machine are incapable of providing. And so we are right to take Dumbledore's warning seriously and not dwell on dreams. It is a warning we should all heed; it is the warning that philosophy makes to all of us. We should pursue knowledge and truth and not linger too long in our dreams and desires while forgetting to live and authentically fulfill them.

8

Kreacher's Lament: S.P.E.W. as a Parable on Discrimination, Indifference, and Social Justice

STEVEN W. PATTERSON

There's an awful lot of discrimination in the Harry Potter series of novels. Nearly all of the time, the discrimination comes out in the behavior of characters who are unequivocally evil. Whether it is Draco Malfoy's classist hatred of the Weasleys, Voldemort's racist lust to destroy all "mudbloods," Lucius Malfoy's maltreatment of Dobby and other house-elves, or Dolores Umbridge's xenophobic disdain for Hagrid, the message is clear: discrimination is something practiced by *evil* people. Nobody we would consider *good* discriminates. But is that so? The answer to this question, I think, turns on what we think discrimination is.

In this chapter we shall explore this question by taking a closer look at the moral impact of discrimination against house-elves, and the response to that discrimination launched by Hermione: the Society for the Promotion of Elfish Welfare, S.P.E.W. for short. In the picture it offers of how discrimination can survive "below the moral radar," so to speak, of good people, the story of S.P.E.W. offers an invaluable lesson for pluralistic cultures such as our own, which yet bear the social burdens that are the legacy of discrimination. The main argument will have three parts. First, by way of general introduction, the concept of discrimination will be outlined. Having settled the question of what discrimination means, morally, we will investigate the moral basis for thinking that such discrimination is wrong. Next, we will consider the question of whether indifference to the plight of those who suffer discrimination is itself morally wrong. Finally, it will be argued that indifference to discrimination is not only a moral failing, but practically unwise as well.

Discrimination and Prejudice

Philosophers like to be careful with their words, so let us begin by noting something general about the word 'discrimination'. 'Discrimination' has both a morally loaded and a morally neutral usage. It's important to keep clear about the difference lest we fall into the error of *equivocation*—using a word with two different meanings without specifying which meaning we intend. (Equivocation is the blast-ended skrewt of philosophical mistakes. Just when things seem settled they turn up and incinerate even the most carefully crafted of arguments. The only remedy in both cases is to proceed with extreme care!)

'Discrimination' in the morally neutral sense just means, roughly, 'the ability to tell things apart'. This usage is common enough. We say, for example, that gourmets are people with *discriminating* palates, meaning that their ability to detect subtle flavors and methods of preparation in food is highly tuned. Similarly, we might say that when it comes to practical jokes, there are no more discriminating judges than the Weasley twins. Discrimination, in this sense, morally is neither here nor there. It is a purely descriptive term, hence we shall call this the *descriptive* sense.

The sense of 'discrimination' in which we are interested here, by contrast, stands in stark contrast to the descriptive usage. This sense of 'discrimination', the *moral* sense, we shall define as 'the treatment of moral equals as moral inferiors'. This sense, unlike the descriptive sense, *isn't* morally neutral. We can see the difference quite easily. If we say that someone has a discriminating character, and we are using the word in the descriptive sense, then we have made no judgments about his character. By contrast, if we are using the word in the moral sense, then we have made a rather strong negative comment about his character. But what, exactly, will we have said?

What Is Wrong with Prejudice?

In order to answer the question just posed, we shall first need to answer another. What is wrong with prejudice, precisely? The most ready-to-hand account is that prejudice is wrong simply because no one deserves to be treated that way. In short, prejudice is wrong simply because *everyone is deserving of basic moral respect*, and basic moral respect is incompatible with any form of prejudice. This sort of argument is a popular one today, but its roots are very old, lying in the moral philosophy of that illustrious Enlightenment thinker, Immanuel Kant. Kant believed that all rational beings, Muggles or otherwise, are entitled to basic moral equality simply on the basis that they are rational and have a will of their own. He expressed this idea in a form he called the Categorical Imperative: *One should always act so as to treat humanity, whether in one's own person or in that of another, as an end in itself and never as a mere means.*[1] Now what Kant meant was that every rational being has a will of its own, and therefore the innate freedom to choose its own acts as well as its larger commitments in life. It is wrong to deprive persons of that freedom by forcing them to serve not their own interests, but the interests of someone else. In fact, Kant believed, it is not merely wrong, it's *irrational*.

It is irrational to treat a person as a mere means and not as an end in themselves (as a fully rational and autonomous being with a full complement of moral rights) because the moral permissibility of an act depends upon its being the kind of act that one would allow anyone to do. Kant's word for this kind of act is 'universalizable'. If an act is universalizable, then it is permissible. As it turns out, acts which are impermissible are acts which are not universalizable without contradiction. All of this seems more complicated than it actually is. The following example should demonstrate how Kant's moral philosophy works.

Suppose Malfoy wants to sabotage Neville's cauldron in potions class, so that Snape will throw Neville out of class in a frustrated rage. Kant would say that Malfoy's plan embodies the following policy: *It is morally permissible to sabotage the cauldrons of people I don't like for my own amusement.* Kant would next consider whether this is the sort of act that one would be willing to allow anyone to do whenever they wanted—whether it is universalizable. So, to do the test we imagine what things would be like if the act were always allowed. We begin by

---

[1] Immanuel Kant, *Groundwork for the Metaphysics of Morals* (Indianapolis: Hackett, 1993), p. 36.

rewriting the policy in Malfoy's act of cauldron sabotage to reflect this: *It is morally permissible for* **anyone** *to sabotage the cauldrons of people they don't like for their own amusement.* Now, we ask ourselves, what would the world be like if this were the policy for everyone? There would be a lot of failed potions, no doubt, but the consequences aren't the issue. The issue, Kant would tell us, is that if we agree to this policy, then we are agreeing, in theory, to *others'* acts of sabotage of *our* cauldrons for *their* personal amusement. In other words, we would be agreeing to be treated as a *mere means* (not as a fully rational being but as an instrument) to the end of *others'* amusement! Clearly we wouldn't allow this in our own case, since the categorical imperative requires us never to treat humanity, be it in our own persons or that of others, as a mere means. The result is that we cannot affirm Malfoy's cauldron sabotage rule without committing ourselves to a contradiction.

Malfoy's likely response would demonstrate this nicely. If we told him everything we now know about Kant's ethics he would very likely say, "That's not what I want!! I want to upset Neville's cauldron! And no one had better upset mine!" In effect, then, Malfoy would be agreeing to a rule which allows people to be treated as mere means, while at the same time claiming an exception for himself. What he would fail to see is that rules that apply to humanity as a whole are all-or-nothing proposals. Someone who tries to make an exception of his own case is thus guilty of a contradiction. He affirms that the rule does not apply to himself, but that it does apply to everyone else, but since he is as human as everyone else, he ends up believing both that the rule applies and does not apply. Hence he winds up in a contradiction, and as any sensible person knows, it is clearly irrational to believe a contradiction.

If Kant is right, then, we have two good reasons to think that prejudice is wrong. It is wrong in the first place because it violates the humanity of those who suffer it. Secondly, it is wrong because no one could rationally agree to a rule that allowed prejudiced behavior. For such rules violate the categorical imperative, and as Malfoy's mistake shows, this leads to a contradiction. Hence prejudice isn't just immoral, it is irrational. It's plain bad business all the way 'round. So now that we may know why prejudice is wrong, we should be able to take up the question of whether *indifference* to prejudice is wrong. The case of Hermione's attempt to rescue Dobby and the other house-elves from servitude will help show that it is.

Why S.P.E.W. Doesn't Work

We first become acquainted with the house-elves in *Chamber of Secrets*, when Lucius Malfoy's house-elf, Dobby, comes to warn Harry of coming dangers at Hogwarts. Dobby appears wearing a ripped pillowcase for clothing (house-elves in bondage are not permitted to wear real clothing), alternating between delivering his warning and attempting to punish himself for delivering it against what he knows to be the wishes of his master (CS, pp. 12–20). It is one year after Dobby receives his freedom as a result of a clever trick on Harry's part that we see the emergence of Hermione's "Society for the Promotion of Elfish Welfare" (hereinafter, S.P.E.W.) in *Goblet of Fire*. S.P.E.W.'s stated aims include "to secure house-elves fair wages and working conditions" as well as, in the long run, to change "the law about non-wand use, and trying to get an elf into the Department for the Regulation and Control of Magical Creatures" (GF, p. 224). These sound like noble goals, but strangely, they don't catch on. Ron's first reaction to them is instructive: "Hermione," he says, "open your ears. They. Like. It. They *like* being enslaved" (GF, p. 224). We learn not too much later that this sentiment is widespread, hampering S.P.E.W.'s efforts to gain momentum among the student body of Hogwarts.

Although they are fictitious, house-elves, it would seem, exhibit all the signs of having a will of their own. Dobby visits Harry to deliver his warning against the wishes of his master, knowing that doing so can bring him death. Dobby's sister Winky suffers banishment from her house in order to protect her master, and eschews wages out of a sense of pride while working at Hogwarts (GF, p. 376). The other house-elves shun Dobby after his independence (GF, p. 378). Even the pathetic Kreacher, servant of the household of Sirius Black, shows free will in his attempts to resist Sirius's efforts to rid his mother's house of the artifacts of her allegiance with the Death Eaters (OP, pp. 109–110). Thus we can say that house-elves "count" as the sort of rational, autonomous beings that matter in Kant's ethics. If house-elves were real, then we would owe to them every moral protection that we would owe to other human beings, because like us, they have the ability to reason. Once we see this, it becomes clear that from a moral point of view, the enslavement of such beings is morally wrong.

What then do we say about the indifference to the plight of the house-elves shown by Ron, and to a lesser extent, by Harry and the rest of Hogwarts (with the very notable exception of Dumbledore)? Are Harry and Ron prejudiced too? If so, then it would seem to suggest that even people who are otherwise good can be prejudiced (without, it seems, even being aware that they are). This would (and probably should) create a certain amount of tension. We are led to believe that only evil people like the Malfoys, Voldemort, and Umbridge are prejudiced. Ron and Harry, by contrast, are supposed to be good, and if they end up being prejudiced too, then we will either have to recognize a certain moral tarnish on our heroes or we shall have to revise our image of discrimination as something practiced only by evil people. The tension can be resolved if the following question can be answered: If the enslavement of house-elves is immoral, is it also immoral for others to sit idly by and do nothing to end their servitude? If we can answer this question negatively, then Ron and Harry will have a defense. If not, we shall have to revise our idea of prejudice slightly.

There are at least three arguments that indifference is permitted, despite the obvious immorality of house-elf enslavement. The first goes like this: As bad things go, the enslavement of the house-elves is not that bad. Some house-elves suffer terrible conditions, sure, but not all do. Some, perhaps many, are as well cared for as those under the kitchen of Hogwarts. It's not as if they're all going to die if nothing is done. Surely in a perfect world there would be no house-elf slavery, but this isn't a perfect world and there are bigger fish to fry, so to speak, what with Death Eaters running loose and such. So we have to keep our moral priorities straight. House-elf slavery is nearer to the bottom of the list of wrongs to right.

Secondly, it's true that the house-elf enslavement is a bad thing, but just because it is a bad thing doesn't mean that others have a duty to prevent it. After all, it's unreasonable to hold everyone to a duty to make the world a perfect place. People have to live their lives and can't go around crusading all the time. We have no more of a moral duty to prevent house-elf slavery than we do a duty to see that no one ever dies of heat exhaustion, or gets the flu. We must face the fact that there are some unpleasant features of life that we have to live with. It is simply too much to ask of people to require such altruism as would be needed to remedy such pervasive unpleasantness.

Thirdly, there is Ron's argument. House-elves seem to *want* to be enslaved. Winky, for example, is positively *devastated* by her freedom, ultimately turning to drink and becoming absolutely useless outside of the system of slavery. If house-elves want to be enslaved, then where do we get off freeing them? They have a will of their own and they could exercise it to live differently if they so chose. Certainly they would ask for their freedom if they wanted it, but they don't want it. We know this because they never ask for their freedom. Since they have a will of their own and don't want to be free, it is wrong of us to force them to be free against their will. Just because Dobby seems to enjoy his freedom doesn't mean any other elf will, and it is just wrong to assume otherwise, no matter how good our intentions might be. We have a duty to respect their autonomy and not to interfere with their servitude.

Now it's important to understand what each of these arguments claims. The first claims that although we have a duty to help the house-elves, that duty is weak and is outweighed by more pressing concerns. The second argument claims that we have no duty either way to help the house-elves, and the third claims that we have a duty *not* to "help" them. Any of these arguments, if successful, would give reason for thinking that indifference to the plight of the house-elves is morally permissible. As we shall see, however, each of these arguments fails. We shall begin with the last argument first.

Ron argues that house-elves do, in fact, want to be slaves. But given that they are rational creatures, how could that be? There is a phenomenon that could explain the apparent desire of the elves for slavery consistently with their rationality. This phenomenon has been observed to happen in the case of groups that suffer extended periods of prejudice. Over time, the self-image of these groups comes to resemble the image of them held by those that keep them in bondage, and the resulting lack of self-respect does more than any chain to maintain their state. This phenomenon has been noted among African Americans at least since W. E. B. DuBois's watershed 1903 work, *The Souls of Black Folk.* The African American, DuBois says:

> is a sort of seventh son, born with a veil, and gifted with second-sight in this American world, —a world which yields him no true self-consciousness, but only lets him see himself through the revelation of the other world. It is a peculiar sensation, this double-consciousness, this sense of always looking at one's self through the eyes of others. . . . One ever feels his two-ness . . .[2]

Commenting on what he takes to be its occurrence among African Americans in their struggle to outgrow the legacy of institutional prejudice of the early to mid-twentieth century, philosopher Cornel West echoes DuBois when he observes, "The uncritical acceptance of self-degrading ideals that call into question black intelligence, possibility, and beauty not only compounds black social misery but also paralyzes black middle class efforts"[3] at reform. West's point is that the efforts of black Americans to improve their lot is hampered by the task of overcoming the stereotypes not merely thrust on them by racists, but actually internalized over many decades of enslavement and second-class citizenship.

The observations of West and DuBois help us understand why, as Ron observes, the house-elves don't seem to want to be free. Judged only on the basis of appearances, Ron's observation is right. His mistake is to infer from this that there is no duty to free them, let alone a duty *not* to free them. On the contrary, their resistance to their freedom is an indication not of the depths of their hearts' desire, but of the depth of their bondage. So the first argument fails.

But perhaps the second argument holds. On this argument there is agreement that the house-elves' enslavement is a bad thing, yet disagreement that it is bad enough to create a duty on our part to do anything about it. After all, so many bad things happen that we cannot seriously be expected to prevent them

---

[2] W.E.B. Du Bois, *The Souls of Black Folk* (New York: Dover, 1994), p. 2.

[3] Cornel West, *Race Matters* (New York: Vintage, 1993), p. 98.

[4] For the general character of the reply to this argument I am relying on a portion of Simon Blackburn's very lucid reply to a similar objection in his *Being Good* (Oxford: Oxford University Press, 2001), pp. 48–49.

all. No sensible morality could require so much. The reply to this argument is twofold.[4]

First, we may note that while this reply might be sensible with respect to large-scale evils that cannot be prevented, there is something a little disingenuous about applying it to problems for which human beings are not only responsible but which are susceptible to correction. The house-elves, one could point out, were not always enslaved. The statue of the races in the Ministry of Magic is evidence that, nominally at least, house-elves were accorded equal status in the past (OP, p. 127). Thus it isn't so easy for the wizarding world to wash its hands of the matter. Secondly, it must be emphasized that requiring that something be done about the enslavement of the house-elves is not the same thing as requiring that everyone become a moral saint. The claim that the house-elves are entitled to their freedom doesn't require perfect altruism, it simply requires that house-elves be freed, and there's plenty of room between the two. Certainly there is sufficient room for the claim that there is a duty to free the house-elves. Careful attention to the claim made on behalf of those suffering the effects of prejudice and slavery should defeat this argument.

This brings us to the last, and perhaps the most persuasive, of the three arguments. This argument is most persuasive because it acknowledges all the important features of the elves' claim to freedom from slavery. It acknowledges the slavery as an evil, and that there is a duty (ultimately) to end the slavery. What it claims is that the end of house-elf freedom isn't as important or as pressing as are other claims, such as those arising out of the need to fight the Death Eaters. This stage of our hypothetical argument presents us with a choice: given limited social resources do we strive for social justice or work for the more pressing demands of security? The reply to this argument is that, in the final analysis, social justice *is* a matter of security. The final section of this chapter will be devoted to explaining why.

Indifference, Security, and Social Justice

The third argument for overlooking indifference to the plight of the house-elves is the strongest of the three considered. In essence, this argument confronts us with a dilemma. Are valuable time and resources to be spent fighting prejudice when far greater evils are loose in the world, or should the greater portion of our efforts be focused on the eradication of the worst, most threatening evils? To put it in terms of our running example, should Harry and Ron be spending their time freeing house-elves who resist freedom, or should they be fighting Voldemort and the Death Eaters instead? The question is difficult, and an answer can only be outlined here, but what I want to suggest is that the choice between dealing with overt threats and struggling for social justice is, in fact, something of a false dilemma, and that the struggle for social justice is in fact just another front in the struggle against the greater evils in the world.

We see this in no uncertain terms with respect to the house-elves. In *Order of the Phoenix*, it is the corrupt house-elf Kreacher who delivers Harry's godfather, Sirius Black, to his ultimate demise. After the battle's end, when Dumbledore and Harry are discussing this sad turn of affairs, Harry blames Kreacher for his complicity in Sirius's death. Dumbledore rebuffs him, saying:

> I warned Sirius when we adopted twelve Grimmauld Place as our headquarters that Kreacher must be treated with kindness and respect. I also told him that Kreacher could be dangerous to us. I do not think that Sirius took me very seriously, or that he ever saw Kreacher as a being with feelings as acute as a human's. . . . Kreacher is what he has been made by wizards, Harry. . . . Yes he is to be pitied. His existence has been as miserable as your friend Dobby's. He was forced to do Sirius's bidding, because Sirius was the last of the family to which he was enslaved, but he felt no true loyalty to him. And whatever Kreacher's faults, it must be admitted that Sirius did nothing to make Kreacher's lot easier. (OP, p. 832)

In this passage Dumbledore reveals quite clearly how the prejudice and maltreatment suffered by Kreacher have made him an instrument of the dark powers that ultimately killed Sirius Black. Dumbledore's speech continues, however, and it is near the end that the passage most relevant to our immediate concerns occurs.

> Sirius did not hate Kreacher. He regarded him as a servant unworthy of much interest or notice. Indifference and neglect often do much more damage than outright dislike. . . . We wizards have mis-

treated and abused our fellows for too long, and we are now reap-
ing our reward. (OP, pp. 833–34)

One important thing to see in this passage is Dumbledore's
equation of indifference and neglect with mistreatment and
abuse themselves. Another is Dumbledore's recognition that
wizard-kind is paying the price of its mistreatment of house-
elves and the other magical races in the course of their struggle
against Voldemort. So, with respect to the question of whether
Ron and Harry are wrong to be indifferent to S.P.E.W., the
answer would seem to be, in Dumbledore's eyes, *yes*. But what
about in *our* eyes? Is there a lesson for us to draw from
Dumbledore's assessment of Kreacher's role in Sirius's death?

I believe that there is, but that to see the lesson one must first
grasp an analogy that stretches back to antiquity.[5] Suppose that
society is like a human being. It has parts and divisions, systems
and subsystems, and various functions that it can perform. It can
also deliberate, set goals for itself, and change those goals.
Furthermore, it can observe and react to its environment in
response to threats. Now suppose that as health is to the human
being, so justice is to the society, and that as ill health is to the
human, so injustice is to society. The threats to both the body
and the society are numerous, are produced by many causes,
and come in many forms. Threats posed by evil men, like Death
Eaters, bank robbers, and terrorists, are to society what threats
like animals, microbes, and human enemies are to the person.
All these threats are external, and come more or less unbidden.
Prejudice and its effects, like those visited on the house-elves,
are not like this. Prejudice in all its forms is to the society something more akin to what total indifference to health is to the person. It is a form of ignorance which can weaken to the point of
death. A person who has no regard for his health might eat
spoiled foods, ignore illnesses and persistent pains, or neglect to
keep himself in the physical condition necessary for maintaining
his life. Unlike threats of the first sort, these are within the scope
of the person's control. A person who lets himself slide into ill

---

[5] The analogy permeates Plato's *Republic*, but receives its most focused treatment in Book IX. It's worth noting that the philosophical life of the analogy
between persons and societies outlasted Plato by quite some time. Thinkers as
late as Hobbes and Hegel make explicit use of it as well.

health in this way pays a price not only in terms of his overall quality of life, but in his ability to handle external threats as well. When confronted with an external threat, such a person will be much less likely to meet that threat successfully than a person who is in good health. Thus the man who neglects his health makes the job of his adversaries easier. Likewise a society that is indifferent to the effects of prejudice on its members, a society that bears the burden of a certain amount of injustice instead of trying to eliminate it, is a society which will find itself weakened in the face of its adversaries.

The upshot of this analogy is that the person who is indifferent to the injustices resulting from prejudice is a lot like the person who ignores his health. Both jeopardize their integrity unnecessarily. The situation of the person who is indifferent to the injustices of prejudice is a bit worse, though. This is because prejudice is *immoral*. Someone who is indifferent to prejudice is negligent of the good of their society at best, and at worst, they may be complicit in its downfall—just like Sirius's treatment of Kreacher makes him partially responsible for his own death.

So what about Harry and Ron? Are they wrong not to care about S.P.E.W.? Probably they are. Does this make them bad people? It's hard to say, but the intuitive position seems to be that they are good people with a kind of moral blind spot attributable to youth. Certainly we can see the moral difference between Harry and Ron's indifference and the outright hostility of Voldemort and the Malfoys. Unlike those clearly evil characters, they don't actively hate other races. Like most people, they are simply too distracted by what appear to be bigger concerns to see the connection between those concerns and social justice. For it seems to be just as Dumbledore says: "indifference and neglect often do much more damage than outright dislike." If Dumbledore is right it is because, for most of us, indifference and neglect often don't register on our moral radar until it's too late. Thus injustice is allowed to creep silently along like an undiagnosed cancer. By itself, indifference to injustice may not make one a bad person, but it surely isn't wise.

If all of the preceding is right, then the story of S.P.E.W., like so much else in the Potter novels, is worth a second thought. If we are careful, we shall be able to see that it tells us something very valuable about prejudice and injustice. It is commonly held that prejudice is wrong, and we condemn it rightly and readily when we see it overtly exercised. But the more dangerous form of prejudice, the kind that often slips in without our notice, is just as damaging, if not more so. For indifference doesn't announce itself in the ugly words or deeds of easily spotted and denounceable people. Instead, it stealthily corrodes the bonds that hold us together while hiding in plain sight under the best possible cover—our own ignorance.

Slytherin

*Knockturn Alley and
the Dark Arts*

9

Is Ambition a Virtue? Why Slytherin Belongs at Hogwarts

STEVEN W. PATTERSON

Suppose that you and three friends got together and decided to form a school of witchcraft and wizardry. You all have certain traits that you think make for good witches and wizards, so to encourage those traits in your trainees, you decide to divide your school up into four houses. All students will train under instructors from all the houses, but only one house shall be the home of each student. This system will ensure that students of like temperament and character have an opportunity to bond, form friendships, and support each other through the rigorous educational program that your school will offer. This is a fine idea, and you and your friends take up the task of drawing up the central traits you wish to encourage. Here's how the conversation might go.

You, going first, say that as you are a courageous wizard, you would like to see your house as a place to nurture young wizards and witches who are unafraid to pursue their craft, and to be at the forefront of the wizarding world as leaders and heroes. Your friend says that as she is intelligent, and finds that to be the key to sound wizarding, her house shall be home to students whose intellectual gifts set them apart as a breed unto themselves. After her comes your third friend, a hard worker by nature whose diligence in her work reflects a deeper loyalty to all that she holds dear. She, naturally, says that her house will be a haven for those whose natural gifts of courage and intelligence may be found wanting at times, but whose unswerving fidelity to the principles of good and responsible wizarding—as well as to their fellow classmates—will make them worthy to stand by the bravest and cleverest in any house. Finally, all have gone except your last friend: the brooding, sometimes scary, but undeniably talented fellow with the dark, narrow eyes and well-groomed goatee. "What kind of students will your house foster?" all ask. He smiles thinly and replies in a throaty hiss, "Give me the evil ones from old families."

Think about the above conversation for a minute. It shouldn't take long for you to see that your last friend's answer is terribly out of sync with the others. If your friend really was sincere about creating a house for evil wizards and witches, why would you and the other two want to start a school with him? Who could possibly want to take students who are already known to be evil and make them more powerful by educating them in the finest wizarding techniques available? The idea seems absurd. Nonetheless, the picture portrayed by the brief sketch given above is precisely the image many have of the Hogwarts School of Witchcraft and Wizardry. Hogwarts has four houses: Gryffindor, Ravenclaw, Hufflepuff, and Slytherin. Each house seems to be attached to a character trait that most people would consider desirable. Gryffindor's hallmark is courage, Ravenclaw's is intelligence, Hufflepuff has diligence, and Slytherin has . . . well . . . not much going for it in the way of desirability, it would seem. All the other schools are populated with characters we either love, as with the Gryffindor of Harry and his friends, or with sympathetic characters, like Cedric Diggory of Hufflepuff or Cho Chang of Ravenclaw. Slytherin, by contrast, is full of bad guys like Draco Malfoy and the baddest of them all, the evil Lord Voldemort, as well as those who if not bad, are at least mean, like Potions instructor Severus Snape. Now if we are to understand Hogwarts as basically a good place (and it certainly seems that we are), then the question that naturally arises for us is this: What is Slytherin, with its rogues' gallery of malicious students, outright villains, and generally unpleasant folk, doing at a place like Hogwarts? The answer to this question will tell us something not only about Slytherin's place in Hogwarts, but something rather worth considering about ourselves and our own society as well.

Aristotle and the Sorting Hat

Our investigation begins with the Sorting Hat scene from *Sorcerer's Stone*. This scene is the reader's first introduction to the four houses of Hogwarts, so it is appropriate for us to begin our investigation here. In this scene the first-year students are led into the Great Hall so that they may be sorted into their houses by the Sorting Hat—a ragged old wizard's hat that introduces itself in song. Roughly the last half of this song is what interests us. It runs:

> You might belong in Gryffindor,
> Where dwell the brave at heart,
> Their daring, nerve, and chivalry,
> Set Gryffindors apart;
> You might belong in Hufflepuff,
> Where they are just and loyal,
> Those patient Hufflepuffs are true
> And unafraid of toil;
> Or yet in wise old Ravenclaw,
> If you've a ready mind.
> Where those of wit and learning,
> Will always find their kind;
> Or perhaps in Slytherin
> You'll make your friends,
> Those cunning folk use any means
> To achieve their ends. (SS, p. 118)

The song plainly shows us that each house is inhabited by students with certain *traits of character*.

What are traits of character? Why are they important? One answer to these questions is provided by the ancient Greek philosopher Aristotle. Aristotle, whose reputation for greatness in the history of philosophy is rivaled only by a handful of others, develops his moral philosophy around just these concepts. According to Aristotle, traits of character are qualities of a person's soul (we might today prefer 'personality') which are revealed in their actions—particularly in the sort of actions they tend towards on the whole. Traits of character are important because they tell us about a person's *moral* qualities. Our knowledge of someone's being good or virtuous depends on our being able to observe him performing good or virtuous actions regularly enough that we could rightly call him *virtuous* or *good*. A person is virtuous—and our calling him virtuous or morally good is correct—when he meets the following three criteria:

1) He knows what is morally good and what it requires of him,

2) He chooses to do what is morally good *because* it is morally good, and

3) His morally good acts are done out of a firm disposition to act in such ways.[1]

In order to understand how this model of moral goodness works, let us consider an example from *Goblet of Fire*. The backdrop for the events of this book is the Triwizard Tournament, a wizarding competition between three great schools of witchcraft and wizardry. Harry, of course, finds himself drawn into this difficult and dangerous competition as a representative of Hogwarts. One of the challenges in the competition involves rescuing a loved one from apparent drowning at the hands of Mer-People who live at the bottom of a lake on the grounds of Hogwarts. Harry must save Ron, and he does, but while doing so he notices that the sister of Fleur Delacour, one of his fellow competitors, seems likely to go unsaved. Harry risks his life to save Fleur's sister, even though doing so is dangerous, is not required by the rules of the competition, and will likely set him back in the competition. Harry saves her anyway because he believes that if he doesn't, then no one else will (GF, p. 503). If we look at Harry's action from Aristotle's point of view, we can see that his act exhibits the virtue of bravery. Harry knows what must be done and he chooses to do it—not because it will make him a hero or because it will benefit him (at the minimum the action threatens to hurt Harry in the competition)—but because it is the right thing to do. In short, Harry saves Fleur's sister because it is what is *morally required*. Readers of the Harry

---

[1] Aristotle, *Nicomachean Ethics*, Book II, Chapter 4, in *The Basic Works of Aristotle*, ed. Richard D. McKeon (New York: Random House, 1941).

Potter novels will have no trouble at all recognizing that this is the sort of action that Harry does habitually. Thus we can see that, according to Aristotle's criteria at any rate, Harry is a brave person. He knows what he must do, he chooses it for its own sake, and does so consistently. He has, as a trait of his character, the moral quality of bravery or courage.[2]

Harry's performance in the Triwizard tournament is a good example of the virtue of courage, but this example naturally leads us to the following question: What are virtues? Surely not every habitual action is a virtue. Only the morally good ones are. So what are those? What are the character traits that a person must have in order to be considered virtuous? Aristotle's answer to this question is that virtues are qualities that display *wisdom in the conduct of life*. Aristotle argued that what sets people apart from other living things is their capacity to think, and to acquire wisdom. This unique ability of ours is what he calls our *proper function*. By this he means only that thinking is what makes us what we are; it is what we do. We are most human when we think, and we are best when we think well, and attain wisdom. Aristotle noted that we do not consider evil people wise, even when we consider them intelligent. Rather, wisdom and the virtues go hand in hand, and we may see the effects of them in a certain quality they bring to the life of the person who has them. For Aristotle believed that it is only through wisdom, including the "practical" wisdom of the virtues, that a person can achieve that form of happiness called *eudaimonia*: the sense of harmony with self and with others that arises naturally out of virtuous activity in the soul. Those who are *not* wise and *not* virtuous—no matter how intelligent they may be—cannot attain this state.

This distinction is illustrated nicely by the contrast between Albus Dumbledore and Voldemort. Both are intelligent, but of the two we could only say that Dumbledore really enjoys anything like happiness. Even in the worst of times, as when he is cornered by Ministry agents who wish to arrest him and take him off to the dread of Azkaban (OP, p. 620), and even when he is facing the Dark Lord himself (OP, p. 813), Dumbledore's

---

[2] Tom Morris's opening chapter in this book explores this issue of Harry's courage.

demeanor is even and pleasant. He smiles at his enemies as well
as his friends, and shows no sign of hatred, malice, or even mild
discontent when confronted by foes. Aristotle describes the virtuous person as having just this kind of cool and even-tempered
character.[3] Voldemort, by contrast, is probably the least happy
person in the entire series of books. His joys are fleeting and
temporary, and he is most often in a bad mood. This is because
his joy lies not in the performance of good acts, but in the performance of bad acts. He lives only for the pain of others, and
so seems himself to be in a near-constant state of agitation and
anger. Now of course these traits are important parts of his character—he wouldn't be much of a Dark Lord if he went around
smiling at everyone—and we can say the same about
Dumbledore's happiness. From a literary point of view, we are
supposed to like Dumbledore and dislike Voldemort, and so
their characters are pleasant and unpleasant, respectively. To
object on these grounds to the idea that their characters are
good illustrations of how a person's moral qualities may relate
to the type of life he has is, nevertheless, to miss an important
component of the reason why we are drawn to one and repelled
by the other in the first place. It's perhaps sensible to think that
at least part of the reason why Dumbledore's character is so
appealing is that he *does* represent that kind of ideally wise person so sadly lacking in contemporary life. At least a part of the
reason that Voldemort is so terrifying is because we see in his
character the literary reflection of the worst evil that the real
world has to offer—the evil that results when intelligence and
ability are put into the service of malicious ends.

There is one last point we must note about Aristotle's
account of the virtues. Aristotle recognized that all of our important choices in life take place in emotional contexts. What we
feel, emotionally, can have an effect on our choices, and good
choices are those in which a person gives an appropriate weight
to his emotions, neither denying them altogether, nor allowing
them to subvert his process of reasoning. A reasonable person
gives his emotions the appropriate weight, and chooses his
actions in the way which best fits his capabilities and circumstances. Aristotle believed that to be virtuous was to observe

---

[3] Aristotle, *Nicomachean Ethics*, Book III, Chapter 7.

what he called the *Doctrine of the Mean*.[4] This just means that a virtuous action is one which represents a kind of *middle course* between what would be an excessive response (one in which too much weight is given to the emotions) and what would be a deficient response (one in which too little weight is given to the emotions). In either the excessive or deficient cases, a person's acts will be out of step with his capabilities and circumstances because of his failing to deal with his emotions properly.

Once again, we can see this in the books. If we take Harry's emotions into account when thinking of his actions, we may notice that his courage isn't the absence of any feeling of fear. Rather, it is a *type of response* to the feeling of fear. As we see when Harry confronts Tom Riddle's Basilisk (CS, pp. 318–320), when he duels the dementors to save his godfather (PA, pp. 383–85), and when he faces the resurrected Voldemort for the first time (GF, pp. 662–69), Harry feels fear. But he doesn't allow his fear to master him. Neither does he ignore it and charge ahead as if he were an all-powerful wizard, heedless of any danger. Rather, remaining aware of his limitations and the disparity in power between himself and his foes, he does what he has to do to protect himself and his friends. In short, he displays the virtue of courage. With the account of virtue thus complete, we may now proceed to the question of just what Slytherin's virtue might be.

The Virtue of Slytherin House

So what is Slytherin doing at Hogwarts? It may be that Slytherins exhibit a quality not traditionally thought to be a virtue, but which suits our own time quite well. We need only recall the words of the Sorting Hat to find out what it is: "Those cunning folk use any means to achieve their ends." This suggests that Slytherins are *ambitious*. Ambition completes the quartet of moral qualities represented by the houses of Hogwarts. The suggestion that ambition is a virtue will at once strike some as doubtful. Nevertheless a little careful thought, with the help of the framework for understanding virtues that Aristotle gives us, will show that ambition *is* a virtue both in the wizarding world

---

[4] Aristotle, *Nicomachean Ethics*, Book II, Chapter 6.

of Harry Potter and in our own world as well. I shall begin by illustrating the positive effects of this virtue in the actions of one very prominent Slytherin: Professor Severus Snape.

From the very first book we find out that Snape is ambitious. One of the first things we learn about him is that he covets the position of instructor in Defense Against the Dark Arts (SS, p. 126). Later we find out that he has earned Dumbledore's trust in his capacity of double agent Death Eater (GF, p. 713)—and if that's not using cunning to achieve one's ends, it's hard to imagine what could be! Snape's persistent struggle to promote Slytherin's efforts to win the house cup throughout all of the books also reveals an ambitious side to his character. In order really to appreciate Snape's character it must be noted that Snape has other virtues as well, particularly loyalty to Dumbledore. We may not like Snape, but by the end of *Order of the Phoenix*, we have, if not a little sympathy, at least some grudging respect for this unlikely member of the Order. The lesson is an important one—people are not always what they seem, morally, to be, and sometimes people are unfairly judged by their demeanor rather than by their moral character.

Apart from Snape's character there are other places in the novels where respect is granted, even if reluctantly, to the Slytherins' achievements. Perhaps most obviously, Harry nearly finds himself sorted into Slytherin—the house which, according to the Sorting Hat, "can aid him on the way to greatness" (SS, p. 121). Indeed, Harry's own ambitions—his desire to prove himself, and to live up to the memory of his parents—are some of the most intriguing aspects of his character and drive some of the key events in the books.

There are other instances as well where we see a respect shown for ambitious undertakings. In Harry's first visit to the Wand Shop in Diagon Alley, Ollivander, the proprietor, tells Harry that Voldemort had done great things, "terrible, but great" (SS, p. 85). This grudging respect for the Dark Lord's achievements, which finds an echo in none other than Dumbledore's willingness to call Voldemort's knowledge of magic "perhaps more extensive than any wizard alive" (OP, p. 835), suggests that we can appreciate the scope of people's knowledge or achievements even if we think that they themselves fail to have a good character overall. And this seems right. After all, who but a Caesar could have crossed the Rubicon? Who but Bill Gates could have built the Microsoft empire? We do not always like ambitious people, but there is no denying that many great and historical things would not have come to be (and will not in the future come to be) without them. It is also worth pointing out that quite often our moral paradigms, our saints, are just as ambitious as our paradigm sinners. Was Gandhi not ambitious when he undertook to gain independence for India? Was King not ambitious when he organized and led the fight for racial equality in the 1960s? Ambition comes just as frequently in forms we admire as in forms we do not admire.

So we can see that the level of ambition a person has is only one part of his character, which we must weigh along with all the others. The thing to remember is that it isn't one virtuous quality alone that makes a person morally good, it is a *complex* of moral qualities. This is implied by Aristotle's notion of the virtuous person being *wise* in the conduct of life. For Aristotle, wisdom is a sort of master virtue, and those who have it have more than simple bravery or ambition alone. Those who have wisdom have the coordination of knowledge, action, and virtue that gives a person a truly good moral character. It is admirable to want to do great things, but it is even more admirable to be wise (and hence virtuous) in the course of doing them.

Ambition as a Virtue

But why should we think that ambition is a virtue? This objection can be answered if it can be demonstrated that ambition fits perfectly well into the Aristotelian model of a virtue. Recall that a virtue is a midpoint between an excess and a deficiency in terms of taking account of one's emotions, abilities, and circumstances. If this is the case, then we ought to be able to give an account of the excess and deficiency that might sit on either side of ambition. Let's begin by specifying the emotion relevant to ambition. It is the *desire to excel*. This is an emotion that is common to those who achieve great things. In arenas as diverse as athletics, scientific research, and international business, those at the forefront of their fields are those who have the will to be there, to set the new record, to achieve the latest breakthrough, or to win the largest market share. In such competitive endeavors, it's a truism that those without the will to persevere to the end seldom reach the top ranks. That drive is the desire to excel, and it is the emotional context for the virtue of ambition. Comparison with the cases of excess and deficiency with respect to this emotion will help to complete our picture of the virtue of ambition.

Consider first the deficiency. The person whose desire to excel is deficient would fit under the heading of that suggestive neologism of our time, "slacker." We usually use this word to describe a person with no desire to do anything. It could just as well be applied to one who lets his desire for achievement be compromised by preferences for easiness and freedom from struggle. In order for slacking to be a vice, it has to be the case that the emotions of the person who is insufficiently desirous of excellence are out of step with what he could achieve in his circumstances. Consider, for example, a person who has a 4.0 GPA but who shuns college because he would rather stay at his parents' house, watch daytime talk shows and professional wrestling, and drink beer. He knows he could do better, and in fact sometimes does want to do better, but he cannot shake himself free from the convenience of his life as it is. This sort of person might have other virtues, to be sure, but there is no doubt that he lacks the virtue of ambition, and would be described accordingly by those in a position to know.

The case of excess is likewise easy to describe, as it is typically what people have in mind when they think of ambition. This is the image of the ultimately self-seeking person who allows his desire for greatness to override all of his other virtues. Such a person is single minded in his desire for advancement, and doesn't tolerate competition. He has no sense of his own limitations and will use others to get what he wants when he cannot achieve it himself. Friends, family, and colleagues are mere means to his ends, and he knows no loyalties beyond their usefulness to him. This person—let us call him the "climber"— is like the photographic negative of the slacker. The slacker will not act on his ambitions, the climber won't act on anything *but* his ambitions. Both are defective, from the moral point of view. The virtuously ambitious person falls in between their extremes.

The virtuously ambitious person wants to do great things, and seeks to do them, but does not become mastered by his ambitions. He keeps things in perspective, as it were, and maintains his other moral qualities, never letting emotions overpower reason, but never shutting himself down to emotions either. He is reasonable, but emotionally aware. He chooses good goals for their own sake and pursues them diligently, all the while maintaining an awareness of his capabilities and context. His expectations are high, but not unreasonable, and barring tragedy, he can be happy in the broad sense of enjoying harmony with self and others. This is the picture of the virtuously ambitious person that Aristotle would paint.

Of all the characters in the Harry Potter novels, Hermione Granger perhaps best represents the qualities of virtuous ambition. Her desire to excel in her studies drives her to work harder than anyone else to master the arts of magic. Yet despite her drive for academic success, she remains loyal to her friends and supports them in the manner of a true friend. Harry and Ron couldn't make it through Hogwarts without her.

What We Can Learn from Slytherin House

We've seen that the moral core of Slytherin House is ambition. Even if very few Slytherins actually seem to be capable of virtuous ambition, we may still see that Slytherin House belongs at Hogwarts, in a moral sense. If we pay careful attention to the moral characters of the Slytherins, we may learn a valuable lesson: a modicum of ambition is morally healthy, but when allowed to rule us, it can turn us into monsters like the Malfoys or Voldemort. This is something worth keeping in mind in a culture such as ours, where such a premium is put on achievement. The Harry Potter novels aren't, strictly speaking, morality plays (and we may be glad of that—they would be nowhere near as entertaining as they are if they were!), but they *can* be morally instructive. Even Aristotle would have agreed.

10

A Skewed Reflection: The Nature of Evil

DAVID and CATHERINE DEAVEL

Why is there evil in the world? To answer that, we need to know what evil is. The Potter books' dramatic portrayal of a fight between good and evil gives a general outline of what evil is, particularly moral evil. The books portray evil by using three main concepts: 1) evil is a privation, or a deformity parasitic on something good; 2) evil, due to this weakness, must accordingly mask itself by deceit; and 3) moral evil can only really exist as the result of free choice.

Evil Doesn't Exist

The first thing we learn from the Potter books is that evil does-n't really exist. Evil does not really exist in itself, but is a privation, a lacking in what something is supposed to be. It is a lacking of what is good.

Before we show how the books present this idea, let's clar-ify what it means to say that an evil is a lack of something. People lack lots of things, but are these lacks really evils? What if Hermione were to say, "I don't have wings, which are good things to have: *that, Harry, is an evil*"? Augustine of Hippo (354–430) knew someone might ask this and made the distinc-tion between an *absence* and a *privation*.[1] Hermione's lack of

---

[1] *The Confessions*, Book 7, especially xii and xiii. René Descartes explicitly makes use of this same distinction in his *Meditations on First Philosophy*,

wings is a lack of something good to be sure, but not a lack of a good that is part of the normal, healthy state of being human. A wingless human is a bit like a dog without a savings account; they both lack something, but not something part of the proper state of human-ness and dog-ness. Hermione's winglessness is an absence of a particular good, but not a privation.

If, however, Harry's friend Neville Longbottom were to accidentally use the spell *Petrificus Totalus!* on himself, we would be callous to say his paralysis is not an evil because un-charmed statues cannot move their limbs at all either. This is true, but beside the point since Neville is not a statue. When something that is part of being a healthy, flourishing human (or house-elf or whatever) is lacking to it, then we have not just an absence, but a privation.

Non-physical evils. Of course these examples have been mostly instances of physical evil, a lack of some physical trait or ability that is proper for a human being. But for humans (and for any other rational beings in the world of fantasy), to talk about evil is not just to comment on whether people's bodies are working properly. It's also to talk about whether people's hearts and minds are working properly. To be fully human is to do the right things, love the right things, and care for the right things. To do evil or to be evil in a certain case is really not something definite, but is a failure to do, love, or care for the right things.

How do these books show that evil is a privation? Let's talk about three ways in which the Potter books teach that evil is really a lack of something good: Boggarts, Dementors, and Voldemort.

Boggarts

Professor Lupin explains that boggarts like "dark, enclosed spaces. . . . Wardrobes, the gap beneath beds, the cupboards under sinks—I've even met one that had lodged itself into a grandfather clock" (PA, p. 133). Something like the bogeymen we feared under our own beds, boggarts appear as whatever they think will frighten a passerby the most. For Neville what is

---

Meditation 4, and Thomas Aquinas also uses this distinction as the basis for his analysis of evil (see *De Malo* (On Evil), I, 3: "If some lack is natural to a thing, it cannot be said to be evil for it").

most fearful is Professor Snape, while for Ron Weasley it is an enormous spider. The shape-shifting boggart can look like almost anything.

No one knows what a boggart looks like when it is alone, or even whether it looks like anything at all. Professor Lupin says that a boggart sitting in the darkness "has not yet assumed a form" (PA, p. 133). Does this mean that the boggart doesn't have a physical form at all? It would be mightily odd if it didn't have a form since most everything we know in either our world or the world of Hogwarts has a form. Even ghosts like Nearly Headless Nick take a form that is visible (though a bit disgusting). If we were to surprise a boggart, we don't know what we'd experience. We see and feel things that have shapes. Would we feel simply a presence in the dark, as people who claim to have encountered ghosts simply got a chilling feeling? Or would we feel nothing at all? Do two boggarts alone in a room know that another is present? And interesting as these questions are, what do they tell us about evil?

Well, they tell us that boggarts are parasites. Boggarts can't seem to be "themselves" without something else. In order to move around and interact with the world they must "feed" off something else. What makes the boggart not a pleasant pet, but a pest and an evil for other creatures, is that it feeds from the fear of other living things. To say they feed off fear means *boggarts don't seem to be able to be anything without the fear and unhappiness of others.* It's not clear how a boggart determines one's greatest fear and then benefits from it, but a boggart clearly thrives on the psychological turmoil that it taps into and exploits. Without the fear of others, it simply goes back to dark, enclosed spaces and sits alone.

Dementors

These horrible creatures are less ambiguous than boggarts. They have a form that shows exactly what kind of creature they are, down to their clothing: "Where there should have been eyes, there was only thin, gray scabbed skin, stretched blankly over empty sockets. But there was a mouth . . . a gaping, shapeless hole, sucking the air with the sound of a death rattle" (PA, p. 384). That skin, also described as "rotting," is covered by a hooded cloak. Dementors glide soundlessly, inches above the ground. The dementor seems a cross between the Grim Reaper, a ringwraith from *Lord of the Rings*, and the character in Edvard Munch's painting, "The Scream." The dementor's entire form says "death," and death itself does not exist except as the parasite on and destroyer of life.

It is not just physical appearance that tells us about dementors. In *Order of the Phoenix*, Harry defends Dudley from dementors who have entered Little Whinging. For the use of magic by an under-age wizard off school property, Harry must have a hearing with the Ministry of Magic. The lone witness to the attack, Mrs. Figg, describes the dementors: "I felt them. Everything went cold and this was a warm summer's night, mark you. And I felt . . . as though all happiness had gone from the world . . . and I remembered dreadful things . . ." (OP, p. 145). The dementors' very presence brings a physical sensation of cold—the feeling of corpses—and the feeling that the presence of ghosts is traditionally described as bringing. More importantly, it floods the mind with numbing unhappiness, the memory of "dreadful things," as Mrs. Figg says.

How do dementors bring these memories back? Not through any positive means, but only negatively. Dementors can survive only by taking the happiness out of a person's mind. The absence of happiness forces human beings to remember only unhappiness, horrible things, and especially the reality of death—the absence of life. Lupin tells Harry, "If it can, the dementor will feed on you long enough to reduce you to something like itself . . . soul-less and evil. You'll be left with nothing but the worst experiences of your life" (PA, p. 187). Unlike boggarts, dementors literally feed off human happiness. They survive as parasites, soul-vampires who destroy the spiritual and psychological well-being of their victims for their own survival and pleasure. This is why they have gotten into the prison business, to have people sent to them by legal means so that they can have a sort of perpetual feast. Sirius Black recounts how he survived his stay in, and eventually escaped, their prison, Azkaban: "I think the only reason I never lost my mind is that I knew I was innocent. That wasn't a happy thought, so the dementors couldn't suck it out of me . . . but it kept me sane and knowing who I am . . ." (PA, p. 371).

While it is not clear that the boggarts do anything more than temporarily paralyze those who come near them, the dementors actually take away happiness, rendering their victims insane. Insanity means a lack of health in mind and soul. If a person lacks all health, he is dead. Many people go completely insane in Azkaban, and many of them just die. Because the mind and body are so connected, a lack of health in mind leads to a lack of health in body. (This connection between mind and body is also shown in the effectiveness of chocolate to remedy a close encounter with dementors. As chocolate soothes the bodily senses, it restores one's spirits as well.)

The most horrifying aspect of the dementors is their "soul kiss." Although they generally feed slowly from the human souls in Azkaban, they are also able to swallow a soul whole through that "gaping, shapeless hole of a mouth." Lupin explains that the Dementor's Kiss reduces the victim to a terrible, drained state "much worse than [death]": "You can exist without your soul, you know, as long as your brain and heart are still working. But you'll have no sense of self anymore, no memory, no . . . anything. There's no chance at all of recovery. You'll just—exist. As an empty shell" (PA, p. 247).[2] That these soul suckers survive on the complex emotions of humans and human-like creatures makes them a classic portrayal of an evil being, one that harms not only the body, but takes instead the interior lives of persons. But even the horrific dementors are not the most terrifying portrayal of evil as a parasite. The most frightening picture is . . .

Voldemort

Voldemort is most frightening because he is human. Although boggarts and dementors chill us because of the kind of creatures they are, Voldemort chills us most because he is one of us and represents the possibility of choosing evil freely. He represents a choice to forsake living a life of abundance, giving and receiving love, for a life of simply taking by force or deceit from another's life. Therefore, we fear most hearing from him what Luke Skywalker heard from Darth Vader in *The Empire Strikes*

---

[2] Many philosophers, including Plato, Aristotle, Augustine, and Thomas Aquinas, argue that the soul is what gives a thing life. If they are correct, then the soul-less life described by Lupin is technically impossible: a soul-less thing is a dead thing (or an inanimate thing). In the imaginary world of Harry Potter, however, this literary device effectively conveys the horribleness of the dementors and serves as a vivid metaphor for the destructiveness of evil.

Back: "I am your father"—I am of the same flesh as you. But we will discuss the role of choice later. First, let's see how Voldemort fits this description of evil as privation and parasite.

The first reference to Voldemort in the books gives us an insight into what is wrong with him. In the wake of Voldemort's defeat at the hands of the infant Harry, Professor McGonagall remarks that Dumbledore is the only wizard Voldemort ever feared. Dumbledore replies, "You flatter me . . . Voldemort had powers I will never have." How odd. If evil is a privation, an inability, a weakness, how can Dumbledore say that Voldemort has powers that he not only doesn't, but will never have? McGonagall answers this question, "Only because you're too—well—*noble* to use them" (SS, p. 11). What appears as weakness on Dumbledore's part is revealed to be strength, the nobility that Voldemort lacks. While "noble" sometimes means famous or upper-class, McGonagall means by "nobility" greatness of character and high moral ideals, qualities needed by a powerful person to act consistently for the good—and check baser impulses. While Voldemort's power to manipulate things magically is amazing, he seems unaware that this is not the only kind of power, or even the most important kind. Voldemort has powers Dumbledore will never have, but the opposite is also true. Dumbledore has the power of nobility, a good character and high moral ideals. He can see the world clearly in a way that is completely impossible for Voldemort.

Voldemort was unable to see what accounted for his defeat at the hands of Harry. He was a more powerful wizard than Harry's parents, even more so than a mere infant. But though he was able to kill James and Lily Potter, he was not able to defeat them or kill their baby. He was unable to do this because he encountered in them the very thing he lacked, love. This love, more powerful than the death curses he hurled at the infant Harry, deflected them back at himself, leaving him lacking even more as a person.

In *Sorcerer's Stone* we encounter the defeated Voldemort weak as a boggart but as horrifying as a dementor. Voldemort himself explains what resulted from that attack: "'See what I have become?' the face said. 'Mere shadow and vapor . . . I have form only when I can share another's body . . .'" (SS, p. 293). Like the boggart, Voldemort seems to have no "him" there. Unlike the boggart, Voldemort doesn't just use fear, he actually uses someone else's body. The face of Voldemort, "the most terrible face Harry had ever seen," is "chalk white with glaring red eyes and slits for nostrils, like a snake"—and bulges out of the back of Professor Quirrell's head (SS, p. 293)! Voldemort is literally a parasite on Quirrell's body. But living by taking another person's life is not enough; Voldemort must gain strength by feeding, via Quirrell, from the blood of unicorns, those one-horned symbols of purity. Voldemort has no qualms about slaughtering innocent unicorns, just as he had no qualms about attacking the infant Harry or parasitically sapping Quirrell's life.

It is one thing to live because of someone else's willing self-sacrifice, as Harry does because of his parents, and another to live because one sacrifices others for one's own gain. Voldemort doesn't understand this, but Dumbledore explains that this is why Quirrell feels tremendous pain when he touches Harry: it is "agony" to touch someone marked by something so good as sacrificial love (SS, p. 299).

Quirrell had "learned" about good and evil from Voldemort who taught that only power matters (SS, p. 291). Quirrell learned this "truth" at a great price since Voldemort ultimately abandons Quirrell to die. As Dumbledore says, ". . . he shows just as little mercy to his followers as to his enemies" (SS, p. 298). Notice Dumbledore doesn't say "friends" but "followers." To have friends one must be a friend; not to understand love is to make friendship—and life itself—impossible.[3] Dumbledore also notes, "not being truly alive, he cannot be killed" (SS, p. 298).

Voldemort eventually gains a body. Initially weak as a baby, it has the form of a "crouched human child" but is, Harry sees, like no other child ever: "It was hairless and scaly-looking, a dark, raw, reddish black. Its arms and legs were thin and feeble, and its face—no child alive ever had a face like that—flat and snakelike, with gleaming red eyes" (GF, p. 640). For all of Voldemort's use of others' lives—Quirrell, the unicorns, and the people he killed simply because they were not useful to him—his life is still a half-life. Voldemort plots to regain his adult body by means of an ancient spell that requires three sacrifices—first, bone from Voldemort's Muggle father, whom he hated and murdered; second, the sacrifice of Wormtail's hand, severed in fear and desperation by this servant himself; and, third, blood from

---

[3] For more on what makes friendships possible, see Chapter 3 in this volume.

Harry, Voldemort's enemy. This terrible restoration shows us again the parasitic character of evil. Unlike a true human child, the weakened Voldemort could not grow to flourish as an adult; he regains an adult body through a potion concocted from the elements of others' bodies. His new bone, flesh, and blood are gained through fear or force at the expense of other people.

Evil Protects Itself and Grows through Deception

If evil is a privation, then it will always have a weakness. Its power flows not from true strength but from the manipulation and distortion of what is good. Truth and goodness will always be stronger in and of themselves. In their completeness, they expose evil's lack—lack of love, lack of health in mind and body, lack of hope, and lack of clear-sightedness. In order to gain the upper hand, evil's best strategy is to disguise itself. Often, we find Voldemort or his followers trying to convince others that Voldemort is irresistible in his power and that the moral principles that might inspire one to oppose the dark lord are empty shams, the hollow wishes of weak and foolish people.[4] In the Harry Potter books, evil masks itself by deceit.

Regarding creatures, the boggarts and dementors make use of deceit to paralyze their victims. Boggarts take on false forms to confuse and overwhelm opponents through fear. The heart of the boggart's effectiveness is its ability to fan a person's fears through its shape-changing. The only way to win against a boggart is to keep firmly in mind that the boggart's form is in fact false; then one can use the boggart's ability to read thoughts against the creature. A boggart is ultimately repelled by laughter. The trick is to use the *Riddikulus* charm—which forces the boggart to take on an amusing shape or circumstance. For example, when a boggart appears as Professor Snape, Neville defeats it by imagining that Snape is wearing Neville's grandmother's clothing.

---

[4] Friedrich Nietzsche praises "genuine philosophers" (as Voldemort praises genuine leaders) for rejecting objective moral principles and instead "creating" and "legislating" morality. There is no truth to be discovered, despite our desire for truth; so, we should pursue instead our "will to power" (*Beyond Good and Evil*, VI, 211). Only those who are "limited" in intellect and ability cling to the illusion of moral principles and fearfully resist the "free" thinking and action of those less limited (*Ibid.*, VII, 219).

The *Riddikulus!* charm requires strong concentration, however, a difficult task in the face of the embodiment of one's
greatest fear. When Mrs. Weasley faces a boggart in *Order of the
Phoenix*, she breaks down in tears because the boggart takes on
successively the shapes of her husband, her children, and Harry,
all sprawled dead at her feet. This visual lie is powerful because
it is drawn from the very real fears of a good person: the boggart paralyzes Mrs. Weasley because it has turned her love for
her family and Harry and her worry for their safety into
weapons against her. Despite herself, Mrs. Weasley is drawn into
the grim illusion that the boggart presents. A boggart is dangerous precisely because it attempts to deceive us into believing
that our greatest fears have come true. The boggart's victim will
only be able to use the *Riddikulus!* charm effectively if she can
see through the physical deceit and laugh at the boggart.

When Harry first encounters the dementors, he is much more
affected by them than his classmates because, as Lupin explains,
Harry has more horrors in his life than other people. When the
dementors "drain peace, hope, and happiness" from Harry, they
leave him with only sadness and misery (PA, p. 187). This is the
key to the dementors' brand of deceit: they take away not only
happiness and peace, but hope—the virtue that allows one to
be open to peace and happiness in the future. This offense
against hope is essentially an offense against truth. Whether
Harry's happy thoughts and feelings have been sucked away or
not, it is simply not true that Harry's past and present life have
not contained the happiness and peace which are the results of
love that Harry has been given and has given to others. That
love is the care and concern of one person for another's well-
being and development as a full human person.

It is precisely in this way that the half-lifed Voldemort is able
to convince people to follow him: he convinces them that there
is no hope. When sad Peter Pettigrew admits to betraying
Harry's parents to Voldemort, his excuses are offenses against
truth and hope: "He—he was taking over everywhere!" and "He
would have killed me" (PA, pp. 374–75). The first excuse is a
falsehood about the present and past. Voldemort had not been
taking over everywhere, a fact that Pettigrew knew well—
Dumbledore always kept Hogwarts as a fortress against
Voldemort. Further, Pettigrew and the Potters were part of the
Order of the Phoenix, a secret bastion of principled resistance

to Voldemort. Pettigrew's fear makes him susceptible to the lie that these efforts to fight Voldemort are futile. The second excuse offends hope because it offends the truth. The truth is that Voldemort surely would have tried to kill Pettigrew as he did kill James and Lily Potter and unsuccessfully tried to kill Harry. But somehow Voldemort had convinced Pettigrew that there would be no escape, that nobody could ever protect him. Worse, Voldemort convinced Pettigrew that his loyalty to the Potters and their love for him were not ultimately worth fighting for. Instead, he betrays both to save his own skin.

Remember Quirrell's "lesson" (SS, p. 291). This is the great lie—that there is no goodness, hence no love; there is no evil, thus no lack of love. But this is simply not true. Pettigrew and Quirrell should have known that there is such a thing as love in the world because they experienced it. Presumably their parents raised their boys not because they were too weak to seek power, but because they cared for these children enough to seek their good at the expense of their own power and plea-sure. The experience of being raised as a human being, assum-ing that there is no abuse or neglect, should be enough for anyone to know that there is such a thing in the world as good-ness, such a thing as love. Even Voldemort should know this. He is human, too.

But this is where we see the lie goes deeper. Voldemort and his Death Eaters don't want to acknowledge that they are human. The Death Eaters always cover up their faces when they appear to others. They apparently want to look like those other hooded deceivers, the dementors. Voldemort is constantly trying to wipe away all traces of his humanity and appear as something more than human. He kills his own father and grandparents, to erase the living memory of his own humanity. He has no wife and chil-dren, signs of hope for the future if there are any. (Here, one might note that none of the Death Eaters seems to have more than one child at most; by contrast, the Weasleys, who embody hope in the face of horrible circumstances, are a large family.) Voldemort changes his name from Tom Riddle, another reminder that he is human (Tom is his father's name) into the horrifying name that means something like "Will to Death." This title is itself a lie, because he doesn't have a death wish. Like almost all humans he is afraid of death. But in his case, he will do anything to avoid it, including taking the lives of others.

Why, in the face of reality, do people buy these lies? Why are they deceived by the unreality when reality has been all around them? Why, we ask again, is there evil in the world? The answer is difficult, but what is frightening is that it seems to be the result of a free choice.

Evil Is a Result of Free Choice

One of the scariest aspects of Rowling's view of evil is that people can and do choose it. They choose the lie of evil rather than the truth of goodness. Of course, as we noted, they don't choose it *as evil*. Nobody says outright, "I choose to forego love, happiness, and peace for a dreary, friendless, loveless world in which I seek power alone, power that will probably destroy me along the way." Nobody, or almost nobody, reaches the stage where he courts evil as evil, incompleteness, and death. Even Voldemort must keep telling himself lies about the world in order to pursue his own agenda. But it is true that people in the end must choose lies or truth.

One lie about evil is that people are simply predestined for evil because of their ancestry, the alignment of the stars, or some other characteristic necessitating a "destiny" to head to the dark side. In other words, the last deceit of evil is that one has no choice whether to succumb to it or not. Like Peter Pettigrew, it blames outside forces for one's own choices. This theme runs throughout the series. From the very beginning Harry worries that he will be in Slytherin, Voldemort's old house, because it is his "destiny" (SS, p. 130). When he discovers in *Chamber of Secrets* that he (like Voldemort) speaks parseltongue, the language of snakes, Harry worries that not only is he destined for the dark side, but that he is the heir of Slytherin who will unleash doom on all Hogwarts.

Harry's fears are understandable since he is assaulted constantly by the notion that there is no freedom for the individual. Muggles like Uncle Vernon and Aunt Petunia insinuate that Harry is bad simply because of his magical powers. Aunt Marge, ignorant of Harry's powers, has a more general theory: "If there's something rotten on the *inside*, there's nothing anyone can do about it" (PA, p. 25). All three seem to believe that people are born "bad" or "good" and that life is simply a working out of this fundamental nature or fate.

Many wizards hold a similar fatalism, ranging from those who follow astrology to those who believe that it is the *non-magical* people who are inferior or simply bad. Sibyll Trelawney, the flaky Divination teacher, is only known to have made one or two accurate predictions in her life, but she influences students nonetheless with her own view that people have no choice about their lives, but are instead acting out a fate decreed by the stars. Other wizards think that the stars have little to do with it, but that the purity of wizard blood does. The Malfoy family is obsessed with this theory that an individual's worth has to do with being "pure-blooded"; Draco often refers to Hermione as "mudblood," an insulting term for one who has both Muggles and wizards in her family tree. Sirius Black's family (whose motto is *toujours pur*—"always pure") shares the belief. Finally, Cornelius Fudge, the archetypal ineffectual administrator who heads the Ministry of Magic, also seems to believe this theory. When, in *Goblet of Fire*, large numbers of wizards realize Voldemort has returned and is making alliances, Fudge hesitates to contact the giants because they are hated by much of the wizarding community. His assumption that wizards are superior in kind to other rational magical creatures as well as to non-magical people is reflected in the statues displayed at the Ministry of Magic: stone renderings of assorted magical creatures gaze up adoringly at a wizard and witch.

Dumbledore, the constant voice of wisdom, spends much of his time refuting these fatalistic views of the person. Of prediction of the future, he tells Harry that because "the consequences of our actions are always so complicated, so diverse, that predicting the future is very difficult business indeed. . ." (PA, p. 426). Dumbledore's logic depends upon the freedom of the individual and the fact that our choices will have unforeseen consequences, in part because our actions affect the options and motivations of others as they make their own choices. For example, the cruelty of the Malfoy, Crouch, and Black families toward their house-elves has unexpected consequences, just as Harry's kindness to Dobby (the Malfoys' house-elf) earns him a humble ally who helps him in surprisingly important ways. Further, as Dumbledore suggests, Harry's mercy toward Pettigrew (now a Death Eater) may prove pivotal in a future encounter with Voldemort. People are not puppets, acting out a script written in the stars by an impersonal fate. We cannot simply consult the stars and find out what kind of people they are or determine how they will react to a given action or event.

Nor can we simply find out about the person's abilities, whether they are magical or non-magical, and then determine their character. To discern the kind of person we are dealing with we must look elsewhere. In *Chamber of Secrets*, Dumbledore reminds a worried Harry that though he shares many characteristics and even talents with Voldemort, he is not like him:

> "It [the Sorting Hat] only put me in Gryffindor," said Harry in a defeated voice, "because I asked not to go in Slytherin. . . ."
>
> "*Exactly,*" said Dumbledore, beaming once more. "Which makes you *very different* from Tom Riddle. It is our choices, Harry, that show what we truly are far more than our abilities." (CS, p. 333)

Harry had considered his place in Gryffindor to be a dodge of the Sorting Hat's proper decision, a decision it would presumably have made without Harry's input. He thought his request "interfered" with the hat's judgment. In direct contrast, Dumbledore asserts that this view treats Harry's choice as external to the course of Harry's life rather than the central determining factor it truly is. Despite their similarities, Harry and Voldemort's choices set them decisively apart.

Our choices, not astrologers' charts and certainly not our bloodlines, show what we are in the here and now. But the choices we make also change us and make us what we are and will be. Dumbledore tells the "race-conscious" Cornelius Fudge, "You place too much importance, and you always have done, on the so-called purity of blood! You fail to recognize that it matters not what someone is born, but what they grow up to be! See what that man [the son of a prominent wizarding family] chose to make of his life!" (GF, p. 708). We are what we choose to make our lives. We are evil only if we choose evil. Here, the Potter books again follow Augustine and Thomas Aquinas: moral evil results from free choice of the will. Our choices involve privation when we choose lesser goods over greater goods.[5]

---

[5] This formulation follows Augustine (cf. *Confessions*, Book VII, iii, vii, and xvi). Augustine and Thomas Aquinas differ slightly in their precise explanations of

Of course, since choosing evil is to choose something less, it's much easier to choose it. That's why human beings, says Dumbledore, "have a knack for choosing the worst" (SS, p. 297). It's easier to go along with an angry crowd, a corrupt institution, or even your own emotions, than to stop, determine what the truth is, and then make the decision it entails. Peter Pettigrew illustrates that this decision for good is especially difficult when it could require great personal sacrifice. Harry learns that he and his parents were protected from Voldemort by the Fidelius Charm, which "involv[es] the magical concealment of a secret inside a single, living soul" (PA, p. 205). As the name of the charm implies, the Potters' protection depended on the fidelity, the faithfulness of this friend:

> The information is hidden inside the chosen person, or Secret-Keeper, and is henceforth impossible to find—unless, of course, the Secret-Keeper chooses to divulge it. As long as the Secret-Keeper refused to speak, You-Know-Who could search the village where Lily and James were staying for years and never find them. (PA, p. 205)

Peter Pettigrew was the Potters' Secret-Keeper. Voldemort is powerful, but he could never have found the Potters unless Pettigrew chose to betray them. In the end, Pettigrew's fear of Voldemort and desire to save his own life outweighed his devotion to the Potters. Pettigrew desperately claims that he had no choice—Voldemort was too powerful, he himself would have been killed. In response to Pettigrew's protests, however, Sirius Black reminds Pettigrew he *did* have a choice. Even in the worst-case scenario, Pettigrew had the choice of saving his own life or the lives of the Potters. He chose the easier and lesser path; he chose to betray his friends to their murderer and to save his own life. Pettigrew feared Voldemort for good reason. The choice to resist Voldemort often demanded great sacrifice as the consequence: many wizards died for their defiance of Voldemort, and Neville Longbottom's parents were tortured to

---

the origin of moral evil (compare Augustine's explanation in *City of God*, Book 12, vi and viii with Thomas's in *De Malo* I, 3); however, their theories are more similar than different and their emphasis on free will in moral evil is clearly echoed in the Potter books.

the point of insanity. Pettigrew's choice also has far-reaching consequences but of a different sort. In saving his own life, he has radically changed it. His choice loses him his other friends, forces him into years of hiding, and eventually binds him to Voldemort as a slave. An individual's choice for good or a choice for evil shapes this person and brings lasting consequences for oneself and for others.

Seeing Clearly, Acting Bravely

Throughout the series, Harry is learning how to recognize good and evil and how best to act on this knowledge episode by episode, in bits and spurts, as Voldemort's power increases and the stakes grow. What makes the plot so dynamic is that it follows the complicated pattern of real life. Neither Harry nor any of the other characters, including Dumbledore and Voldemort, is either all good or all evil. As Sirius tells Harry, "[T]he world isn't split into good people and Death Eaters" (OP, p. 302). For example, Professor Snape, a former Death Eater who can barely hide his dislike for Harry's father and, largely by association, for Harry, has chosen to renounce past ties and fight with Dumbledore against Voldemort's return. On the other side, as Harry is dismayed to learn, his father and Sirius Black could be cruel and arrogant when they were teenage students at Hogwarts, and the adult Sirius remains impulsive to a fault. But both grew into men of great courage, and both chose to risk their lives to battle Voldemort and to protect those whom they loved. Even a Death Eater can choose to act for the good, and good people are not entirely perfect people.

These characters and others who populate the Potter books help to clarify the task set before Harry and his friends. Part of growing up is taking seriously the importance of seeing clearly, of recognizing good and evil for what they are, and trying to act for the good and against the evil. Just like humans in real life, Harry and his friends do not always judge properly or act properly in every situation despite what are generally earnest efforts to do so. They sometimes jump to conclusions or act impulsively or emotionally before they have made a proper judgment. Again, just like real humans, these mistakes can harm others; for example, Harry's admirable desire to help Sirius in *Order of the Phoenix* inadvertently puts Sirius and others in danger. This was because Harry didn't learn to guard his mind from the influence of Voldemort. The stakes are real for them and for us. But the key is to keep trying to clear one's vision and set one's heart in the right direction.

There are some who will simply try not to judge at all. They bury their heads in the sand and try not to make a decision. Cornelius Fudge refused to take action simply because he refused "point-blank, to accept the prospect of disruption in his comfortable and ordered world—to believe that Voldemort could have risen" (GF, p. 707). This is the easy way. Try not to make a decision. But the decision will need to be faced eventually. And it will be a harder, sadder decision. Perhaps we should heed Dumbledore's word. His speech to the school in *Goblet of Fire* serves as a clarion call:

> Remember Cedric. Remember, if the time should come when you have to make a choice between what is right and what is easy, remember what happened to a boy who was good, and kind, and brave, because he strayed across the path of Lord Voldemort. Remember Cedric Diggory. (GF, p. 724)

When the mask of evil is ripped off, it is death that we find, not life. When the choice of evil seems "easy," remember Cedric Diggory.

11

Voldemort, Boethius, and the Destructive Effects of Evil

JENNIFER HART WEED

The Dark Lord Voldemort viciously murders Harry Potter's parents before turning his wand on Harry himself. Miraculously surviving the attempt on his life, baby Harry is placed in the custody of his Aunt Petunia and Uncle Vernon, who subject him to an indifferent and abusive childhood. In one instant, Voldemort changes the course of Harry's life forever. Harry suffers the loss of his parents, while Voldemort seemingly is benefited by the absence of the Potters. Even worse, Voldemort continues living a life filled with malicious activities.

If one takes a closer look at Voldemort's life after he murders the Potters, however, it becomes clear that he receives something other than the benefit of having two less wizards to oppose him. A physical transformation occurs in Voldemort that is both deforming and frightening, which seems to be the result of his evil actions. While Voldemort's deformities cannot ease Harry's suffering, they can provide some assurance that Voldemort is negatively affected by his misdeeds.

The view that evil actions have a destructive effect on an evildoer has a rich history. Indeed, such a view is found in the writings of the fifth-century philosopher Boethius.[1] According to Boethius, an individual determines his character by virtue of the

---

[1] The self-destructive nature of evil is not an exclusively Christian idea. One can find similar observations about evil in the writings of Aristotle and Rabbi Moses Maimonides, for example.

actions that he performs, and so it is up to him either to better or worsen his character depending on the decisions that he makes and the actions that he performs. Evil will always be self-destructive to the evildoer despite appearances to the contrary, although such self-destruction does not alleviate the suffering of an evildoer's victims.

Boethius and the Destructive Effects of Evil

The portrait of evil that is manifested in the character of Voldemort exemplifies the account of evil given by the philosopher Boethius. Anicius Boethius (around A.D. 480–524) wrote his most famous work, *The Consolation of Philosophy*, while he was awaiting execution by the Ostrogothic king, Theodoric. Boethius had held the privileged position of consul to Theodoric, but had been denounced as a traitor and placed under house arrest. Although the circumstances surrounding his arrest and execution are unclear, Boethius claims to have been accused of treason unjustly amidst a life of loyal service.[2] Like Harry, Boethius mourned his separation from his family, and so to comfort himself, Boethius wrote a story about the nature of evil and the effects of evil on evildoers.

Boethius says evil is "parasitic" on goodness, a characterization that he borrows from St. Augustine. According to Augustine, goodness is prior to evil. Evil is not a thing that exists on its own; evil exists as a parasite on goodness. For example, the love that Petunia Dursley has for her son, Dudley, is good. But her habit of indulging Dudley's every wish and whim to the point of spoiling him is bad. In this sense, spoiling Dudley is an example of a mother's love gone wrong. She cannot spoil Dudley without first loving him. Her love for Dudley, however, has become misplaced and misdirected to the extent that she no longer provides limitations to his childish desires, such as his unhealthy preoccupation with the number of his birthday presents. The act of spoiling Dudley is parasitic on her love for him.

Other evil actions can be similarly explained. Augustine suggests that one way of thinking about evil as a parasite on

---

[2] Boethius, *The Consolation of Philosophy* (London: Penguin, 1969), translated by Victor Watts, Book I, Chapter 4. This text also includes a brief biography of Boethius by Victor Watts.

goodness is to view some evil actions as the result of turning away from higher goods in favor of lower goods. He offers the following example:

> [The will] turns to its own private good when it desires to be its own master; it turns to external goods when it busies itself with the private affairs of others or with whatever is none of its concern; it turns to goods lower than itself when it loves the pleasures of the body. Thus a man becomes proud, meddlesome and lustful; he is caught up in another life which, when compared to the higher one, is death.[3]

An example of turning away from a higher good in favor of a lower good can be found in the character of Voldemort. He prizes above all else political power and influence, which are not in themselves bad things. Because he so values power, he attempts to annihilate all those who oppose him. Rather than pursuing higher goods, such as love and friendship, Voldemort turns to murder and deceit to ensure his rise to power.

Boethius takes the Augustinian definition of evil as parasitic on goodness and applies it to his own view of human nature.[4] According to Boethius, human beings differ from animals inasmuch as human beings possess the capacity for rational thought.[5] Moreover, human beings have the ability rationally to control their physical desires and to direct all of their behavior towards the highest good. According to Boethius, the highest good for human beings is happiness. Human beings can, however, pursue happiness in a variety of different ways. Boethius argues that the good person pursues happiness through virtue while the evil person pursues happiness through other desires:

> Now the highest good is the aim of good and evil men alike, but good men seek it by natural exercise of the virtues, whereas evil men try to acquire it through desires of one kind or another, and not through the natural faculty of attaining the good.[6]

---

[3] St. Augustine, *On Free Choice of the Will* (New York: Macmillan, 1964), translated by Anna S. Benjamin and L.H. Hackstaff, Book 2, Chapter XIX.
[4] Boethius, Book IV, Chapter 2.
[5] This view of human nature is not unique to Boethius; it is shared by Aristotle, Maimonides, and St. Thomas Aquinas, among others.
[6] Boethius, Book IV, Chapter 2.

Boethius argues that happiness, since it is a good, cannot be achieved through evil acts. Happiness can only be achieved through virtuous activity.[7] At least one effect of evil on the evil-doer is that it prevents him from achieving his ultimate goal in life: true happiness. Draco Malfoy, for example, consistently taunts and bullies Harry, Hermione, and Ron. Boethius would argue that these actions prevent Draco from achieving happiness. In this way, Draco not only injures his classmates, he also injures himself by acting in such a way as to impede his own happiness. It seems clear from Rowling's books that Draco is an unhappy character.

The loss of happiness, nevertheless, is not the same thing as self-destruction. One might wonder how evil actions are self-destructive to an evildoer. Boethius answers this question in the following passage:

> Observe now the nature of this punishment which attends the wicked, by contrasting it with the situation of the good . . . . Whatever departs from the good ceases to exist, so evil men cease to be what they had been before. Of course, the very appearance of the human frame which they still possess shows that they were men; thus by resorting to wickedness they have lost their human nature as well. Since goodness alone can raise a person above the rank of human, it must follow that wickedness deservedly imposes subhuman status on those whom it has dislodged from the human condition . . . . In this sense he who abandons goodness and ceases to be a man cannot rise to the status of a god, and so is transformed into an animal.[8]

Boethius concludes that just as evil diminishes a human being by causing him to lose his natural goal, happiness, so evil dehumanizes the evildoer. In other words, evil actions transform an evildoer from a human being into an animal, not literally of course, but figuratively. Remember, in Boethius's view it is the ability to reason that differentiates human beings from animals. Human beings have the capacity to rationally control their desires and their actions so that they can achieve happiness. When a human being commits evil acts he is abandoning

---

[7] *Ibid.*

[8] *Ibid.*, Book IV, Chapter 3.

happiness, which is the natural goal of his rational capacity. So the evildoer is a defective human being. He does not rationally control his desires and he abandons his pursuit of true happiness. As a defective human being the evildoer resembles an animal, who lacks this capacity altogether.

Evil acts have a dehumanizing effect on a human being; they cause the human being to resemble an animal. For example, it is revealed in *Prisoner of Azkaban* that Peter Pettigrew told Voldemort the location of James and Lily Potter, enabling their murder. Peter subsequently disguises himself as a rat in order to hide from the Potters' friends. We can interpret the physical transformation of Peter into a rat as indicating the moral state of his character. Peter "rats out" the Potters to Voldemort, and then Peter physically *becomes* a rat. Rowling seems to treat Peter's act of betrayal symbolically, diminishing him from a human being to an animal.

Augustine argues that evildoers eventually lose their ability to distinguish between right and wrong: "The man who does not act rightly although he knows what he ought to do, loses the power to know what is right."[9] If Augustine is correct, then another way in which an evildoer is dehumanized is through losing the ability to make moral judgments. Without the ability to tell the difference between right and wrong, the evildoer begins to resemble an animal, since animals lack this ability also. There are significant differences between an evil human being and an animal, however. For example, Peter Pettigrew is morally worse than a rat because a human being is supposed to be able to tell good from evil and choose the good, while a rat never has this ability. Human beings only lose their ability to differentiate between good and evil when they voluntarily commit evil actions. So their loss of this ability is their own fault.

According to Boethius, an evildoer abandons his own proper nature in committing evil actions. In the very act of abandoning his nature as a rational animal, the evildoer abandons the best part of himself. The very act of rejecting part of himself leads only to an internal division in the evildoer, which in turn leads to misery and greater self-destruction; it can never lead to happiness. The evildoer destroys himself by rejecting part of him-

---

[9] Augustine, Book 3, Chapter XVIII.

self and by failing to live up to his potential. So, truly, the evil-doer undergoes a "dehumanizing" and self-destructive transformation when he commits evil acts. With every evil act the self-destruction becomes greater as the evildoer consistently rejects his own nature. Voldemort experiences this kind of spiraling self-destruction after he attempts to murder the whole Potter family.

Voldemort and the Destructive Effects of Evil

Lord Voldemort is both a terrible and powerful wizard, sowing "discord and unrest" among the other characters (GF, p. 725). Many of the Potter plots center on Voldemort's schemes to achieve world domination and the efforts of the virtuous wizards, including Harry, Hermione, and Dumbledore, to stop him.

In the first book, *Sorcerer's Stone*, we are introduced to Voldemort as a murderer. Hagrid, Harry's friend, explains that it is Voldemort who murdered Harry's parents and who tried to murder Harry, too (SS, p. 54). Voldemort is an attempted child-killer, a "wizard who went bad" (SS, p. 54). The indifference with which he treats human life is evidence of his corruption. He does not recognize the humanity and the worth of those around him; all he sees are obstacles on his own path to power. His willingness to murder Harry displays his callous refusal to distinguish between innocent "non-combatants" and his enemies (SS, p. 291). All who stand in Voldemort's way will be destroyed, regardless of their age or innocence.

Voldemort denies the very existence of good and evil (SS, p. 291). In this respect, Voldemort mirrors the Augustinian-Boethian account of evildoers who begin to resemble animals in their decision making. Voldemort either refuses to distinguish between good and evil or he lacks the ability to make such a distinction, just like an animal. Indeed, Voldemort deems all things permissible in his quest for power, including killing children. Harry's schoolmates are understandably terrified of Voldemort and they refuse to pronounce his name, choosing rather to call him "You-Know-Who" (PA, p. 106).

As the only human being to escape from Voldemort, Harry is marked by Voldemort's hatred. Harry has a lightning bolt scarred on his forehead, which is the sign of Voldemort's attempt to murder him (SS, p. 55). But Harry's scar is not the only effect of

Voldemort's attack. Voldemort himself explains the strange turn of events that occurred the evening that he murdered Harry's parents:

> My curse was deflected by the woman's foolish sacrifice, and it rebounded upon myself. Aaah . . . pain beyond pain, my friends; nothing could have prepared me for it. I was ripped from my body, I was less than spirit, less than the meanest ghost . . . . but still, I was alive. What I was, even I do not know . . . . I had no body. (GF, p. 653)

Through Lily's love for her baby, the curse that Voldemort had used with the intention of murdering Harry was turned back on Voldemort himself. He was reduced to "something barely alive," a creature not quite human and yet not quite a ghost, either (GF, p. 20). In this transformation we see a dramatic, literal portrayal of the self-destructive effects of evil. Through his attack on Harry, Voldemort is physically reduced to something less than human, something that requires care and support from his followers to survive.

One would think that the loss of Voldemort's body and the resultant suffering would be enough to cause him to re-think his activities and his choices. Given the fact that it was his own quest for power that motivated him to attack the Potters in the first place, Voldemort might blame himself for his sorry state. There is no evidence, however, that he considers this possibility or that he learns any kind of moral lesson from his ordeal. Voldemort's lack of introspection on this matter, as on others, is another self-destructive effect of evil. His self-deception about his own moral failings is interesting given his attempts at deceiving those around him (SS, p. 294).[10] He is blind to the true cause of his own dehumanization; he blames the Potters for the loss of his body (GF, p. 653). Far from accepting the blame for his own suffering and mending his ways, Voldemort becomes obsessed with getting his body back in order to continue his quest for world domination.

In his attempts to regain his human shape, Voldemort somehow attaches himself as a parasite on Professor Quirrell's body (SS, p. 293). He also manipulates Quirrell into killing a beautiful

---

[10] For more on the morality of self-deception, see Chapter 2 in this volume.

unicorn for its life-giving blood, only compounding his self-destruction. As the centaur Firenze explains:

> It is a monstrous thing, to slay a unicorn . . . Only one who has nothing to lose, and everything to gain, would commit such a crime. The blood of a unicorn will keep you alive, even if you are an inch from death, but at a terrible price. You have slain something pure and defenseless to save yourself, and you will have but a half-life, a cursed life, from the moment the blood touches your lips. (SS, p. 258)

Once again, Voldemort does not distinguish between his enemies and innocent "non-combatants" such as the unicorn. The unicorn's life is expendable, as are the lives of all those who oppose Voldemort's rise to power. Voldemort does not return to life unscathed, however. His cursed life is manifested both in his actions, which grow progressively more barbaric, and in his physical appearance. During a confrontation with Quirrell, Harry catches his first glimpse of Voldemort: "Where there should have been a back to Quirrell's head, there was a face, the most terrible face Harry had ever seen. It was chalk white with glaring red eyes and slits for nostrils, like a snake" (SS, p. 293).

Voldemort typifies the parasitic nature of evil that Augustine identified. Bereft of his body and the ability to survive on his own, Voldemort's only option for survival is to draw life from the body of another human being. Far from appearing attractive or beautiful, Voldemort is hideous and snake-like. He acts without any regard for the safety of Professor Quirrell or Harry (SS, pp. 291–95). In fact, Voldemort leaves Quirrell to die when it is clear that Quirrell has outlived his usefulness, further illustrating Voldemort's view that the lives of other human beings are both worthless and disposable.

As if signifying his internal decay, Voldemort's appearance worsens and becomes more grotesque throughout the stories. In a disturbing scene near the beginning of *Goblet of Fire*, Voldemort murders an innocent Muggle named Frank who just happens to enter the house in which he is hiding (GF, p. 15). Just prior to his murder, Frank catches a glimpse of Voldemort. This glimpse is so frightening, Frank screams uncontrollably until Voldemort kills him. Voldemort's appearance also frightens Wormtail, his disgusting little minion, as Voldemort says, "I revolt you. I see you flinch when you look at me, feel you shudder when you touch me" (GF, p. 9). If even his evil fol-lowers are revolted by the sight of him, Voldemort's appearance must be frightening indeed.

The destruction that Voldemort experiences at each stage of his life is linked with his own choice of actions. First, he attacks the Potters and consequently loses his body. Next, he becomes a parasite and manipulates his host into killing a beautiful uni-corn for its blood. Consequently his life is forever cursed. After leaving Quirrell to die, Voldemort disappears in search of another source of life (SS, p. 298). His condition and his dispo-sition are so frightening at this point, however, that most of his followers abandon him, as Professor Trelawney intuits:

> The Dark Lord lies alone and friendless, abandoned by his fol-lowers. His servant has been chained these twelve years. Tonight, before midnight . . . the servant will break free and set out to rejoin his master. The Dark Lord will rise again with his servant's aid, greater and more terrible than he ever was. Tonight . . . before midnight . . . the servant . . . will set out . . . to rejoin . . . his mas-ter. . . . (PA, p. 324)

Voldemort's dependence on his followers indicates the extent of his own self-destruction. Once again, his helplessness could have been an opportunity for reflection or for redemption. Voldemort, however, seems oblivious to the fact that he is the cause of his own destruction and, further, that he is capable of correcting it. He ignores any possibility of reforming himself, becoming more and more violent and more and more intent on revenge. We can only predict that Voldemort will decay still fur-ther in the books to come. Barring any attempts to change his ways, Voldemort's evil activities will probably result in his total destruction.

Voldemort and Moral Education

The effects of evil extend far beyond one's victims or one's com-munity; the effects of evil are also received in the person of the evildoer. Voldemort's progressive worsening throughout the sto-ries should serve to teach readers about the self-destructive effects of evil and the ugliness of a wicked character. This self-destruction can be explicitly connected with Voldemort's choice of actions, for example his murderous attempts, his manipulation of the weak, or his killing of animals. This self-destruction stands in contrast to the virtues manifested by Harry, Dumbledore, Ron, Hagrid, and Hermione, virtues such as courage, friendship, and love.

It is clear from the stories that both Voldemort and Harry are responsible for their own moral characters. Their actions and their choices determine the kinds of people that they become. Voldemort's choices lead to his own ruin and suffering as well as the suffering of others, while Harry's choices lead to his development into a courageous young man who is fiercely loyal to his friends. Although Voldemort's self-destruction is not enough to alleviate Harry's grief over the loss of his parents, it provides some measure of justice. The murder of the Potters serves to affect Voldemort negatively and to cause him to suffer.

As Boethius and Augustine point out, evil affects both the evildoer and the victim of evil. Through his own actions, the evildoer causes his own suffering. Although Rowling is probably not deriving this idea from Boethius and Augustine, she seems to agree with them. Voldemort's progressive worsening seems to be a kind of suffering. Based upon the dehumanization and the self-destruction that attends the evildoer, the choice between the subhuman murderer and the courageous young wizard is an easy one, or ought to be. It is better to be the virtuous schoolboy than the more menacing, dehumanized Dark Lord.

12
Magic, Muggles, and Moral Imagination

DAVID BAGGETT

The vastly different attitudes toward a particular young wizard are truly remarkable. While shattering one publication record after another, the Potter series also elicits angry protests, hitting number one in the American Library Association's list of the books most commonly challenged in school districts and public libraries in the United States. Some literary critics are among the series' detractors, panning it as insignificant fluff, while others hail it as a minor classic. More than one critic has written that the books leave no room for the transcendent and numinous, while countless others level the charge that the books desensitize children to occult influences. Some view the books as contrary to Christian thought, while others see a deep congruence. Still others think of the Potter series as deeply moral, while certain vocal critics accuse it of advancing a highly subjectivist moral relativism. Just as Harry is amazed to discover his fame in the wizard world, he would be amazed to discover himself in a swirl of controversy among Muggles.

The Devil Made Harry Do It

The astounding success of the Potter series, particularly among children, has without question had the salutary effect of drawing huge numbers of young people into reading. This widespread influence, however, is part of the reason why many adults have such grave qualms about it. The stories are about wizards and witches, spanning several aspects of real-life occultism, from charms to numerology to ancient runes. It's no small concern that impressionable children may be unduly drawn to occultism, whether it's Wicca, Satanism, or variants of New Age theology.

Undoubtedly, many people immediately dismiss such allegations as worthy of serious consideration only by the likes of Ned Flanders, conspiracy-minded fundamentalists, and moralists. Some of the criticisms of the Potter series have indeed been humorless and contentious, as well as inadequately gracious and informed, none of which conduces to cordial debate. But neither does the condescension and dismissiveness expressed by some of the Potter supporters in the face of such criticisms. What's needed is not name-calling and inflammatory rhetoric, but the kind of cool-headed and respectful analysis of the allegations in a spirit of friendly discourse that Dumbledore is famous for.

Most of those issuing the accusations not only believe in the reality of the spirit world, but also believe that not all spiritual forces are benign. Those who are skeptical about the supernatural understandably find it difficult to sympathize. If someone is doubtful of God's existence, he is certainly less prone to take seriously Satan or demonic spirits, stuff thought best relegated to a pre-modern, superstitious past and a naïve, unscientific view of the world.

Detractors of the series are most concerned that the stories, wildly popular with children, tend to glamorize the occult, piquing kids' curiosity about it and desensitizing them to its dangers by making it appear as harmless fun. Stirring children's curiosity in this way, it is argued, makes them vulnerable to dark spiritual forces. Again, a charitable rendering of this view requires that we remember that such critics are neither agnostic nor skeptical about the existence of sinister supernatural influences.

It is not unduly difficult, with a little imagination, to feel the force of this objection. Children, our most valuable resource and investment, are impressionable and are susceptible to being misguided. A healthy process of socialization is vital to their emotional well-being and social adjustment. Such a process should carefully steer clear of those influences that carry inordinate risks of doing more harm than good. The possibility of the

Potter series effecting such damage, many would argue, is ample cause for serious concern. Even a minor likelihood of such damage is enough to raise suspicion, given the potential seriousness of the consequences that early interest in the occult may incur.[1]

Defenders of Potter are likely at this point to remind us that the books are, after all, fiction, not to be confused with real life. But features of the books, it has been contended, blur the line between fantasy and reality. One of those features is among the books' real virtues: their ability to engage the reader in identifying with the characters. Children's imaginations are caught up in Harry's world, identifying with his struggles, envisioning Hogwarts as real, and wishing to be part of such a place. The suggestion is that it is only a short step to believing that magic, too, is real and its resources available to the reader. Trips to most major bookstores may bolster critics' suspicions, as they peruse shelf after shelf of books on occult themes. Such sections on witchcraft and magic often now overshadow those on philosophy.

Rowling admits that about a third of the magic-based material appearing in her books are or were actual historical beliefs. Children, the argument goes, can't be expected to make the subtle distinctions between fiction and reality that more discerning adult readers can. So the perhaps unwitting effect of this confusion between fantasy and reality, especially among the youngest readers ill-equipped to tell the difference between what is real and what is not, could be a whetting of the appetite for the occult.

What's Wrong with Harry?

Before assessing the quality of that case, let's lay out another case that's been made against Potter, this one on moral grounds.

---

[1] Those who don't have such a take on New Age and Wiccan theology should insist that an argument be provided here. Though they are right to insist on such an argument, giving that argument would take us too far afield for present purposes. Such a critique, were it to be provided, might focus on such theology's instances of unprincipled syncretism, the way it attempts to put together pieces of theological systems that are composed of mutually exclusive truth claims.

Although some have applauded the series for the way it extols the virtues, others have lambasted it for promoting the worst sorts of moral relativism and egoism. Richard Abanes, for example, accuses Rowling of projecting a morally ambiguous vision, in which infractions of rules often go unpunished, lying is an acceptable way to avoid trouble, and the distinction between good and evil is blurred.[2] He thinks that morality is often complex and multi-faceted, but that the Potter books do nothing to contribute to such a nuanced understanding. In articulating such concerns, Abanes represents a significant number of Potter critics who sense danger lurking.

Abanes sets out to construct a cumulative case to show the morally dubious nature of the Potter series. Examples of rule-breaking abound in the books, he reminds us. Harry is said to show an almost Slytherin-like disregard for the rules, and Harry's behavior confirms it. Harry is not legalistic when it comes to school rules or the guidelines governing the wizarding world. For example, to find out the identity of Nicholas Flamel, he sneaks into the restricted section of the library using his invisibility cloak, and he follows Professor Snape into the Forbidden Forest.

Harry's lovable friend Hagrid is also notorious for rule violations, performing spells when he isn't supposed to, and asking Harry and his friends to help smuggle his dragon out of Hogwarts (SS, p. 237). Hagrid had raised the dragon—Norbert—against the 1709 Warlock's Convention law prohibiting dragon breeding in Britain (SS, pp. 230—33).

Those most concerned about the rules, Abanes points out, are often the mean characters like the Dursleys, Professor Snape, or Hogwarts caretaker Argus Filch. Indeed, Harry and the readers are convinced throughout much of *Sorcerer's Stone* that Snape is completely evil. Only at the end do we find that the gentle Professor Quirrell is the real villain in cahoots with Voldemort. This sort of reversal recurs when, for example, Mad-Eye Moody in *Goblet of Fire* turns out to be impersonating the real Moody or when Voldemort's minion Pettigrew turns out to have been living for twelve years in rat form as Scabbers (Ron's

---

[2] Richard Abanes, *Harry Potter and the Bible: The Menace Behind the Magick* (Camp Hill: Horizon, 2001), p. 96. Abanes designs his spelling of "magick" here to distinguish occult magick from sleight-of-hand magic.

family pet). This distinction between appearance and reality is an object lesson in the difficult task of obtaining true knowledge, since we have to rely on appearances that may be misleading.[3] But in a story of this nature, such reversals might be thought to blur the line between good and evil.

Violations include not only minor infractions of school rules, but also significant moral rules, such as prohibitions against lying. Recall, for instance, Hermione's "downright lie" about the troll in *Sorcerer's Stone* to get the boys out of trouble. Hermione, normally the last one to violate any rules, lies and claims she has broken a rule (pp. 177–78). Or consider Dumbledore's assertion that truth is *generally* preferable to lies (GF, p. 722), which prompts Abanes to emphasize that this shows inadequate commitment to truth, a point he thinks is generalizable to most of the characters in the novels. Even Dumbledore himself lies to protect Harry in *Order of the Phoenix* (p. 618).

Harry all too often lies to conceal facts that might otherwise cause him harm. Rowling writes, "Excuses, alibis, and wild cover-up stories chased each other around Harry's brain, each more feeble than the last. He couldn't see how they were going to get out of trouble this time" (SS, p. 242). In *Goblet of Fire*, Harry lies to Hermione (p. 443), a house-elf (p. 408), Hagrid (p. 456), Snape (p. 516), Trelawney (p. 577), and Fudge (p. 581), all without negative consequence.

In fact, Harry's infractions of the rules often go unpunished— for example, when Fudge doesn't punish Harry for inflating his aunt in *Chamber of Secrets*, or when Dumbledore doesn't punish him for finding the Chamber. When Mr. Weasley finds out his sons, to rescue Harry, flew the enchanted car without permission, his first response is, "Did you really? . . . Did it go all right?" (CS, p. 159). Indeed, sometimes misbehavior is actually rewarded, such as when McGonagall puts Harry on the Quidditch team after he violates Hooch's directive not to fly while she is away on an errand (SS, pp. 148–152).

On the same day, Harry agrees to fight Draco in a "wizard's duel" at midnight in the school's trophy room. Such a fight is

---

[3] Epistemology is the branch of philosophy that studies the nature of knowledge, traditionally defined as true, justified beliefs, although the right account of knowledge is a difficult question. Shawn Klein's chapter in this book elaborates on the challenge of securing knowledge in a world of appearances.

against Hogwarts rules and would require Harry to be out of his dorm at night, a second violation of the rules, and hard to justify morally, no matter how much readers might like to see Draco get a sound drubbing.

Since Harry isn't always punished, critics think the series thereby promotes ethical relativism. Relativism makes morality a matter of preference, either of a group or of an individual. Philosophers usually call morality made subject to individual whim ethical subjectivism, and Abanes seems to focus his accusations on such subjectivism when discussing relativism. Relativism of this kind denies that there are universal moral rules and instead assigns to individuals the capacity to determine the contents of morality. Since we like Harry, the argument goes, whatever Harry does is ultimately okay. No matter how many violations of the rules he might commit, his ends justify his means.

Moreover, what motivates the characters' moral choices, Abanes wishes to suggest, is crass self-interest. Whether Voldemort or Harry, the underlying motivation is the same: doing what they want to do. "Voldemort wants what he wants, as does Harry. The only difference between them rests in the rules they choose to break, the lies they choose to tell, and the goals they choose to pursue."[4]

Here the actual charge isn't exactly relativism so much as egoism. As a psychological theory, egoism says that all of us are motivated by self-interest all the time. As an ethical theory, it says that self-interest ultimately *should* function as our only motivation. Presumably, Abanes is suggesting that Rowling depicts the characters in her novels as egoistically motivated, "good" characters and "bad" alike. Since both sides "lie when it is expedient and break rules whenever those rules do not serve their needs . . . both sides are technically 'evil' or sinful, even though their agendas might be vastly different."[5] By endorsing such motivations, Rowling, the argument goes, is embracing and approving such ethical egoism, which contributes to the morally confused message of her books.

"In short," Abanes concludes, "Rowling's moral universe is a topsy-turvy world with no firm rules of right and wrong or any

---

[4] Abanes, p. 136.
[5] *Ibid.*, p. 88.

godly principles by which to determine the truly good from the truly evil."[6]

Answering the Moral Charge

Let's address this charge. Starting with Harry, it's important for us to admit that he isn't perfect. He's willing to violate school rules and to lie on occasion, liable to be insensitive to the enslavement of the house-elves, and susceptible to fits of moodiness and anger. But a heroic or virtuous character need not be perfect, and occasionally will fail. Harry isn't always a moral exemplar, but he is learning as he goes, and he clearly exhibits a sort of character and integrity distinctly different from the villains. Harry, for one thing, cares about other people. He often acts to save a friend, and sometimes even an enemy, as when he saved Dudley in the beginning of *Order of the Phoenix*. Harry is willing to risk his life in order to prevent an innocent person from suffering. And none of this moral motivation is to be found in the villains. Harry *is* what he *consistently does*, Aristotle would remind us; his occasional failures don't define him.

This undermines the charge that Harry is really no better than Voldemort, since Harry breaks rules, occasionally lies, and does what he wants to do. Abanes insists the fact that Harry and Voldemort want different things is incidental; it's what they hold in common—an essentially egoistic motivational structure— that's most important here.

Surely, though, the contents of Harry's and Voldemort's desires *do* matter! To imply that what they want is not as important as the simple fact that they happen to pursue what they want is confused. It leaves out of the picture one of the most important morally differentiating factors of all. Consider Harry and Voldemort for a moment. Harry battles evil forces and desires to see justice prevail. Voldemort desires to crush anyone he has to on his way to achieving power. They both pursue what they want, but that hardly entails moral equivalence. The nature of a person's desires reflects the kind of person one is.

What Abanes calls topsy-turvy morality may simply be a bit of genuine moral complexity. Good and virtuous characters

---

[6] *Ibid.*, p. 244.

have feet of clay, make mistakes, and may break the rules from time to time. It isn't moral subjectivism to acknowledge, as Solzhenitsyn[7] did, that good and evil cut through each of our hearts. Each of us is capable of being lured to evil, of sacrificing others at the altar of our own selfishness.

Moral complexities don't entail that everything ethical is colored gray and up for grabs. That a character like Harry may have flaws doesn't mean he's not a hero or virtuous. That a rule (such as a prohibition against lying) may admit of exceptions doesn't mean it ought not be followed. That moral dilemmas may require us to choose the lesser of two evils doesn't mean that there's no moral difference between them.

Moreover, Harry shows mercy by sparing Pettigrew's life, which eventually leads to the reemergence of Voldemort and the murder of Cedric Diggory. And Sirius inadvertently breaks Ron's leg attempting to get Harry to follow and learn the truth about Pettigrew. Abanes thinks the fact that good deeds are cast as bringing about evil results and harmful deeds as bringing about positive results further confuses the moral message of the books. However, that good consequences might come from bad actions doesn't mean that bad actions are to be generally encouraged. That bad consequences might result from good actions doesn't mean that good actions aren't to be encouraged. That moral appearances can sometimes deceive us doesn't mean we can never discern the difference between right and wrong.

It irks critics that rules are habitually broken in the Potter books, even by good characters, and that such infractions too often go unpunished. But not all violations of rules merit punishment. Sometimes violations of rules are justified, which is why Dumbledore didn't make good on his promise in *Chamber of Secrets* to expel Harry if he broke any more rules (pp. 330–31). Sometimes a higher law beckons. This is why Abanes probably wants to emphasize that some of the violations in the Potter books are more serious in nature than infractions of school rules or Ministry directives that may admit of legitimate exceptions. Some of the infractions violate ethics itself, like the moral rule against lying.

---

[7] Alexandr I. Solzhenitsyn, *The Gulag Archipelago 1918–1956* (New York: Harper and Row, 1975), p. 612.

Certainly truth-telling *is* an important virtue, and kids really do have to learn that it's not an acceptable practice to try evading responsibility or punishment by lying. Immanuel Kant was a philosopher whose ethical theory dictated that lying on all occasions is wrong. He thought that lying is motivated by a principle that can't be consistently generalized. A rule like "It's morally permissible to lie whenever doing so is in your best interest" won't work. Such a universal rule would undermine the truth-telling and promise-keeping on which we all rely when insisting we're telling the truth or that we'll keep a promise. For Kant, reason's foundation for ethics affords no exceptions to such a prohibition against lying, no matter how advantageous or beneficial a particular lie might appear. It is not the consequences of our actions that count.

Although Kant makes sense, the right moral theory needs to take into account at least some consideration of consequences on occasion, even if we have reservations about reducing morality only to a matter of consequences as the great philosopher John Stuart Mill and other utilitarians do. Although we can never fully anticipate every last consequence of our actions, there are times when we can reasonably foresee what they're likely to be, such as when protectors of Jews during the Holocaust or of slaves during the days of the underground railroad were asked for their whereabouts. Given the intrinsic value of life and the particular moral goods at stake on such occasions, lying seems justified, and indeed a moral responsibility! This reminds us that ethics is about more than just rigidly obeying inflexible rules; it's about the kind of person one is and the sorts of moral goods one cherishes, such as human dignity, freedom, and life. Some nonnegotiable moral rules undoubtedly hold, like the inherent wrongness of torturing children (even Draco) for fun, but lying, even if nearly always wrong, does seem to admit of legitimate exceptions.

We can at least well understand Harry's failure always to be entirely forthright with those less than trustworthy. And Harry's infractions *do* sometimes land him in hot water. Ironically, in *Order of the Phoenix*, Harry's *commitment* to telling the truth lands him in detention with Umbridge to endure a particularly unjust and painful punishment, about which, incidentally, he never complains.

It was an eye-opener for Harry to learn in *Order of the Phoenix* that his Dad had been far from morally perfect while a student at Hogwarts. That Harry's Dad could grow up and improve reminds us that Harry, too, is on his way to becoming the man he's capable of being. Harry, as his father did, is morally maturing.

Is Hogwarts a Wiccan Academy?

Critics level the charge that Rowling's books are based in the occult. They write as though fictionalized accounts of occult practices that bear a similarity to actual practices blur the distinction between real life and fantasy. Moreover, they claim, this will only confuse young people who can't be expected to maintain careful distinctions between fiction and reality. If Rowling uses examples of divination in her books, and if real-life occultism historically does so too, then occultism lies at the foundation of her books.

This argument rests on a mistake. Arguably it's the critic, not Rowling, who's blurring real life and fantasy here. Surely there's a crucial distinction between reading or writing fiction about a practice on the one hand, and engaging in the practice itself on the other. Communicating with the dead is biblically forbidden, but does that mean those who take such teaching to heart ought to decry Charles Dickens' *A Christmas Carol* because it involves a fictional tale of just such a thing? Or C.S. Lewis's *Chronicles of Narnia* because they include reference to astrology? Unlikely, and for good reason. Writing fiction about a practice is not engaging in the practice itself, and care needs to be taken not to use the term "occult" so freely as to encompass both.

It's true that Rowling is more susceptible to this charge because she borrows freely from real-life accounts, but she draws from a lot of sources and mythologies, from the Arthurian legends to Homer, not just the occult. What she weaves from these sources is something creative and new, even if it incorporates a range of elements drawn from history and literature. To criticize Rowling's eclecticism fails to appreciate her books on their own terms, a principle necessary for evaluating any literary work fairly (and thereby a moral requirement). Identifying elements from the stories and then infusing them with significance

not attributed to them by the stories themselves results in reckless leaps of logic and, potentially, an unnecessarily harsh and
uncharitable spin on her work.

As several chapters in this book make clear, the Potter books
do anything but glamorize evil, painting it instead in only the
most negative terms. Contending that these books should be
suspect on the basis of their using occult symbols is misguided.
Those liable to launch such accusations typically make an
exception for the sort of magic in works by traditional Christian
writers such as C.S. Lewis and J.R.R. Tolkien. Indeed, Abanes
questionably distinguishes the subtle differences between the
magic in Lewis's *Chronicles*, for instance, and Rowling's Potter
novels. But Abanes seems to be fighting a losing battle. On the
one hand, he insists that kids who read Potter aren't sophisticated enough to distinguish real life from fiction. Yet on the
other hand, he seems to think that the subtle distinctions
between the magic found in Rowling and Lewis won't be lost on
those very same young readers.

Imagination and Morality

Critics strategically accentuate occult connections, possible pit-
falls, and macabre wit, while overlooking the potentially positive elements in the Potter books and the possibility of more
constructive engagements with this incredible series.

Rowling likes to describe her fictional creation as a world of
the imagination—a phenomenon of which Mr. Dursley does not
at all approve (SS, p. 5)—and a world essentially moral. At the
same time, she makes it clear that it wasn't her intention to teach
ethics, which reminds us of an important qualifier before we talk
about her books and morality. The primary purpose of fiction
isn't to make us better people. Even Tolkien rejected the view
that literature is mainly about inculcating ethics. Mark Twain did
as well, and put readers of *Huckleberry Finn* on notice that any
persons attempting to find a moral in it are to be banished. That
Tolkien's work and Twain's have been instrumental nonetheless
in shaping readers' moral views doesn't change the fact that this
wasn't their main intention or primary function.

There is, however, a connection between literature and
morality. Philosopher Martha Nussbaum has mounted an elaborate argument for the role of literature in our moral develop-

ment.[8] Good yarns, such as Rowling's, appeal to both the head and heart, eliciting from us the right sorts of emotions, and providing for us vivid moral paradigms that Aristotle thought were essential to moral education. More suggestive than dogmatic, they teach us to empathize with the sufferings of others, enhancing our capacity for seeing the world through another's eyes.

As Potter junkie and public philosopher Tom Morris writes:

> The Golden Rule, as it is stated properly, appeals to our imaginations. It tells me to treat another person the way I would want to be treated if I were in his position. I can't be guided by it without imagining what it would feel like to be in that other person's situation, with all her morally legitimate concerns and desires. The Golden Rule directs me to use my imagination in such a way as to create empathy for others. I believe that the imagination is the single greatest natural power in human life. And so I think it's no coincidence that the greatest moral rule appeals to exactly that power.[9]

By drawing so many young people back into reading, the Potter books are igniting the imaginations of countless kids. A powerful imagination functions centrally in any commitment to morality, because so much of ethics consists in having the right kinds of emotional and intuitive responses to situations as they arise. Being truly ethical is largely about having the appropriate feelings, the proper sorts of imaginative capacities and properly empathetic tendencies. Rowling is performing a powerful service in drawing kids back into the imaginative exercise of reading.

Imagination and Faith

A few years ago a television special debunking a number of enduring mysteries, from crop circles to the Loch Ness monster, aimed at heightening the viewers' commitment to a careful examination of the evidence. The more I watched, though, the more concerned I became that it was doing more harm than good with its persistently skeptical tone. The biggest obstacle for beginning philosophy students is often their unwillingness to

---

[8] Martha Nussbaum, *The Fragility of Goodness: Luck and Ethics in Greek Tragedy and Philosophy* (Cambridge: Cambridge University Press, 1986).

[9] Tom Morris, *If Aristotle Ran General Motors* (New York: Holt, 1997), p. 148.

suspend both disbelief and skeptical doubt to exercise their imaginations. They resist engaging in thought experiments meant to stretch their creative limits and challenge their thinking to higher levels. A reluctance to imagine, cloaked as skepticism, tends to produce more arrogant cynicism than genuine wisdom. The philosopher's task is not merely to mow down superstitions. It's also to irrigate intellectual deserts.

Not only is a vivid imagination crucial to morality, it's integral to religious faith. The nature of religious truth claims is not such as to appeal to the unimaginative or narrowly empirical. We are called to believe in an invisible God, battle unseen forces, and do good to those who harm us. On the face of it, this is definitely stuff that calls for a great imagination. It requires an openness to more than what the eyes can see, a willingness to believe passionately in more than the senses, a capacity to consider a broader array of evidence than a narrow scientism would admit as legitimate. Such imaginative openness to life's deeper realities may well require a cultivation of imagination; a great imagination may well prove valuable in our quest for knowledge. If the basis of one's decision about religion is just wishful thinking, following fashions, or a failure of imagination, one's rejection (or acceptance) is less likely to track the truth. Philosophy calls for a real and honest openness to what evidence is available, not a dogmatic assumption from the outset that one side or the other is outside the range of possibility.

Those interested in pushing the importance and legitimacy of classical religious faith should perhaps be more careful not to discourage kids from reading books like Rowling's, at least if such reading is done with discernment. Such apologists of the faith may need to think out of the box, as it were, more expansively about their task as defenders of faith, and encourage the reading of all kinds of imaginatively vivid literature. In particular, they ought to endorse the reading of morally potent fairy tales that enliven the imagination, give readers fresh eyes to see through, and open minds. Such openness is not enough, but it may well be necessary for religious hypotheses to retain plausibility and remain, in William James's phrase, a "live option."[10]

---

[10] See "The Will to Believe" in William James, *The Will to Believe and Other Essays in Popular Philosophy* (Cambridge, Massachusetts: Harvard University Press, 1979). For an insightful analysis of Jamesian "liveness" and religious

Religiously motivated critics of Potter may wish to think twice before launching criticisms of something that may well do more for their cause than they currently imagine.

We began by talking about the widely different perspectives on Rowling's series. Aristotle had the insight that the truth often resides between the extremes, and this is likely the case with Potter. The books may not be suitable for six-year-olds, but that doesn't mean they're not suitable for nine-year-olds (not to mention most adults of all ages). The books may well broach moral complexities, but that doesn't mean they're morally ambiguous. They may not be the greatest literature ever written, but that doesn't mean they're not good. They remain infinitely better than many books that tout a kind of worldview that offers little encouragement to think seriously about anything at all. The Potter books are well-written, not to mention incredibly fun, stories that generate conversation well worth having.

---

belief, see Hunter Brown, *William James on Radical Empiricism and Religion* (Toronto: University of Toronto Press).

Ravenclaw

*Many-Flavored Topics
in Metaphysics*

13

Finding Platform $9\frac{3}{4}$: The Idea of a Different Reality

GARETH B. MATTHEWS

> We picture the actual world—indefensibly—as the one solid, vivid, energetic world among innumerable ghostly, faded, wispy, "merely" possible worlds.
>
> —DAVID LEWIS

Some of the most exciting stories we can read introduce us to a reality very different from the humdrum world with which we are so familiar. To get to this different reality the characters in these stories may travel, or be taken, to some far distant place, perhaps to a place on the other side of the world, or to a planet in outer space. Or the characters in the stories may discover, perhaps quite by accident, some magical point of entry, such as a special kind of mirror, or a secret door.

We could call such stories "metaphysical," since metaphysics is that branch of philosophy that concerns itself with the nature of reality. But the stories are not themselves works of philosophy. What they do is raise, sometimes in gripping and unforgettable ways, intriguing questions about whether there might be realities very different from anything we have ever experienced.

It will be useful to compare the Potter stories with two other popular story series, one American and one English. The American series, by Frank Baum, is about the Land of Oz and the English series, by C.S. Lewis, is about a place called Narnia.

The Oz Stories

Think about Dorothy, who in the most famous Oz story, *The Wonderful Wizard of Oz,* is lifted up by a cyclone in Kansas and dropped down, with her dog, Toto, on the other side of the world, in the Land of Oz. What Dorothy finds in Oz is quite different from what she knew in Kansas, but it is not *completely* different. She can go on speaking English and understand, and be understood by, the inhabitants of Oz. She can even recognize the Scarecrow as a scarecrow, and the Tin Woodman as a woodman, even though she had never before met a talking scarecrow, or a man made of tin, let alone a scarecrow or tin figure she could actually have for a friend and companion.

Part of the fun of reading *The Wonderful Wizard of Oz*, or of seeing the movie, comes from following the adventures of Dorothy in this strange place. The story is funny and dramatic. It's filled with surprises. It's a good yarn.

Yet there is much more to the *Wonderful Wizard* and the later books in the Oz series than the fact that they tell us about strange and surprising adventures in a faraway place. These stories also make us think! Consider, for example, the autobiography of the Tin Woodman. He began his life, he tells us, as a creature of flesh and bones, like Dorothy. He was gradually transformed, he explains, by a succession of accidents and repairs. A wicked witch had enchanted his axe so that it chopped off one of his legs. To replace his missing limb he had a tinsmith fit him with a tin leg. Then the enchanted axe chopped off the other leg, which, again, he had replaced by a tin limb. The process continued until the Woodman was all tin.

"Could that really happen?" you might ask yourself. Could it even begin to happen? Could a person who had lost an arm or leg really get a tin replacement? If so, what is the limit to the number or kind of replacements for limbs and body parts that someone could get and stay alive?

The Ship of Theseus

The idea of piece-by-piece replacement is well known to philosophers through the old story of the Ship of Theseus. For convenience's sake, let's call the original Ship of Theseus, *Athena*. Let's suppose that *Athena* was made up of nine hundred separate boards and other wooden pieces. And let's suppose further that the ship's carpenter began to replace each of these nine hundred boards and pieces, one at a time, with a new board or piece. When would *Athena* cease to exist? After the first plank was replaced with a new one? After the 451st board or piece was replaced? Or not until the last, the nine hundredth, board or piece was replaced? Would it matter whether the boards and pieces, after they had all been removed, one at a time, were reassembled in another location to form a whole ship? And, if that happened, which of the two ships would be *Athena*—the one that was the result of piece-by-piece replacement, or the one produced by putting all the old pieces together again to form a ship?

The story of the Ship of Theseus comes down to us from ancient times. Yet it raises questions that we can still puzzle over today. For example: What do I have to know about the bike I got back from the repair shop to know that it is really and truly my old bike, and not just a patchwork bike, with parts from the old bike, perhaps most of its parts, or perhaps only the handlebar, or the seat? And what allows my own body to continue to be my own body from day to day, even though the cells that make up my body are constantly being replaced? Why don't I get a new body every time my body gets a new cell, or loses a cell?

The autobiography of the Tin Woodman adds two new elements to the old story of the Ship of Theseus. For one thing, the woodman, unlike the Ship of Theseus, gets replacement pieces that are of a different material from the original. The ship got a new wooden piece to replace each old wooden piece, whereas the Tin Woodman gets a tin piece to replace a piece of flesh and bones. Is this change of material important? If so, why is it important?

Once we consider replacement with parts of some different material, we can modernize the story of the Tin Woodman to allow for, say, plastic replacements for hearts, lungs, and skin, titanium replacements for bones, biochemical replacements for blood, and so on. We can even think of replacing networks of nerves with computer circuitry. A modernized woodman could become the Bionic Man, constructed by replacing organs and body parts, one at a time, including even the brain.

A second thing that makes the story of the Tin Woodman different from the old story of the Ship of Theseus is the fact that the Woodman is able to *remember* and *tell others* his story of what it was like to become, gradually, all tin. Unlike the ship, he can, it seems, recognize himself as himself in his new material. Exactly why that should be important is also worth thinking about.

We can see with only this one example—and there are many, many more interesting examples—that the Oz stories take us to another place with a different reality in such a way that we are prodded into thinking freshly about our own familiar world. The world of Oz is enough like, but also enough different from, our own world, to raise intriguing questions about our familiar world, and about whether we really understand it.

The Narnia Chronicles

Some stories, however, introduce us to another reality by having their characters get to another place, not by a cyclone, a balloon, or a spaceship, but by magic. In C.S. Lewis's *The Lion, the Witch, and the Wardrobe,* the child characters discover that they can walk into a wardrobe in a strange old house and end up in a completely different place, a land called "Narnia." It is a place with its own climate, its own creatures, and even its own time! We realize that the time is different when we learn that Lucy and her friends can spend weeks and months in Narnia and yet, when they return through the wardrobe to the house they had been exploring, no time in that world has passed at all!

The Narnia tales, like the Oz stories, are engrossing yarns. They are books that both adults and children find it hard to put down. But do the Narnia chronicles, like the Oz stories, offer us any help in thinking about or understanding our own familiar reality? Or are they just an escape, even if an exciting escape, from the boring things we are already so familiar with?

In fact, *The Lion, the Witch, and the Wardrobe*, and the other Narnia tales that follow it, are supposed to tell us something important about our own lives. The drama that Lucy, Edmund, Peter, and Susan are drawn into, and become central participants in, is meant to help us understand the religious significance of our own lives. The writer of these stories, C.S. Lewis, was quite clear about this purpose. Thus, for example, he meant for his readers to realize that the lion in Narnia, Aslan, is a Christ figure, and that part of what happens in *The Lion, the Witch, and the Wardrobe*, is a retelling of the biblical story of the crucifixion of Christ. Lewis carried on a correspondence with some of his child readers and he reported, with obvious satisfaction, that many of them had understood the religious meaning of the stories, sometimes better than adults do.

There are, of course, many readers of the Narnia chronicles who do not realize that C.S. Lewis meant to be writing a religious epic that could be enjoyed by kids. No doubt there are some readers, whether adults or children, who can enjoy these gripping stories without even being interested in the religious meaning their author assigned to them. Nevertheless, it's true that the author intended to present another reality, not just as a diversion, but as a story version of what he considered a great cosmic battle between good and evil. It is also true that he thought this religious epic is what gives meaning to our own ordinary circumstances of being born, growing up, having a family, getting old, and dying.

Hogwarts

What, now, about the Harry Potter stories? They, too, present the reader with a different reality from what we think of as the reality of our ordinary lives. It is a world of witchcraft and wizardry, of magic potions, spells, and transfigurations, a world of flying broomsticks and messenger owls. Do they present this world in a way that is like the Oz stories, or in a way that is like the Narnia tales, or in some other, perhaps completely different way?

A first thing to say is that the Harry Potter world of Hogwarts is meant to be a separate reality that is nevertheless *coordinated with* our familiar everyday world. It is certainly not just a faraway place, like Oz—something you might use a balloon, or a jumbo jet, or a spaceship, to reach. Nor is it something that runs on a time system that is different from ours. Hogwarts itself is, presumably, somewhere in England, though we won't be able to find it on an ordinary map, that is, on a Muggle map.

There is, of course, a standard way to get to Hogwarts. It is to go to King's Cross Railway Station in London, which is otherwise the mainline station for trains from London to

Cambridge, Ely, and points beyond. To be sure, you won't get to the right platform for the Hogwarts Express, Platform $9^{3}/_{4}$, unless you push your baggage cart resolutely toward the barrier between Platforms 9 and 10 (and Dobby hasn't bewitched the barrier!). But a certain physical and entirely public (that's to say, Muggle) location is a point of entry into the Hogwarts world.

Hogwarts and Narnia

So far, Hogwarts is a bit like Narnia in that there is a locatable entry point for reaching this other reality. But does the business about Platform $9^{3}/_{4}$ sufficiently resemble the wardrobe in the Narnia story to make the world of Hogwarts very much like the world of Narnia? Here are some important differences.

First, once Harry gets past the barrier and the Hogwarts Express comes into view, what he sees is a scene much like that of other trains taking kids to English boarding schools. The story continues in this vein. There are, of course, constant reminders that things are also different in the wizard world. Thus the kids on the train munch chocolate frogs, rather than gummi bears, and trade witch and wizard cards rather than football cards. But the similarities are as obvious as the differences.

Second, some people in the Muggle world know something about the world of Hogwarts, even though they have never themselves been through the "door" to wizard reality. They may, like Harry's aunt and uncle, fear and reject the wizard world, but still acknowledge it even as they try not to. Some Muggles, like Hermione's parents, seem happily reconciled to the existence of the magical world, sending her to Hogwarts and shopping with her in Diagon Alley.

Third, there is plenty of movement back and forth between the Muggle world and Hogwarts. Messenger owls appear with messages from Hogwarts. In fact, when Harry and Ron discover that they have missed the Hogwarts Express, Ron leads Harry to his father's Ford Anglia, which has been parked on a side road near King's Cross Station and, since the car is enchanted, they can use it to fly to Hogwarts. Once they take off, they can see the whole of London, "smoky and glittering, below them" (CS, p. 70).

Fourth, and this may be the most interesting point of all, the school subjects at Hogwarts are the various "sciences" and "disciplines" of witchcraft and wizardry. There is a library of volumes on these topics, there are textbooks on them, there are specific classes in potions, transfigurations, etc., and, of course, final examinations. I shall return to this observation later on.

So far we have noted four points of difference between the wizard world of Hogwarts and Narnia. What about the religious significance of the Potter stories? As we have already said, the Narnia chronicles are meant to be stories about another world that give us the religious meaning of this world. The Potter stories are not meant to do that. However, there is a strong sense of evil in them, personified, of course, in the figure of Voldemort. And Harry's life is clearly a battle of courage and decency against darkness and depravity. So, although the Potter stories are not a religious allegory, they do dramatize the battle of good against evil that is central to a religious view of our "earthly existence."

Hogwarts and Oz

What now about Hogwarts and Oz? As we have said, the Oz stories encourage us to reflect on the reality we already know and, perhaps through that reflection, to come to understand our common world better than we did before. Do the Potter stories encourage us to reflect on interesting ideas and concepts we already make use of?

In fact they can, although in ways that may not be entirely obvious. Consider, for example, Hermione's idea that she, Ron, and Harry might "get inside the Slytherin common room and ask Malfoy a few questions without him realizing it's us" (CS, p. 159). Ron and Harry find that idea preposterous, since they would be recognized immediately. But Hermione's idea is that they could be changed into three of the Slytherins by drinking something called "Polyjuice Potion."

The notion that Polyjuice Potion transforms one person into another is extremely puzzling. What would it be like for you to become the kid next door? Would the kid next door then become you? If not, would two people become simply one person? And what would that be like?

When Hermione, Ron, and Harry begin to carry out their plan, it emerges that what is about to happen is something rather different from one person's becoming another. Hermione puts a "simple Sleeping Draught" in each of two chocolate cakes (CS, p. 213), which Crabbe and Goyle eat. While they are asleep, Ron and Harry take hair samples from them (pp. 214–15). Hermione pours the Polyjuice Potion into the glasses. She adds a hair sample from Millicent Bulstrode to one glass, a hair sample from Goyle to the second, and one from Crabbe to the third (pp. 215–16). The procedure seems to be something a little like cloning, in which a hair sample might supply the DNA for a fertilized egg. But to produce a clone of, say, Crabbe, is not to turn anything or anybody into Crabbe. It is to make a Crabbe look-alike, someone distinct from Crabbe himself who, nevertheless, looks like Crabbe. This is the outcome that is suggested when Hermione says, "And we also need to make sure the real Crabbe and Goyle can't burst in on us while we're interrogating [Malfoy]" (p. 213).

If the products of these transformations are supposed to be something like clones, then the question arises, 'What knowledge and memories will they have?' Clearly they will not be able to carry out their mission unless the person who used to be Harry still has the knowledge and memory Harry had before his transformation and the person who used to be Ron still has the knowledge and memory Ron had before his transformation. But does that mean that Polyjuice transformations just change one's appearance without affecting one's memory or one's knowledge? Apparently. Then taking the potion is more like growing a skin suit that makes one resemble someone else than it is like becoming a clone of someone, let alone being actually transformed into another person.

What the Polyjuice episode brings up is a bushel of intriguing questions about personal identity, about cloning, and about disguises. It doesn't present us with a neatly packaged puzzle, the way the autobiography of the Tinman in the *Wizard of Oz* does. But it gives us the materials for raising a number of fascinating and important questions. What would it be like to have drunk the Polyjuice Potion? Would it be like awakening in a hospital room with amnesia? Or would it be like awakening after your own brain had been transplanted successfully into the body of another person? Or would it be like gaining thoughts and memories you couldn't fit together with earlier memories?

Hogwarts and Our World

There are also other ways in which the Potter stories might help us think about the world we knew before we picked up our first Potter book. For one thing, the very coordination of the wizard world with the Muggle world should invite us to think about the fact that people around us, perhaps even our own relatives or very best friends, may have, for all we know, very different belief systems from our own. Here is an analogy to bring home this point.

The psychiatrist, Ian Stevenson, has been perhaps the world's leading researcher into evidence that people around us may seem to remember having had a previous life, perhaps only a few years ago in a town or village nearby, or perhaps a very long time ago in a faraway place. Stevenson began his researches with trips to India, where belief in reincarnation, or, as it is sometimes put, "transmigration of souls," is relatively common. In some of the families he visited it was no big deal for a child to speak of having once lived as a member of another family, in another village.

Some of Stevenson's most interesting cases have been Native Americans in Alaska, whose culture includes belief in reincarnation, but who have married non-Indians without any such beliefs. Thus an Indian wife, who grew up in the belief that she had already lived another life, might marry someone with no such belief—indeed, someone who would think it totally weird to believe he had had a previous life. The Native American wife might never share her belief in having had a previous life with her husband for fear he would think she was crazy. And thus, unknown to him, her belief system would be very, very different from his.

Many people in our (real!) world believe in ghosts, poltergeists, UFOs, aliens from other planets, and paranormal phenomena of all sorts. The Harry Potter stories should remind us that the person sitting next to us in a train station or airline terminal may have a very different belief system from our own. For all we know, the person in the next seat may expect to be met at her destination by a space alien, though she would never admit this fact to a total stranger, or perhaps even to her best friend!

Seeing but Not Noticing

Here is another way in which the Potter stories may help us think about what we take reality to be. Harry Potter sometimes wonders how Muggles can fail to notice the magical happenings that, it would seem, ought to be observable to them as well as to him. The explanation, apparently, is that Muggles are, in general, very unobservant. What they see and hear is pretty much restricted to what they have become accustomed to think they will see and hear. Whatever falls outside this sphere of expectation is easily dismissed as illusion or even hallucination. Thus when Harry is suddenly picked up by the Knight Bus near the beginning of *Prisoner of Azkaban*, he asks Stan, the bus conductor, "How come the Muggles don't hear the bus?"

> "Them!" said Stan contemptuously. "Don' listen properly, do they? Don' look properly either. Never notice nuffink, they don'." (PA, p. 36)

Have you ever seen something that you might have counted as evidence of the landing of an Unidentified Flying Object of some sort—*if you believed in, say, space ships from other planets*? Many people have. But we promptly dismiss the evidence, since we don't believe such things visit the earth.

Should we pay more attention to the odd experiences we have, the ones we cannot integrate easily into our accepted view of what is real and what is not? Perhaps. But at least this much is clear. We should know that what we see and what we hear is shaped by what we *expect* to see and hear. And what we count as real is heavily influenced by what we have been socialized to count as real. The Harry Potter stories underscore this point.

Science and Alchemy

Here is a final point, something we already touched on briefly. The curriculum at Hogwarts School of Witchcraft and Wizardry "normalizes" what we might otherwise call "paranormal phenomena" by including among school subjects such topics as spells, the history of magic, magic theory, potions, and transfigurations. The natural assumption is that any subject that can be taught to students in such a way that their competence in this subject can be tested by examination is a science. This assumption is reinforced by the fact that students at Hogwarts are made to buy textbooks in their (paranormal) academic subjects and by the idea that more advanced research in these fields can be carried out in the school library. It is further reinforced by the various attempts to demonstrate the magical skills, the theory of which is taught in the classroom and the comprehension of which is tested by examination.

An analogy can be found in the present-day attempts to integrate the treatments and remedies of Chinese medicine into the Western practice of medicine. One reason that Western doctors are less likely to disregard Chinese medicine today than they were a few years ago is that some of them have actually gone to China for medical training, to study the science of herbs, acupuncture, and so on. Another is that they have seen for themselves some of the success of Chinese practice, results that, in some cases, they have been able to reproduce in a Western setting. Yet another reason is that they have begun to try to understand the theory that lies behind the practice of Chinese medicine. Many Western medical schools now have departments of alternative medicine where Chinese medicine is learned and taught.

The point is not that all, or even many, of the subjects studied at Hogwarts should, or even could, be incorporated into our school curricula. After all, the great Harry Potter thought experiment is, above all, something that is simply fun to read about and imagine. Nevertheless, these stories may remind us that Sir Isaac Newton, one of the chief founders of modern Western science, spent a considerable part of his life and energy studying what we dismiss today as mere "alchemy." Some of Newton's alchemy seems to have been quite like Hogwarts science!

Newton's idea of gravity—the idea that lifeless bodies, without any thoughts or feelings, attract each other, even at huge distances—struck many of Newton's contemporaries, including the great German philosopher, Gottfried Wilhelm Leibniz, as pure myth and magic. For us today, however, gravitational attraction is as real as the attraction of one human lover to another. Perhaps some day parts of Newton's alchemy will be considered just as descriptive of reality as his physics. Who knows? In any case, we can certainly enjoy, and enjoy thinking about, the magic, witchcraft, and alchemy of the Harry Potter stories without having to take bets on the future of science.

14

Space, Time, and Magic

MICHAEL SILBERSTEIN

Where is Diagon Alley relative to the rest of London and the actual world? *Where* is platform nine and three-quarters? And *where* is Hogwarts relative to the actual world? *How* do wizards travel through space-time shortcuts such as those provided by Floo powder, the Knight Bus, and teleportation (Disapparating/ Apparating) via spells and Portkeys? Of course, these *where* and *how* questions go hand-in-hand.

A key philosophical question regarding any work of fantasy is where and when the fantastical realm in question is relative to the actual world of everyday experience. What spatio-temporal and causal relations do the fantasy world and its inhabitants bear to our own? For example, if the two realms are distinct then how does one travel between the fantasy world and our own? Does time "pass" in the fantasy realm at the same rate it "passes" on Earth? What is the nature of space and time in the fantasy world compared to our own? For example, does the fantasy world allow time travel, teleportation, or other extraordinary events? Is it logically and physically possible for normal humans to replicate these feats by technological (non-magical) means alone? If these things are possible in the real world—which is the concern of metaphysics—does the fantasy world contain space-time phenomena disallowed by the logical or physical laws of the actual world? Do the magical means of manipulating space and time miraculously break or bend the natural laws of the actual world or merely exploit unknown possibilities?

Where and When: The Harry Potter Universe and Our Own World

About any fantasy story, we must ask the question: Where or when is this mythical world relative to our own? For example, in the case of Tolkien's Trilogy, Middle-earth is a forgotten and ancient period in Earth's actual history, a period, according to the story, we now wrongly regard as mythological. By contrast, C.S. Lewis's land of Narnia is a distinct magical realm that can be entered from our own world via certain magical portals. Narnia is a magical land with different laws where time flows at a much faster rate with respect to Earth time. Months might pass in Narnia where only minutes have passed on Earth. The world of Harry Potter is neither a faraway time in Earth's past or future, nor a distinct magical realm, but is Earth's present day. J.K. Rowling makes it clear that the magical world of Harry Potter and the actual world are one and the same. The best way to illustrate this is by asking where are the major "magical" places such as Diagon Alley, platform nine and three-quarters, and Hogwarts relative to "the Muggle world"?

Magical and Non-Magical Places

It would be easy to get the impression that Diagon Alley, platform nine and three-quarters, and other places described in the Harry Potter books, really are distinct magical locations because they are arrived at by secret and magical means. "He [Hagrid] tapped the wall three times with the point of his umbrella. The brick he had touched quivered—it wriggled—in the middle, a small hole appeared—it grew wider and wider—a second later they were facing an archway large enough even for Hagrid, an archway onto a cobbled street that twisted and turned out of sight" (SS, p. 71). This is the passage where Harry first learns how to access Diagon Alley via the back wall of the London pub, the Leaky Cauldron. Take Harry's first encounter with platform nine and three-quarters. After Harry miraculously walks through the wall separating platforms nine and ten he finds himself next to the Hogwarts Express, and a sign overhead says eleven o'clock. He looks behind himself and reads another sign which says *"Platform Nine and Three-Quarters"* (SS, p. 117).

But upon closer inspection we find that while these places are special, they are right here on Earth:

> The trouble is, about a hundred thousand wizards turn up at the World Cup, and of course, we just haven't got a magical site big enough to accommodate them all. There are places Muggles can't penetrate, but imagine trying to squeeze a hundred thousand wizards into Diagon Alley or platform nine and three-quarters. So we had to find a nice deserted moor, and set up as many anti-Muggle precautions as possible. (GF, p. 69)

In this passage we learn from Mr. Weasley that what makes a place "magical" is that "Muggles can't penetrate," not that such places are not part of our space-time continuum. We also learn that for whatever reason magical sites are small and perhaps rare.

What separates magical from non-magical places is that the latter but not the former must be heavily protected by spells in order to keep Muggles from seeing or otherwise finding them:

> 'Seats a hundred thousand' [World Cup stadium], said Mr. Weasley, spotting the awestruck look on Harry's face. 'Ministry task force of five hundred have been working on it all year. Muggle Repelling Charms on every inch of it. Every time Muggles have got anywhere near here all year, they've suddenly remembered urgent appointments and had to dash away again . . . bless them'. (GF, p. 96)

From this passage we learn that the World Cup stadium is not a magical place proper and therefore must be charmed to keep humans away. Additionally, Hermione tells Ron that Hogwarts itself and other schools of wizardry such as Durmstrang are also not magical places but must be protected from prying Muggle eyes by spells and enchantments (GF, pp. 66–67).

There's ample evidence that all the other key places and creatures in the Harry Potter universe are right here on Earth as well, even dragons, as the following passage suggests: "Charlie's in Romania studying dragons, and Bill's in Africa doing something for Gringotts" (SS, p. 107). Indeed, even "magical places" such as platform nine and three-quarters and Diagon Alley, which require magical means to enter are right here on Earth in our space-time continuum. In both Diagon Alley and platform nine and three-quarters, wizards go "through walls" by some magical means in order to enter the hidden areas (SS, pp. 89–94). Moreover, there isn't any suggestion—in either the books or the films—that any sort of teleportation or apparating is occurring. As we shall soon discuss, whenever any sort of apparating occurs in the Harry Potter universe it is accompanied by tell-tale signs such as the feeling of motion, strange colors, sensations, and the like. In the case of both platform nine and three-quarters and Diagon Alley, what wizards experience is continuing into another apparently connected location. Hagrid gives us further evidence for thinking that Diagon Alley is a part of this Earth.

> 'Why would you be mad to try and rob Gringotts?' Harry asked.
>   'Gringotts is hundreds of miles under London, see. Deep under the Underground. Yeh'd die of hunger tryin' ter get out, even if yeh did manage ter get yer hands on summat'. (SS, p. 64)

So, Gringotts is directly under London and we know that the entrance to Gringotts is in Diagon Alley (SS, pp. 71–72). Since apparating or teleportation isn't used to get inside, it must be that Diagon Alley and Gringotts are in the heart of London right here on Earth. But then why is it that Muggles never sense platform nine and three-quarters if it is literally part of King's Cross station, or Diagon Alley if it is literally nestled a wall's breadth away from the rest of that part of London? Because, as we just learned, these are "magical sites," which are undetectable by Muggles.

Consider that in the Harry Potter films one can see Earth's sky in both of these magical places. Note also that in *Chamber of Secrets*—both the film and the book—there is a scene in which we see Hermione's parents in Diagon Alley, which makes it clear that Muggles can enter magical places if they are accompanied by wizards. Also recall the scene in *Chamber of Secrets* where Harry and Ron miss the Hogwarts Express and end up taking the flying car to Hogwarts. The fact that on this flight they are seen by Muggles, that they can find and follow the train and tracks of the Hogwarts Express, and that they can fly directly to Hogwarts just as a normal plane would, all constitute more evidence that everything in the Harry Potter universe is part of Earth's space-time continuum. We can only assume the reason that Muggles do not notice the Hogwarts Express is the same reason they do not see Hogwarts itself. We might well wonder why train transportation is necessary at all, given teleportation and such. The answer, as we are repeatedly told, is that for security reasons apparating is not allowed in or out of Hogwarts (PA, p. 419).

Other key locations, such as the Ministry of Magic and St. Mungo's Wizards Hospital, are in London too (OP, 482–83). Recall that wizards enter the hospital by stepping through an enchanted window display. The location of the Ministry is underground in London and is entered via an old, broken-down red phone booth (OP, pp. 125–26, 768–69). Further evidence that the Muggle world and wizard world are the same world is that time "passes" at the same rate at magical places that it does in London; for example, if it is 11:00 A.M. at King's Cross station then it is 11:00 A.M. on platform nine and three-quarters.

How: Travel by Magical Means

How do wizards travel through space-time shortcuts such as those provided by Floo powder, the Knight Bus, and teleportation (Disapparating and Apparating) via spells and Portkeys? Unfortunately the best answer to this question is, it's magic! None of the descriptions in the books provides us with anything like a detailed explanation. However, some of these methods of travel may not be quite as inexplicable or inconceivable as they seem at first.

Apparating

It turns out that apparating can be quite dangerous and tricky. Potential serious errors include unintended landing sites such as in walls or on top of people or, even worse, getting "splinched" (only half your body teleports away leaving the other half behind). But what does apparating feel like?

> It happened immediately: Harry felt as though a hook just behind his navel had been suddenly jerked irresistibly forward. His feet left the ground; he could feel Ron and Hermione on either side of him, their shoulders banging into his; they were all speeding forward in a howl of wind and swirling color; his forefinger was stuck to the boot as though it was pulling him magnetically onward and then—
>
> His feet slammed into the ground. (GF, pp. 73–74)

So apparating involves motion through some kind of space because apparaters feel as though they are in motion and when they reappear, they are often described as "windswept," "disheveled," and "prone" on the ground. Also, most of the passages describing apparation imply that some time goes by from the point of disappearing in one place and reappearing in another. All of this suggests that apparating does not mean literally disappearing in one place and *instantly* reappearing in another without having traversed *any* space-time. But *where* is the connecting space that has been traversed and *how* do wizards traverse it so quickly? One possibility is that apparating is not so much teleportation (that is, instantly getting from point A to point B without having traversed any intervening space), but rather it is travel by "wormholes" or their magical equivalent. A wormhole is a tunnel made out of space-time, between two different points of space-time.

Imagine, if you will, that space-time is like a very elastic rubber sheet. It might be possible to create a tunnel in the fabric of space-time (for example, with a massive object or by magic) that connects two space-time locations (such as the Weasleys' house and the World Cup stadium) in such a way that the distance between them is greatly diminished. Such a tunnel would be a shortcut between these two points. Such a shortcut could connect two different places or even two different times. Einstein's General Theory of Relativity allows for the possibility of such wormholes. One possible conjecture is that apparating can be explained as the creation and manipulation of very small wormholes by magical means. Such a wormhole connecting different points on Earth could be quickly traversed and would be functionally equivalent to teleportation.

Floo powder

There is also some suggestion that travel via Floo powder is not strictly speaking a form of teleportation, but some kind of extra-physical or magical connection between certain fireplaces:

> 'I had your fireplace connected to the Floo Network, you see—just for an afternoon, you know, so we could get Harry. Muggle fireplaces aren't supposed to be connected, strictly speaking—but I've got a useful contact at the Floo Regulation Panel and he fixed it for me'. (GF, p. 45)

> Harry spun faster and faster, elbows tucked tightly to his sides, blurred fireplaces flashing past him, until he started to feel sick and

closed his eyes. Then, when at last he felt himself slowing down, he threw out his hands and came to a halt in time to prevent himself from falling face forward out of the Weasleys' kitchen fire. (GF, p. 51)

So travel via Floo powder requires that fireplaces be connected in some magical way that is not a mere physical connection (you cannot literally walk from fireplace to fireplace) and yet is somehow more like normal travel between distant points than apparating. We clearly get the impression that traveling via the Floo Network is a wild ride. Perhaps the Floo Network exists for those who cannot yet apparate or for when it is not safe to do so. If so, we may view the Floo Network as a set of pre-connected magical wormholes that are connected via magic.

The Floo Network also serves another function, namely communication between distant fireplaces via "Floo talking" (OP, p. 740). In *Order of the Phoenix* Harry not only sees Grimmauld Place, he is seen by and has a conversation with the disloyal house-elf Kreacher who inhabits it (OP, p. 741). Now we have a real mystery on our hands, for it would seem that Harry's head is in the fireplace at Grimmauld Place and his body is still firmly planted at Hogwarts in Umbridge's office. It would appear that his head and body are still connected, but how is this possible under the circumstances given the large distance between these two places? It seems unlikely that Harry's neck is elongated to the point where it literally traverses all that distance, so it would seem that the connection between his body and his head is a magical and not a physical one.

Time Travel: The Tensed versus the Tenseless View of Time

In *Prisoner of Azkaban*, Hermione makes use of the "Time-Turner"—a device that allows Harry and her to time travel. But before we say more about these events it is important to get straight on some basic facts about time travel in general. First, we need to understand that there is only one conception of time in which *time* travel makes sense, namely, the "tenseless" theory of time. The common-sense view of time is the "tensed" view which holds that time, unlike space, flows or becomes.[1]

---

[1] See Craig Callender and Ralph Edney, *Introducing Time* (New York: Totem Books, 2001) for an ideal historical and philosophical overview of time.

On this view, time, like a river, is a dynamic or changing entity. According to the tensed theory of time, the future is undetermined, unreal, and open. The past is set, but long gone like faded fireworks. Only the present is real on this view, and the present is where the past and future meet. The tensed view of time is not only the common sense-view, at one time it was also widely held by philosophers. Take this passage from Augustine for example: "How can the past and future be when the past no longer is and the future is not yet? As for the present, if it were always present and never moved on to become the past, it would not be time but eternity."[2]

By contrast, the tenseless theory of time holds that the "past," "present," and "future" are all equally real.[3] On this view there is no becoming, no change, and the future is not open. In addition to the three spatial dimensions, time is conceived as a fourth dimension that is very much like just another spatial dimension. Events such as your birth, graduation, and death are all equally real (though not equally present) and we can plot them on a space-time diagram just as we would plot a point on a regular map. On this "block" or "static" picture of time the universe is a "four-dimensional space-time continuum." The notion of "now" or "the present" has no fixed position, according to this view. Indeed, past, present, and future are *relative* notions, relative to where you are on the space-time block. The events of your birth and death, just like Paris and Hong Kong, are equally real, they just exist at different space-time points. The temporal relations among all four-dimensional objects are fixed forever. As evidenced by the following quotation Einstein himself held the tenseless view of time because he believed, as do many philosophers and physicists today, that the relativity of simultaneity implies it: "[t]he distinction between past, present, and future is only an illusion, even if a stubborn one."[4]

From a four-dimensional perspective there is no such thing as change. The universe is like a still-born space-time jewel with many facets (for example space-time points), hence the name

---

[2] Augustine, *Confessions* (New York: Penguin, 1961), p. 253.
[3] Callender and Edney, pp. 33–38.
[4] A.P. French, ed., "On the Electrodynamics of Moving Bodies," *Einstein: A Centenary Volume* (Cambridge, Massachusetts: Harvard University Press, 1979), 281.

"block world." The best way to conceive of change in such a world is by analogy with the illusion of change created by still film frames moving through a projector. In frame one (time t_1), for example, Lupin is a man, in frame two (time t_2) he is part man and part wolf, and in frame three (time t_3) he is a full-blown Werewolf.

It should now be easy to see why time travel only makes sense on the tenseless view of time. On the tensed picture of time neither the past nor the future exist, only the present is real. Therefore there is no past or future to travel to on the tensed view! On the other hand, the tenseless view makes time travel possible, at least in principle, because all space-time points are equally real. In the block universe "past" and "future" (relative to our frame of reference) are fixed forever.

One interesting consequence of all this is that even if time travel is possible, it is not possible to change the past or the future. Thus all time travel stories in which people go back in time and change events that have *already happened* are inconsistent. Of course one can always try to render such stories consistent by claiming that the "new" past or future is really a distinct branch of time, different time line, different world, parallel universe, etc. But it is very different to travel "across" possible worlds as they do in the TV show *Sliders* and to travel in time as they do in the film *Twelve Monkeys*. For example, the film *Back to the Future* is a consistent story about possible worlds travel but an inconsistent time travel story because Marty changes things that have already occurred, such as the past and present events of his parents' lives. There is nothing wrong with this but such stories are better dubbed *possibility* travel than time travel, because one is moving through possibility space and not time within our universe. To put it another way, if you go back in time and perform some action, according to the block world theory, this means you *always* went back in time and performed that action. It cannot be that the past event unfolded the first time without you and then you go back in time and the past event unfolds for the second time with you! If you go back in time and assassinate Hitler before the start of World War II then you were *always* the one to shoot Hitler. This means that you should not bother trying to do this, because it never happened!

You may ask: but what prevents me from shooting Hitler if time travel is possible? People differ about how best to answer this question but since time travel is only possible in the block universe and since Hitler was not shot before the war, then we know that you cannot go back and shoot him now. It would be a contradiction if both Hitler was not shot before the war started *and* Hitler was shot before the war started, and logical contradictions just cannot happen. In short, the only time travel events that are possible (that can exist) are those that do not entail a contradiction.

Time Travel in the Harry Potter Universe

Now we can ask the question: does J.K. Rowling present us with a consistent time travel story in *Prisoner of Azkaban*? The answer is a qualified yes, qualified because we see aspects of both the tensed and tenseless views of time at work in the story: two logically incompatible notions of time. Let's begin with key uses of the tensed view of time by Hermione.

> 'No!' said Hermione in a terrified whisper. 'Don't you understand? We're breaking one of the most important wizarding laws! Nobody's supposed to change time, nobody!' (PA, p. 398)

Hermione continues, "Professor McGonagall told me what awful things have happened when wizards have meddled with time" (PA, p. 399). We see that Hermione, under the tutelage of McGonagall and Dumbledore, is operating with the tensed view of time. That is, why should wizards bother having severe laws against changing the past when time travel is only possible in those worlds in which the past cannot be changed? One need only worry about changing the past if the tensed theory of time is true, but if the tensed theory of time is true then time travel is impossible. Dumbledore further corroborates this mistake when he says to Harry: "Hasn't your experience with the Time-Turner taught you anything, Harry? The consequences of our actions are always so complicated, so diverse, that predicting the future is a very difficult business indeed . . ." (PA, p. 426). The point is that if time travel is possible then the future is fixed, so predicting the future should not be difficult at all for wizards with that ability.

There's another clear-cut use of the tensed view of time in *Order of the Phoenix* when Harry and company are fighting

Voldemort and the Death Eaters in the Ministry of Magic. Wizards at the Ministry of Magic have actually trapped time itself in a jar and when one of the Death Eaters falls into the jar, his head keeps growing alternatively old and young again because it is trapped in the cyclical flow of time within the jar. This suggests that time is a thing in itself which flows and changes. However, none of these events makes sense on a tenseless view of time. Events do not appear, disappear, and change on this view; time is not a force—the universe is just a collection of space-time still frames, so to speak.

In the case of time travel we have to make a distinction between personal time and objective time. In objective time, for instance, people might die before they were born; say you are born in the year 1988 and in the year 2004 you travel back to Dinosaur days and are killed by a *Tyrannosaurus rex*. In objective time you died millions of years before you were born in 1988. However there is no real paradox here, because in personal time you were born, traveled back in time fifteen years later, and died.

Prisoner of Azkaban is ultimately a consistent time-travel story because upon close examination Harry and Hermione do not change events that have already happened. However, unless one reads the book very closely, the natural assumption is that the pair do change an event that has already happened, namely, the death of Buckbeak. We are primed to this misreading by all the tensed view of time oriented dialogue surrounding their trip back in time. Hermione interprets Dumbledore's directive in the following way: "there must be something that happened around now he wants us to change" (PA, p. 396). In *Prisoner of Azkaban* it *appears* that Buckbeak has been beheaded, and that later on Harry and Hermione travel back in time and save Buckbeak "before" he is executed (p. 331). However, this is exactly the sort of thing that the tenseless view of time will not allow, and only the tenseless view of time supports the possibility of time travel. Again, Buckbeak's having both been killed and not killed is a logical contradiction and so is not a possibility. Fortunately the film version of *Prisoner of Azkaban* is very careful, using a number of devices to ensure that the audience understands that Buckbeak was never killed and that it was always the time-traveling Harry and Hermione that saved him. As one example of this, the film version makes it clear that the time-traveling Harry and Hermione were always outside Hagrid's house watching their non-time-traveling selves and waiting to free Buckbeak. Based on the book alone it would be easy to think the sequence of events was as follows:

1) While exiting Hagrid's garden the three hear Buckbeak get executed: "the unmistakable swish and thud of an axe" (PA, p. 331).

2) Hermione and Sirius are rendered unconscious by the Dementors and Harry is surrounded by them. Just as Harry is about to have his soul sucked out by a Dementor's kiss an "animal of light" appears out of nowhere and drives the Dementors away and Harry faints.

3) Harry and Hermione wake up in the Hospital wing of Hogwarts and learn that Sirius is imprisoned upstairs and is about to be administered the Dementor's kiss. Dumbledore sends Harry and Hermione three hours back in time to save Sirius.

4) Harry and Hermione go to the edge of the woods and watch all the same events transpire leading up to Buckbeak's execution but this time they sneak up and rescue Buckbeak.

5) While making their escape, Harry sees the Dementors closing in on his "other self," the unconscious Sirius and "other" Hermione. Harry decides to go and find out who saved him from the Dementors. Harry realizes that it was he (his time-traveling self) who saved himself from the Dementors and he conjures up a patronus in the form of a "stag" which does exactly that.

6) Harry and Hermione save Sirius and get back to the hospital wing just in time to sense Dumbledore sending their "other selves" off to time travel and save Sirius.

From this sequence of events it appears that Buckbeak both is and is not beheaded, yet this is a logical contradiction that cannot occur. However, a close and charitable reading of these passages reveals that in fact Buckbeak was never killed and that the "events" experienced by the non-time traveling Harry and Hermione and their time-traveling counterparts, are in fact the same events. Rowling shows this by cleverly tying together the two events with almost the same language. In the first sequence, there is the "unmistakable swish and thud of an axe" that we are supposed to take as the execution of Buckbeak (PA, p. 331). And in the second sequence, after the time-traveling Harry and Hermione have saved Buckbeak, we hear "a swishing noise, and the thud of an axe" when the executioner swings his axe into a fence (PA, p. 402). In the movie version, we see the exe-cutioner chop a large pumpkin in half to the same effect.

The fact that time-traveling Harry saves his "other self" from the Dementors is certainly strange but it does not violate any known laws of logic or physics. This is an example of what we call "a closed causal loop." In this case the events in the loop are: (A) Harry was saved from the Dementors because he trav-eled back in time and saved himself and (B) Harry was able to travel back in time because he saved himself. Why was Harry saved? Because he traveled back in time. Why did Harry travel back in time? Because he was saved. This causal loop goes round and round because event (A) caused event (B) and event (B) caused event (A). Normally, causal relations between events form a straight chain and not a loop. Causal loops are standard fare for time-travel stories because they are mind-bending and both logically and physically possible.

What We've Learned About Harry Potter's World

We have learned that the world of Harry Potter is our present world and that magical means are used to travel around this world by creating or manipulating the magical equivalent of wormholes. The best explanation we can come up with for Floo powder communication: it's magic! Apparating and the Floo Travel Network might be physically and logically possible, but it is unclear how to explain Floo powder communication except by purely magical means.[5] Time travel is logically and physically possible in our world and thus in the world of Harry Potter. However, time travel is only possible in a block universe (the

---

[5] Roger Highfield, *The Science of Harry Potter* (New York: Penguin, 2002).

tenseless theory of time) in which no events can be changed, erased, or rewritten. Time travel as presented in *Prisoner of Azkaban* is, if charitably interpreted, consistent with the block world that makes time travel possible. However, the frequent warnings throughout the book about the dangers of changing the past, present, or future might lead even the attentive reader to conclude otherwise.

15

Why Voldemort Won't Just Die Already: What Wizards Can Teach Us about Personal Identity

JASON T. EBERL

When Lord Voldemort recounts what happened to him the night he killed Lily and James Potter, but failed to kill their son Harry, he describes himself as having been painfully "ripped" from his body and thereafter existing as "less than spirit, less than the meanest ghost" (GF, p. 653). Despite the loss of his body, Voldemort survives his first encounter with Harry Potter and continues to exist in one of two ways: either as an immaterial spirit, or by possessing the body of an animal or another person.

Voldemort is not the only wizard who is capable of existing apart from the typical bodily fashion. Some wizards survive their body's death as ghosts or poltergeists; for example, Hogwarts Professor Binns, who "had simply got up to teach one day and left his body behind him in an armchair in front of the staff room fire" (CS, p. 148), or Nearly Headless Nick. In addition to disembodiment, wizards can—with the help of certain spells, potions, and magical devices—move their bodies nearly instantaneously between distant places (teletransportation) or change their appearance into animals or other persons (transfiguration).

Many of us Muggles who read J.K. Rowling's Harry Potter books also believe that we may survive the death of our bodies, or experience periods of disembodied existence in some form or fashion while alive. Some of us believe that we may survive death in a different type of body, perhaps the body of an animal, or without a body at all. This possibility raises several questions concerning what philosophers refer to as *personal identity*:

What is it that I am referring to when I say "I"? What makes the "I" that's typing this sentence the same "I" that was reading *Sorcerer's Stone* with my daughter last night? Could I have had a different body than I now have? Could I change from this body to some other? Do I even need a body in order to exist?

As persons themselves, philosophers have been quite interested in proposing answers to these and other related questions for centuries. The views of some philosophers would not allow for the type of disembodied survival that Voldemort and Professor Binns experience. Other philosophers' views do, however, and it is these upon which we'll focus to discover the wizards' survival secret.

Disembodied Survival and the Nature of Persons

Although they are wizards, Voldemort and Professor Binns are also *persons* like you and me. The natural first question when considering wizards' disembodied survival is, "What is a person?", followed by the natural second question, "What makes the same person exist at different times and places?" Answering these questions allows us to approach the final question of concern here, "How can a person exist without a body?"

According to John Locke, in his *An Essay Concerning Human Understanding*, a person is "a thinking intelligent Being, that has reason and reflection, and can consider itself as itself, the same thinking thing in different times and places."[1] What makes persons unique among other types of things in the world, such as rocks, chairs, and cats, is that persons can *think* in a *self-reflective* manner. Persons are able philosophically and scientifically to understand the world around them. Persons are also aware of their own conscious self and can reflect on their thoughts, feelings, and desires.

Locke further states that what accounts for a person persisting as the *same* person throughout time and change is that he has the same *consciousness*:

> For since consciousness always accompanies thinking, and 'tis that, that makes every one to be, what he calls *self*; and thereby

---

[1] John Locke, *An Essay Concerning Human Understanding* (1689) (Oxford: Clarendon, 1975), Book II, Chapter 27, §9.

distinguishes himself from all other thinking things, in this alone consists *personal Identity, i.e.* the sameness of a rational Being: And as far as this consciousness can be extended backwards to any past Action or Thought, so far reaches the Identity of that *Person*; it is the same *self* now it was then; and 'tis by the same *self* with this present one that now reflects on it, that that Action was done.[2]

I am conscious of my presently typing these words on my laptop at home. At the same time, if I stop to think about it, I can be conscious of my past action of having watched the movie version of *Chamber of Secrets*. How do I know that I am the same person who is both typing now and who watched the film two weeks ago? Because I am consciously aware of my performance of both actions.

Defining a person in terms of consciousness, Locke leaves open the potential for a rather sticky dilemma: What would happen if a person lost his consciousness of some past action he had done? This is what happens to Gilderoy Lockhart when he attempts to erase Harry's and Ron's memories in *Chamber of Secrets*:

> "His memory's gone," said Ron. "The Memory Charm backfired. Hit him instead of us. Hasn't got a clue who he is, or where he is, or who we are. I told him to come and wait here. He's a danger to himself." (CS, p. 324)

Years later, when Harry and Ron visit Lockhart in *Order of the Phoenix*, he still has no memory of his life prior to the unfortunate spell. He even appears unable to form new long-term memories as the Healer who cares for him worries about him leaving his room and not remembering how to get back (OP, p. 510). With his memories so disjointed, Lockhart's personal identity has been shattered. There are several different consciousnesses, each defined by its own unique set of memories, that exist successively in Lockhart's body. By constantly forming new short-term memories and then promptly forgetting them, it seems as if a new person comes into existence inhabiting the same body every time Lockhart fails to form a long-term memory!

Locke imagines a similar type of situation:

---

[2] Locke, *Essay*, Book II, Chapter 27, §9.

Could we suppose two distinct incommunicable consciousnesses acting the same Body, the one constantly by Day, the other by Night . . . I ask in the first case, Whether the *Day* and the *Night-man* would not be two as distinct Persons, as *Socrates* and *Plato*.[3]

It seems strange to imagine two persons, with two distinct consciousnesses, inhabiting the same body. Nonetheless, we find this phenomenon occurring in the magical world of Harry Potter, as with Voldemort's parasitical existence in the body of Professor Quirrell:

"See what I have become?" the face said. "Mere shadow and vapor . . . I have form only when I can share another's body." (SS, p. 293)

Voldemort exists as a face on the back of Professor Quirrell's head, and he and Quirrell are thus two persons—two distinct consciousnesses—in one body.

What if two persons come to share *one* consciousness? Do they become one person? To see how this could happen, consider David Hume's understanding of personal identity from his *A Treatise of Human Nature*. Hume, like Locke, understands personhood to be fundamentally a matter of consciousness or, to be more precise, *perceptions*:

For my part, when I enter most intimately into what I call *myself*, I always stumble on some particular perception or other, of heat or cold, light or shade, love or hatred, pain or pleasure. I never can catch *myself* at any time without a perception, and never can observe any thing but the perception. When my perceptions are remov'd for any time, as by sound sleep; so long am I insensible of *myself*, and may truly be said not to exist.[4]

It seems absurd for Hume to think that he ceases to exist every time he enters a dreamless sleep and comes back into existence when he begins to dream or wakes up. At the foundation of his philosophy, though, Hume is a *skeptic* and argues that we should withhold believing in any phenomenon we

---

[3] Locke, *Essay*, Book II, Chapter 27, §23.
[4] David Hume, *A Treatise of Human Nature* (1739) (Oxford: Clarendon, 1978), Book I, Part 4, Section vi.

cannot rationally verify with a great degree of certainty. When Hume rationally reflects on whether there is a *self* named "David Hume," he perceives no such entity. The "self" must be an ever-changing bundle of perceptions.

Personal identity, according to Hume, is the connectedness of various perceptions linked together into one bundle, which I call my "self," by *memory*:

> As memory alone acquaints us with the continuance and extent of this succession of perceptions, 'tis to be consider'd, upon that account chiefly, as the source of personal identity. Had we no memory, we never shou'd have any notion of causation, nor consequently of that chain of causes and effects, which constitute our self or person.[5]

What about when a person enters into a dreamless sleep or a temporary coma? Hume responds that, once we have an idea of our own personal identity through time, we can "extend our identity beyond our memory" and "comprehend time, and circumstances, and actions, which we have entirely forgot, but suppose in general to have existed."[6] So, even though Harry has no memory of his first encounter with Voldemort and his parents' deaths, having heard the story recounted to him on several occasions is enough for him to suppose the encounter took place and thus to consider himself as having existed and experienced that encounter. Of course, Hume would caution Harry to remain skeptical of the story that others had relayed to him since he has no perception of it that he can link by memory to his present perceptions.

This brings us back to the question of whether two persons can share the same consciousness and so become the same person. Think, for example, of when Harry encounters Professor Dumbledore's Pensieve:

> "What is it?" Harry asked shakily.
> "This? It is called a Pensieve," said Dumbledore. "I sometimes find, and I am sure you know the feeling, that I simply have too many thoughts and memories crammed into my mind."

---

[5] Hume, *Treatise*, Book I, Part 4, Section vi.
[6] *Ibid.*

. . . "At these times," said Dumbledore, indicating the stone basin, "I use the Pensieve. One simply siphons the excess thoughts from one's mind, pours them into the basin, and examines them at one's leisure. It becomes easier to spot patterns and links, you understand, when they are in this form." (GF, p. 597)

Harry experiences the Pensieve just prior to Dumbledore's explanation when he is drawn into the stone basin and into one of Dumbledore's stored memories. While inside the Pensieve, Harry does not simply watch Dumbledore's memory, as if it were a movie, but is actually inside the memory itself, as if he had been present at that moment and witnessed the event himself as it happened. Though he is literally "inside" Dumbledore's memory, Harry and Dumbledore do not share the same consciousness. In fact, Harry encounters *two* Dumbledores. One is the Dumbledore of the past who originally had the experience Harry is witnessing in the Pensieve, and with whom he is unable to interact. The other is the present-day Dumbledore who is inside the Pensieve as well in order to re-examine this memory experienced by his past self. Since Harry and Dumbledore (of either the past or the present) do not share the same consciousness in the Pensieve, they do not become the same person. Rather, Harry and "present-Dumbledore" are witnesses to the same event, which is available for them to witness because the original experience of "past-Dumbledore" has been stored in the Pensieve. However, all three persons—Harry, past-Dumbledore, and present-Dumbledore—maintain their own unique *first-person perspective*. Each perceives the event in the Pensieve with his own set of memories, background beliefs, and consciousness of his unique self. Harry doesn't begin to believe he is Dumbledore or *vice versa*. Even present-Dumbledore is viewing the event not through the eyes of his past self, but rather with his own eyes, which now have more years of wisdom and experience behind them.

Harry has another experience that is much more unnerving. In *Goblet of Fire* and *Order of the Phoenix*, he occasionally has the experience of seeing through Voldemort's eyes. At first, the experience is an empathic sharing of Voldemort's feelings (OP, p. 382). As time goes on, however, Harry begins to do more than feel what Voldemort feels. He actually shares Voldemort's first-person perspective. Harry has a dream in which he thinks

he's a snake attacking Mr. Weasley (OP, pp. 462–63) and a recurring dream of breaking into the Department of Mysteries in the
Ministry of Magic (OP, p. 635). After Harry's dream of being a
snake, Dumbledore concludes that Voldemort—who was possessing the snake at the time of the attack on Mr. Weasley—is
influencing Harry's conscious mind through Legilimency, the
magical art of seeing into others' minds. So Dumbledore
instructs Snape to train Harry in Occlumency, which will block
Voldemort from Harry's mind. Harry's experiences indicate that
Legilimency, unlike the experience provided by the Pensieve,
does not allow a wizard merely to experience what someone
else experienced—like watching someone else's home
movies—but actually to enter his mind and share his first-person perspective. Snape explains this concept to Harry:

> "He can read minds?" said Harry quickly, his worst fears con-
> firmed.
>   . . . "Only Muggles talk of 'mind reading.' The mind is not a
> book, to be opened at will and examined at leisure. Thoughts are
> not etched on the inside of skulls, to be perused by any invader.
> The mind is a complex and many-layered thing, Potter . . . or at
> least, most minds are. . . ." He smirked. "It is true, however, that
> those who have mastered Legilimency are able, under certain con-
> ditions, to delve into the minds of their victims and to interpret
> their findings correctly. . . ." (OP 530–31)

Do Harry and Voldemort become the same person in these
experiences? At the time of each experience, they share the
same consciousness and will have the same memory of the
event, for example, of attacking Mr. Weasley as a snake. Thus,
since for Locke and Hume consciousness and memory are the
foundation of personal identity, the conclusion apparently follows that Harry and Voldemort are one and the same person
when they share these experiences. Should we be troubled
that our hero, Harry, and his arch-nemesis and the epitome of
evil, Voldemort, may actually be the same person? No, for they
do not become the same person merely by having a few memories in common. Though they share the same consciousness
at one or two points in time, it does not follow that "Harry
becomes Voldemort" or that "Voldemort becomes Harry," for
the two are not *identical*. According to Gottfried Wilhelm
Leibniz, in his *Discourse on Metaphysics*, for any two things to

be identical, they must share all and only the same properties.[7] In other words, for Harry and Voldemort to be the same person, anything that can be said of one must be able to be said of the other. Voldemort, however, can recall the memory of having killed Lily and James Potter and of having attempted to kill Harry. If Harry were identical to Voldemort, then he would be able to recall the same memory of having killed his parents and having attempted to kill himself (talk about existential angst!), and Voldemort would be able to recall the memory of having lived in a dark cupboard at number four, Privet Drive. Therefore, since it is clear that Harry and Voldemort do not share all and only the same properties, the two cannot be the same person despite their sharing the same consciousness on a few occasions.

In order for Voldemort to exist completely disembodied or for Professor Binns and the other ethereal inhabitants of Hogwarts, such as Nearly Headless Nick, to exist as ghosts or poltergeists, persons must be able to maintain their self-identity without a body. The only feature shared by a wizard's embodied and disembodied selves is his consciousness. What links the two selves are memories of the same events experienced from the same first-person perspective.

Teletransportation and Personal Identity

Aside from having the ability to exist without their bodies altogether, wizards can do various things with their bodies that are rather ordinary to them while quite strange and wondrous to us Muggles. A prime example that bears on the question of personal identity is teletransportation: the instantaneous, or near-instantaneous, movement of one's body between two distant places. A wizard accomplishes teletransportation by using a magical device such as a Portkey or Floo powder, or by the process of Apparition.

Using a Portkey or Floo powder to teletransport oneself does not present any particular challenges to a wizard's persistent personal identity. For the wizard's whole body travels through the process and he even experiences the short lapse of time

---

[7] G.W. Leibniz, *Discourse on Metaphysics* (1686), in *Philosophical Papers and Letters*, second edition (Dordrecht: Reidel, 1969), §9.

between leaving one location and arriving at the other. There is continuity of both body and consciousness in the movement from one place to another. Consider when Harry travels with Ron and Hermione via a Portkey in the form of an old boot (GF, p. 73) or when Harry uses Floo powder to travel from the Weasleys' house to Diagon Alley (CS, p. 49):

> It felt as though he was being sucked down a giant drain. He seemed to be spinning very fast—the roaring in his ears was deafening—he tried to keep his eyes open but the whirl of green flames made him feel sick—something hard knocked his elbow and he tucked it in tightly, still spinning and spinning—now it felt as though cold hands were slapping his face—squinting through his glasses he saw a blurred stream of fireplaces and snatched glimpses of the room beyond—his bacon sandwiches were churning inside him—he closed his eyes again wishing it would stop. . . . (CS, p. 49)

Clearly, Harry's mind and body are intact throughout this journey. Harry experiences vivid physical sensations, including the disquieting gastro-intestinal effects of spinning through hyperspace after having eaten half a dozen bacon sandwiches!

Not all forms of teletransportation, though, go as smoothly or with all of oneself intact. Apparition is a dangerous form of teletransportation, which, unlike the use of a Portkey or Floo powder, is near-instantaneous but has the potential for complication:

> "It's not easy, Apparition, and when it's not done properly it can lead to nasty complications. This pair I'm talking about went and splinched themselves."
>
> Everyone around the table except Harry winced.
>
> "Er—*splinched?*" said Harry.
>
> "They left half of themselves behind," said Mr. Weasley, now spooning large amounts of treacle onto his porridge. "So, of course, they were stuck. Couldn't move either way. Had to wait for the Accidental Magic Reversal Squad to sort them out. Meant a fair old bit of paperwork, I can tell you, what with Muggles who spotted the body parts they'd left behind." (GF, pp. 66–67)

It's not evident in what way the two people in Mr. Weasley's story were "splinched," that is, which body parts were transported and which were left behind. So we can imagine various ways of being splinched. Say Professor McGonagall is splinched such that her head and torso are transported to the Leaky Cauldron, while the lower half of her body is left behind in the Great Hall at Hogwarts. If we asked whether Professor McGonagall is located in the Leaky Cauldron or the Great Hall, a reasonable answer would be that she is in the Leaky Cauldron. This answer makes sense, because the Leaky Cauldron is where her brain is located and the brain, as neurobiological evidence tells us, is linked somehow to a person's consciousness.

Given such a link, an interesting problem arises when we consider a particular way in which a person could conceivably be splinched. Each human brain contains two large hemispheres known as the *cerebral cortex*. Neural activity in these hemispheres, joined together by a bundle of nerves called the *corpus collosum*, is the foundation for consciousness. Now imagine that Professor McGonagall is splinched "down the middle" such that the left half of her body (along with the left cortical hemisphere) is transported to the Leaky Cauldron, while the right half of her body (along with the right cortical hemisphere) is left in the Great Hall at Hogwarts. The cortical hemispheres are, therefore, divided along the corpus collosum. This situation is not as fictional as one might think. In fact, severing the corpus collosum is a form of treatment used to minimize epileptic seizures.

What makes this form of splinching problematic for personal identity is that, while a normally functioning cerebral cortex delegates certain psychological tasks to each hemisphere and the two communicate to each other via the corpus collosum, it's physiologically possible for each hemisphere to take on all of a person's conscious functioning. If your corpus collosum were severed and one of the cortical hemispheres removed from your head, you would remain a fully conscious person. Though you may be cognitively impaired in certain areas for a time, your cortex would eventually learn how to do the job that both hemispheres did previously. Say Neville Longbottom were splinched in this fashion and stayed that way for a long time because the Accidental Magic Reversal Squad found it difficult to undo this particularly nasty form of splinching. Each of Neville's halves would have the same consciousness, the same memories of everything that happened prior to the splinching, and the same sense of self. Each half, one, say, in the Gryffindor dormitory and the other in a vault at

Gringotts, would believe that *he* is Neville Longbottom. Which one is Neville? Is Neville identical to only one of his body's halves? If so, which one? Perhaps Neville is dead and two new persons claiming to be him remain instead.

Neither Locke nor Hume imagined this type of situation occurring, but a more recent philosopher, Derek Parfit, did in his book *Reasons and Persons*:

> *My Division*. My body is fatally injured, as are the brains of my two brothers. My brain is divided, and each half is successfully transplanted into the body of one of my brothers. Each of the resulting people believes that he is me, seems to remember living my life, has my character, and is in every other way psychologically continuous with me. And he has a body that is very like mine.[8]

Parfit rejects several attempts to explain the identity relationship between a person and the two persons that result from his being divided. The problem with establishing personal identity in this case is that the identity relationship is transitive, meaning that if A = B and B = C, then A = C. So, given Hume's criterion for personal identity in terms of psychological continuity, Neville Longbottom is identical to his body's half in the dormitory and also to his body's half in the vault. Since identity is transitive, however, it follows that Neville's bodily half in the dormitory must be identical with his bodily half in the vault. But this can't be true since Neville's halves are obviously not identical, if for no other reason than because they are in different spatial locations. Since it is clearly unacceptable to say that Neville is identical to *both* of his bodily halves, and there is no reason to hold that he is identical to one of them and not the other, it seems that Neville's splinching accident must have resulted in his death and the remaining bodily halves are two new persons. This conclusion, though, raises yet another question: Where did each of these new persons come from if neither one of them is Neville? There seems to be no easy solution to this type of "split-identity" scenario.

Because the relationship of identity entails such a problematic result in this type of case, Parfit says we should put aside our concern with being identical with some future person and

---

[8] Derek Parfit, *Reasons and Persons* (Oxford: Clarendon, 1984), pp. 254–55.

consider "what matters" in our personal survival. What matters, Parfit contends, is simply our being psychologically continuous with a future person:

> Some people would regard division as being as bad, or nearly as bad, as ordinary death [the conclusion arrived at above concerning poor Neville]. This reaction is irrational. We ought to regard division as being about as good as ordinary survival. As I have argued, the two 'products' of this operation [or the splinching accident] would be two different people. Consider my relationship to each of these people. Does this relation fail to contain some vital element that is contained in ordinary survival? It seems clear that it does not. I would survive if I stood in this very same relation to only one of the resulting people [i.e., a single case of psychological continuity]. . . . In the case that we are now considering, my relation to each of the resulting people thus contains everything that would be needed for me to survive as that person.[9]

If Parfit is correct, then Neville can survive his nearly disastrous splinching accident. Though we cannot say that Neville is identical to either of his resulting halves, each has everything that is required for us to say that Neville has "survived" in both the half located in the dormitory and the half located in the vault. Does it matter that we are apparently left with *two* Nevilles now?

At this point, you may be wondering what happens when the Accidental Magic Reversal Squad puts Neville's halves back together. On Parfit's view, just as Neville survives as each of his halves, he continues to survive as the reconstituted singular person who has just one cerebral cortex now—the two hemispheres having been rejoined—and is thereby psychologically continuous with Neville as he existed prior to being splinched.

In the world of Harry Potter, wizards are able to do the amazing things they do, such as survive disembodiment and teletransportation by Apparating, by being persons who are defined as psychological entities. They persist by virtue of their past, present, and future selves being psychologically continuous with one another. This way of understanding the nature of persons and personal identity may be as true in the real world in

---

[9] Parfit, *Reasons and Persons*, p. 261.

which we live as it is in the fictional world created by J.K. Rowling. Perhaps we are best defined as conscious, thinking entities which consist of past and present perceptions connected by memory. If so, then we have an effective way of answering the question of whether you and I can exist without our bodies. So long as my consciousness can exist without requiring a functioning brain—a premise that is challenged by a wealth of neurobiological data linking consciousness with cerebral activity—there is no reason I can't survive my body's death and persist as a non-physical, conscious, thinking entity.[10] Of course, this brief chapter cannot answer the question of whether or not the existence of consciousness requires a brain, nor fully consider the apparent "magic" required for a non-physical conscious mind to interact with a physical brain and body. Nevertheless, our ability to imagine persons surviving disembodiment and significant bodily changes in the world of Harry Potter gives us some insight into the possibility of these wizards' feats in our own world.[11]

---

[10] For various views of the relationship between consciousness and brain function, see Richard Swinburne, *Evolution of the Soul*, revised edition (Oxford: Clarendon, 1997); William Hasker, *The Emergent Self* (Ithaca: Cornell University Press, 1999); David J. Chalmers, *The Conscious Mind* (Oxford: Oxford University Press, 1996); and Daniel C. Dennett, *Consciousness Explained* (Boston: Back Bay Books, 1991). Views represented here are substance dualism, emergent dualism, property dualism, and reductionism, respectively.

[11] I am most grateful to Kevin Decker for supplying me with many helpful references to the Harry Potter books and to the editors of this volume, Bill Irwin, and Greg Bassham for their insightful comments and suggestions.

16

The Prophecy-Driven Life: Fate and Freedom at Hogwarts

GREGORY BASSHAM

We have to believe in free will. We've got no choice.

—ISAAC BASHEVIS SINGER

Think how cool it would be if you had a crystal ball that—unlike Professor Trelawney's—could infallibly predict the future. You could make a fortune betting in the Quidditch pool, know in advance all the questions that will appear on your Herbology final, and never, ever again get shot down in flames when asking that cute witch or wizard from Ravenclaw out for a date.

Some things, of course, wouldn't be so cool about knowing the future. Like knowing exactly when you will die, and how. Imagine if you knew now, for example, that you will die in a fiery flying car crash on June 23rd, 2012. Or that your best friend will be killed by Voldemort on December 5th, 2008. That kind of knowledge would be tough to live with. In fact, if you did learn that something terrible was somehow fated to happen in the future, you would naturally wonder if there was anything you could do to prevent it.

There's a wonderful story philosophy profs often use to get their students thinking about conundrums of fate and free will—and I don't mean the "what will really bake your noodle" scene from *The Matrix*. It's an old Arab fable retold by W. Somerset Maugham in his 1933 play *Sheppey*. The speaker is Death:

There was a merchant in Baghdad who sent his servant to market to buy provisions and in a little while the servant came back, white and trembling, and said, Master, just now when I was in the market-place I was jostled by a woman in the crowd and when I turned I saw it was Death that jostled me. She looked at me and made a threatening gesture; now, lend me your horse, and I will ride away from this city and avoid my fate. I will go to Samarra and there Death will not find me. The merchant lent him his horse, and the servant mounted it, and he dug his spurs in its flanks and as fast as the horse could gallop he went. The merchant went down to the market-place and he saw me standing in the crowd, and he came to me and said, Why did you make a threatening gesture to my servant when you saw him this morning? That was not a threatening gesture, I said, it was only a start of surprise. I was astonished to see him in Baghdad, for I had an appointment with him tonight in Samarra.[1]

The central idea here—that future events will happen no matter what anybody does to prevent them—is a view that philosophers call *fatalism*. According to fatalists, the future is already completely fixed and determined, freedom is an illusion, and we're all just unwitting puppets in a play that was scripted long ago.

Fatalism can seem pretty plausible at times—like when you're wondering whether you might be "fated" to drink that fourth shot of Ogden's Old Firewhiskey—but it's really quite incredible when you think about it. Think what is implied, for example, in saying that you're destined to drink that firewhiskey *no matter what anybody does*. That means that if a gang of Death Eaters zapped you dead with the *Avada Kedavra* curse, you still (somehow) would down that fourth shot. That would be a neat trick even for a resourceful adult beverage drinker like you.

Fatalism, therefore, can be safely tossed in the dumpster. But the idea that future actions and choices are somehow already predetermined, and hence unfree, cannot be so lightly swept aside. There are three major challenges to human freedom and responsibility: the scientific challenge, the religious challenge,

---

[1] Quoted in Theodore Schick, Jr. and Lewis Vaughn, *Doing Philosophy: An Introduction through Thought Experiments* (Mountain View: Mayfield, 1999), p. 140.

and the paranormal challenge. We'll focus mainly on the paranormal challenge, because that is the one raised most clearly in the Potter books. But first let's look briefly at the challenges to freedom posed by science and religion.

The Scientific Challenge to Freedom

Everything is determined, the beginning as well as the end, by forces over which we have no control.

—ALBERT EINSTEIN

Back in the benighted days of yore, people wearing animal skins used to squat in caves and say things like, "Yore, I wouldn't go outside if I were you. Don't you see that lightning? The gods must be angry with us." They attributed all kinds of natural phenomena—rainbows, eclipses, Yore's flatulence—to the arbitrary, mostly unpredictable will of supernatural forces. Nowadays, of course, we have science, and science has been spectacularly successful in showing that we live in an orderly, predictable universe. In fact, science has been *so* successful in this explanatory quest that many people now believe in *causal determinism*—the view that all events, including all human actions and choices, are the inevitable outcome of prior causes. If causal determinism is true, then a sufficiently powerful Intelligence who knew all the relevant facts and laws of nature, could have predicted a hundred years ago that you would be reading this sentence right now.

The catch, of course, is that causal determinism poses an obvious threat to human freedom and moral responsibility. Consider when Ginny Weasley was taken over by Voldemort in the form of Tom Riddle (CS, p. 120). Although it was her hands that wrote in blood the ominous words "The Chamber of Secrets has been opened," she was temporarily possessed and unable to recall any of the events afterwards. Because her actions were determined by forces beyond her control, she wasn't able to do otherwise than she did, and hence, it seems, wasn't acting freely. But, of course, if determinism is true, *none* of us is truly able to act otherwise than we do. Hence the apparent conflict between determinism and free will.

Philosophers disagree whether free will is possible in a fully determined world. *Hard determinists* like B.F. Skinner and John

Hospers say that determinism is true and that free will is impossible in such a world. *Soft determinists* like Jonathan Edwards, David Hume, and John Stuart Mill say that determinism is true but that we can still be free. Like Bernie Bott's Beans, soft determinists come in different varieties but they generally say something like this: free will consists in the ability to do as you choose. If you can do as you wish, if no person, force, or thing is *forcing* you to do something against your will, then your act is free.

Libertarians[2] like William James and C.A. Campbell are unconvinced. Like hard determinists, they think determinism and free will are incompatible. But like soft determinists, libertarians wish to affirm freedom. By "free act," libertarians generally mean acts that are (*a*) caused exclusively by the agent and (*b*) genuinely could have been otherwise than they were. For instance, Harry's generous decision to give his Triwizard Tournament winnings to Fred and George Weasley was a free act according to libertarians, because it was caused solely by Harry's choice, rather than by any past events or compelling internal or external forces, and in exactly the same circumstances Harry could have chosen to do something different than he did, like buying snazzy new Firebolts for the entire Gryffindor Quidditch team. Libertarians deny that, given a particular brain state and all the causal forces at work in the world, only one choice is ever possible. They think that, if somehow we could roll back time and find ourselves in exactly the same causal situation, a different decision could have been made.

So is free will compatible with causal determinism? If, as soft determinists claim, free will is simply the ability to do as one desires, there clearly is no incompatibility. With the exception of prison inmates and parents with small children, most people in this world are often able to do as they please, regardless of whether determinism is true. But is the soft determinist definition of "free will" correct?

The definition works well with standard cases of coerced actions, like when a robber forces you to hand over your wallet at gunpoint. It also works well with many accidental or unintended actions ("I didn't *mean* to turn you into a Chinese

---

[2] Not to be confused with libertarians in the *political* sense—believers in small government and the right to do whatever lamebrained thing you want, so long as you don't violate the liberties or property rights of others.

Chomping Cabbage. Peeves jostled my wand.") According to soft determinists, neither of these kinds of acts is free because they don't accord with your desires. But it doesn't take a Supreme Mugwump to see that the soft determinist definition *doesn't* work for many cases in which a person does what he desires but lacks any effective control over what he desires. Suppose, for instance, Mad-Eye Moody zaps you with an Imperius Curse and orders you to belt out a rousing rendition of the Hogwarts school song, which you do. This isn't like the gunman case in which a person is forced to do something he or she doesn't want to do. The Imperius Curse works by *changing* a person's will, so that the victim does willingly whatever the controlling wizard or witch commands (GF, p. 231). According to the soft determinist definition, therefore, you would freely choose to sing the song. But that seems clearly wrong. And the problem isn't just limited to fanciful examples like those involving Imperius Curses. People who are brainwashed, hypnotized, insane, profoundly retarded, infantile, or driven by irresistible impulses may be doing as they desire. But if they lack at least indirect control over their desires, it's hard to see how their acts can be free, at least in the robust sense of "freedom" required for moral responsibility.[3]

The hocus-pocus of redefining freedom to suit our purposes is as bogus as one of Rita Skeeter's scandal columns. If, as determinists claim, all of our actions are the inevitable product of causes over which we have no control, free will is an illusion.

The Religious Challenge to Freedom

God, from all eternity, did, by the most wise and holy counsel of his own will, freely, and unchangeably ordain whatsoever comes to pass; yet so, as thereby neither is God the author of sin, nor is violence offered to the will of the creatures.

—WESTMINSTER CONFESSION

---

[3] There are, of course, more sophisticated versions of soft determinism than the version I have critiqued. See, for example, Daniel Dennett, *Elbow Room: The Varieties of Free Will Worth Wanting* (Cambridge, Massachusetts: MIT Press, 1984). For a powerful argument that none of these sophisticated versions have succeeded, or ever could, see Peter van Inwagen, *Free Will* (Oxford: Clarendon, 1983).

Challenges to free will can arise from religion as well as from science. In the Christian tradition, for instance, many thinkers, including the great Protestant theologians Martin Luther and John Calvin, claim that God exercises total sovereignty over all earthly affairs, meaning that absolutely everything that occurs happens in accordance with His eternal and immutable will and preordained plan.[4] Clearly, there are massive problems reconciling free will with such total divine control and predestination. But problems exist even if God merely *foreknows* that certain events will occur, even if He doesn't will or cause them to occur.

The problem arises because if God *knows* that a future event will occur, then it *must* occur, because God (being essentially all-knowing) can't possibly be wrong. Now suppose that the future event in question is Harry's courageous decision to rescue Ginny from the basilisk as described in *Chamber of Secrets* (pp. 301–324). We can then formulate the following Argument for the Incompatibility of Divine Foreknowledge and Free Will:

1) If God knows in advance that Harry will fight the basilisk, then it must be the case that Harry will fight the basilisk.

2) If it *must* be the case that Harry will fight the basilisk, then it is not in Harry's power to refrain from fighting the basilisk.

3) If it is not in Harry's power to refrain from fighting the basilisk, then Harry is not free to decide whether to fight the basilisk.

4) So, if God knows in advance that Harry will fight the basilisk, then Harry is not free to decide whether to fight the basilisk.[5]

---

[4] See Martin Luther, "Bondage of the Will," in *Martin Luther: Selections from His Writings* (Garden City: Anchor Books, 1961), p. 181; John Calvin, *Institutes of the Christian Religion*, Volume 2, translated by Lewis Ford Battles (Philadelphia: Westminster, 1960), Book 2, Chapter 2. For a good contemporary defense of this view, see John Feinberg, "God Ordains All Things," in *Predestination and Free Will: Four Views on Divine Sovereignty and Human Freedom*, edited by David Basinger and Randall Basinger (Downers Grove: InterVarsity Press, 1986), pp. 19–43.

[5] For a similar formulation, see Alvin Plantinga, "On Ockham's Way Out," in John Martin Fischer, ed., *God, Foreknowledge, and Freedom* (Palo Alto: Stanford University Press, 1989), pp. 179–180.

There are various ways of responding to this argument, none of them wholly free from difficulties. First, like some Calvinists, you could accept the argument as sound, affirm divine foreknowledge, and deny that any human actions are truly free. The problems with this solution are that 1) it seems to make God responsible for evil and sin, 2) it casts doubt on the justice of God in holding sinners responsible for sin, 3) it calls into question God's own freedom (since He presumably foreknows His own acts as well as those of His creatures), and 4) there are many passages in Scripture that appear to presuppose the reality of free will.

Second, you could opt for the soft determinist tactic of redefining "free will" in such a way that acts can be free even if they are fully determined and could not have occurred otherwise than they do. The problem with this solution, as we have seen, is that the standard soft determinist definition of "free" is a load of old tosh, as Uncle Vernon would say.[6]

Third, you could deny divine foreknowledge, or at least divine foreknowledge of future free choices. Some modern theologians (such as Clark Pinnock) have argued that free choices, by their very nature, cannot be foreknown with certainty. According to such theologians, "future contingent" statements such as "Harry will fight the basilisk" are neither true nor false until the relevant people freely choose whether to perform the relevant action. This is so, it is claimed, because there is no state of affairs or corresponding reality to "ground" such a statement—that is, to make it true. There are two major problems with this solution, however. First, there are many prophecies in Scripture that clearly presuppose that future free actions can sometimes be foreknown.[7] Second, there are some future contingent propositions that can be known to be true, even by fallible mortals such as ourselves. I think I know now, for instance, that my good friend and colleague Bill Irwin won't freely choose to fly to London tonight and sing the Icelandic national anthem

---

[6] Homework for American readers: After consulting at least three dictionaries of British slang, explain the difference between a "a load of old tosh" and a "a load of old bosh."

[7] See Josh McDowell, *The New Evidence that Demands a Verdict* (Nashville: Thomas Nelson, 1999), pp. 164–202. This argument, of course, only has force for those who take Scripture and such prophetic passages seriously.

naked in Trafalgar Square tomorrow morning. Of course, I don't know this with absolute certainty, but it isn't necessary to be completely certain that a proposition is true in order to know that it's true. So, knowing Bill as I do, I know now that Bill won't freely sing the Icelandic national anthem naked in Trafalgar Square tomorrow. And if I know now that Bill won't freely sing the Icelandic national anthem naked in Trafalgar Square tomorrow, then it must be true now that he won't, because it isn't possible to know something unless it's true. And if it's true now that Bill won't freely sing the Icelandic national anthem naked in Trafalgar Square tomorrow, then at least some future contingent statements are true.

Finally, some religious thinkers, following Boethius (around 480–524) and St. Thomas Aquinas (1225–1274), have argued that God can know what we'll do and we still do it freely, because God, being eternal, exists outside of time altogether, and so doesn't strictly *fore*know the future. Rather, God sees all temporal events in one synoptic, timeless vision, like viewing a whole unwound roll of film in a single glance. If this is so, it can be said, the Argument for the Incompatibility of Divine Foreknowledge and Free Will can be answered, because if God doesn't know *in advance* that Harry will fight the basilisk, there is nothing in the past that implies that Harry must fight the basilisk.

This solution, however, also faces serious difficulties. For starters, it's not clear that it's even coherent to speak of an infinitely perfect being that exists outside of time, or that such a conception is consistent with the biblical portrayal of God.[8] For instance, if God exists completely outside of time, it's hard to see how he could be a *forgiving* God, because forgiveness seems to involve change over time (*first* you blame someone, *then* you forgive). Moreover, even if God knows all temporal events in one synoptic eternal *now*, what is true from all eternity seems just as set in stone as what was true, say, a hundred

---

[8] For a balanced discussion of the relevant issues, see Thomas V. Morris, *Our Idea of God: An Introduction to Philosophical Theology* (Notre Dame: University of Notre Dame Press, 1991), pp. 119–138.

[9] Plantinga, "On Ockham's Way Out," p. 183; Scott A. Davison, "Divine Providence and Human Freedom," in Michael J. Murray, ed., *Reason for the Hope Within* (Grand Rapids: Eerdmans, 1999), p. 231.

years ago.[9] In fact, even if God doesn't strictly foreknow the future, the Argument for the Incompatibility of Divine Foreknowledge and Free Will can easily be reformulated to reach the same conclusion. If God eternally knows that Harry will fight the basilisk, then it was true a hundred years ago that God eternally knows that Harry will fight the basilisk. And if it was true a hundred years ago that God eternally knows that Harry will fight the basilisk, then it *must* be the case that Harry will fight the basilisk. And if it *must* be the case that Harry will fight the basilisk, how, then, can his decision be free?

In short, none of these standard ways of reconciling free will with divine foreknowledge is successful. There is, however, a better solution. First, though, let's turn to the paranormal challenge to free will, for the solution to the paranormal challenge and the religious challenge is fundamentally the same.

The Paranormal Challenge to Free Will

Who am I to refuse the promptings of fate?

—Sibyll Trelawney

The Potter books are loaded with examples of paranormal phenomena—that is, mysterious, magical, or supernatural events that apparently exceed the power of science to explain. Examples of paranormal phenomena include things like ghosts, reincarnation, levitation, clairvoyance, tarot cards, psychic channeling, healing crystals, and the current popularity of *The Bachelor* TV show. Among the many varieties of such phenomena featured in the Potter novels is *divination*—the supposed ability to predict the future through magical or other non-natural means. Divination is an ancient art, still widely believed in by people who received "T's" in their high school science courses, and many of the traditional methods of fortune-telling are featured in the Potter books, including crystal balls, palmistry, tea leaves, dream interpretation, astrology, rune stones, and the interpretation of bird entrails.

Interestingly, the Potter novels as a whole offer a generally skeptical view of divination and its practitioners. We are told, for instance, that fortune-telling is "one of the most imprecise branches of magic" (PA, p. 109), that "True Seers are very rare" (PA, p. 109), and that "the consequences of our actions are always so complicated, so diverse, that predicting the future is a very difficult business indeed" (PA, p. 426). In a similar vein, Sibyll Trelawney, the Hogwarts Divination teacher, is presented as a slightly daft old fraud who displays little genuine fortune-telling ability, uses bogus teaching methods, and has the annoying habit of constantly predicting Harry's gruesome and early death. On the other hand, the novels do clearly suggest that genuine divination is possible. We are told, for instance, that Sibyll Trelawney's great-great-grandmother was a "very gifted Seer" (OP, p. 840), and that Sibyll herself on two notable occasions fell into trances in which she made genuine prophecies—first when she predicted, shortly before Harry was born, that he would have the power to vanquish the Dark Lord (OP, pp. 840–41), and later when she prophesied that Wormtail would help Voldemort come back to power (PA, p. 426). In addition, we learn in *Order of the Phoenix* that there are shelves and shelves of prophecies in a tightly guarded room of the Department of Mysteries, at least many of which are presumably genuine, veridical prophecies (OP, pp. 776–780).

In short, Harry Potter's world is a world in which genuine prophetic foreknowledge[10] is possible. Does such foreknowledge pose a threat to free will?

It does, and for exactly the same reason that divine foreknowledge poses such a threat. Suppose, for instance, that Professor Trelawney foreknows on Tuesday that Harry will choose to fight the basilisk on Wednesday. Since Trelawney knows on Tuesday that Harry will fight the basilisk, it must be true on Tuesday that Harry will fight the basilisk, since, as we have seen, it isn't possible to know something unless it's true. So, if it's true on Tuesday that Harry will fight the basilisk on Wednesday, then it *must* be the case that Harry will fight the basilisk on Wednesday. And if it must be the case that Harry will fight the basilisk on Wednesday, then it's not in Harry's power to refrain from fighting the basilisk on Wednesday. And if it's not in Harry's power to refrain from fighting the basilisk on Wednesday, then Harry is not free to choose whether to fight the basilisk on Wednesday. So, if Professor Trelawney knows on

---

[10] Assuming that genuine *knowing* is involved and not merely intelligent guesswork.

Tuesday that Harry will fight the basilisk on Wednesday, then Harry is not free to choose whether to fight the basilisk on Wednesday.

Readers not suffering from a Memory Charm will recall that this argument is exactly parallel to the argument for the Incompatibility of Divine Foreknowledge and Free Will. Thus, prophetic foreknowledge raises the same basic challenge to free will as that posed by divine foreknowledge.[11]

Reconciling Freedom and Foreknowledge

> Men are not prisoners of fate, but only prisoners of their own minds.
>
> —Franklin D. Roosevelt

Fortunately, the religious and paranormal challenges to free will can be met. In fact, the basic solution to both was laid out over six hundred years ago by the great medieval thinkers St. Thomas Aquinas (around 1225–1274) and William of Ockham (around 1295–1349).

What Aquinas and Ockham noticed is that a statement such as

> If God knows in advance that Harry will fight the basilisk, then it must be the case that Harry will fight the basilisk

is ambiguous. It can be interpreted as saying either

> (1a) Necessarily, if God knows in advance that Harry will fight the basilisk, then Harry will fight the basilisk

or

> (1b) If God knows in advance that Harry will fight the basilisk, then it is necessary that Harry will fight the basilisk.[12]

---

[11] Some claim that divine foreknowledge raises greater challenges than prophetic foreknowledge, owing to God's being essentially all-knowing. See, for example, John Martin Fischer's "Introduction: God and Freedom," in Fischer, *God, Foreknowledge, and Freedom.*

[12] Cf. *ibid.*, p. 180.

These two statements may seem similar but in fact they are radically different. (1a) is obviously true—in fact, true by definition, since whatever God (or anyone else) *knows* is true must indeed be true, because it is impossible (by definition) to know anything that is false. (1b), however, is far from obviously true. (1b) asserts that if God knows in advance that Harry will fight the basilisk, then Harry will fight the basilisk in all possible universes that God could create. That seems clearly false, since it denies God's freedom by claiming that if God creates Harry in one possible universe, He must create him in all.[13]

So (1) is either true by definition or it's obviously false. If it's obviously false, of course, then the Argument for the Incompatibility of Divine Foreknowledge and Free Will can't even get off the ground. So let's consider the second possibility, that (1) is true by definition.

As Aquinas points out, if (1) is true by definition, the only necessity it asserts is the "necessity of the consequent"—that is, the fact that the consequent (the *then*-part of an if-then statement) follows logically from the antecedent (the *if*-part of an if-then statement). In other words, the *then* part *must* be true if the *if* part is true. But notice now the kicker: this *must* is a purely *logical must*, not a *causal must*. The only necessity involved is a purely logical necessity—a matter of one thing following logically from another. And as Aquinas and Ockham pointed out, unless God's foreknowledge (or eternal knowledge) of an agent's free choice somehow *causes* that person's choice, there is no true constraint on that agent's freedom.

Consider an analogy. You're sitting in the stands watching a Quidditch match between Gryffindor and Slytherin. You see Harry and Malfoy on broomsticks speeding madly after the

---

[13] God's knowing that I will reread *Sorcerer's Stone* tomorrow doesn't mean I will reread it in this and all possible worlds. But of course that doesn't entirely answer *how* God could know such a proposition's truth value in advance—a point even more obvious when the future actions in question are more realistic possibilities than Irwin's revealing ditty in Trafalgar Square tomorrow. Divine omniscience extending comprehensively to every future contingency remains a big mystery to solve.

snitch, clearly on a collision course, and now only inches away from each other. You see that, no matter what they do, they will definitely collide. Does your foreknowledge of the collision in any way *cause* the collision or diminish the freedom or responsibility of the two seekers? It does not. Given that you *know* that the seekers will collide, then it *must* be the case that they will collide. But because your foreknowledge imposes only a "necessity of the consequent," rather than a causal necessity, it does not in any way affect the freedom or responsibility of those involved.

Free will, then, is consistent with both divine and prophetic foreknowledge so long as the only kind of necessity implied is a purely logical necessity of the consequent.[14] Even if God (or Sibyll Trelawney) foreknows that Harry will fight the basilisk, Harry is free with respect to fighting the basilisk so long as (*a*) the causal chain that terminates in his decision begins with Harry himself and (*b*) he is genuinely able to do otherwise given exactly the same causal conditions. The fact that Harry could not have done otherwise *given* the foreknowledge in no way compromises his free will, since this is merely a conceptual or definitional necessity that in no way imposes causal constraints on his ability to choose.

Thus, the religious and paranormal challenges to freedom can be successfully answered. The scientific challenge, however, remains. Are there, in fact, good scientific grounds for thinking that all of our choices are the inevitable outcome of factors such as heredity and environment? Or does science still leave room for free will, moral responsibility, and the sense of dignity and inherent worth that these entail?

J.K. Rowling leaves no doubt where she stands on these issues. In the memorable scene in *Sorcerer's Stone* involving the Sorting Hat, the hat hesitates whether to put Harry in Slytherin or Gryffindor. Rowling writes:

---

[14] Some kinds of foreknowledge may be possible only if causal determinism is true. Astrology, for example, seems to assume that human destiny and personality is causally influenced or determined by the position of the stars, planets, and Moon at the moment of one's birth. But foreknowledge need not presuppose causal determinism. God, for example, in virtue of His essential omniscience, may be able to foreknow all human choices even if those choices are not determined. And if God can foreknow them, He can reveal them to others. Hence the possibility of prophetic foreknowledge.

Harry gripped the edges of the stool and thought, *Not Slytherin, not Slytherin.*

"Not Slytherin, eh?" said the small voice. "Are you sure? You could be be great, you know, it's all here in your head, and Slytherin will help you on the way to greatness, no doubt about that—no? Well, if you're sure—better be GRYFFINDOR!" (SS 121)

Like our own, Harry Potter's world is one of power and mystery in which, ultimately, the one truly decisive voice is our own.[15]

---

[15] Thanks to Dave Baggett for coaching me on proper gnome-tossing technique, and to Bill Irwin for teaching me the Icelandic National Anthem.

Hogwarts Emeritus Faculty

Thales (*circa* 624–546 B.C.E.)
"Know thyself."

Lao Tzu (*circa* 604 B.C.E.)
"Knowing others is intelligence; knowing yourself is true wisdom. Mastering others is strength; mastering yourself is true power."

Confucius (*circa* 551–479 B.C.E.)
"The man of wisdom is never in two minds about right and wrong; the man of benevolence never worries about the future; the man of courage is never afraid."

Buddha (560–480 B.C.E.)
"Believe nothing, no matter where you read it, or who said it, even if I have said it, unless it agrees with your own reason and your own common sense."

Socrates (470–399 B.C.E.)
"I desire only to know the truth, and to live as well as I can."

Plato (428/7–348/7 B.C.E.)
"There are three classes of men; lovers of wisdom, lovers of honor, and lovers of gain."

Aristotle (384–322 B.C.E.)
"I count him braver who overcomes his desires than him who conquers his enemies; for the hardest victory is over self."

Epicurus (341–270 B.C.E.)

"You don't develop courage by being happy in your relationships everyday. You develop it by surviving difficult times and challenging adversity."

Seneca (4 B.C.E.–65 C.E.)

"The philosopher: he alone knows how to live for himself. He is the one, in fact, who knows the fundamental thing: how to live."

Epictetus (50–130)

"We cannot choose our external circumstances, but we can always choose how we respond to them."

Marcus Aurelius (121–180)

"I seek the truth . . . it is only persistence in self-delusion and ignorance that does harm."

Plotinus (205–270)

"All things are filled full of signs, and it is a wise man who can learn about one thing from another."

Boethius (470–520)

"If chance is defined as an event produced by random motion without any causal nexus, I would say that there is no such thing as chance."

Peter Abelard (1079–1142)

"We call the intention good which is right in itself, but the action is good, not because it contains within it some good, but because it issues from a good intention."

Thomas Aquinas (1225–1274)

"Man has free choice, or otherwise counsels, exhortations, commands, prohibitions, rewards and punishments would be in vain."

Francis Bacon (1561–1626)

"Fame is like a river, that beareth up things light and swollen, and drowns things weighty and solid."

Thomas Hobbes (1588–1679)

"The right of nature . . . is the liberty each man hath to use his own power, as he will himself, for the preservation of his own nature; that is to say, of his own life."

René Descartes (1596–1650)

"In the matters we propose to investigate, our inquiries should be directed, not to what others have thought, nor to what we ourselves conjecture, but to what we can clearly and distinctly see and with certainty deduce, for knowledge is not won in any other way."

Benedict Spinoza (1632–1677)

"Men are deceived if they think themselves free, an opinion which consists only in this, that they are conscious of their actions and ignorant of the causes by which they are determined."

John Locke (1632–1704)

"Where Law ends, Tyranny begins."

Gottfried Wilhelm Leibniz (1646–1716)

"Although the whole of this life were said to be nothing but a dream and the physical world nothing but a phantasm, I should call this dream or phantasm real enough, if, using reason well, we were never deceived by it."

François-Marie Arouet de Voltaire (1694–1778)

"May God, if there is one, save my soul, if I have one."

Benjamin Franklin (1706–1790)

"If you know how to spend less than you get, you have the philosopher's stone."

Thomas Reid (1710–1796)

"This, indeed, has always been the fate of the few that have professed scepticism, that, when they have done what they can to discredit their senses, they find themselves, after all, under a necessity of trusting to them."

Adam Smith (1723–1790)

"Perils and misadventures are not only the proper school of heroism, they are the only proper theatre which can exhibit its virtue to advantage, and draw upon it the full applause of the world."

Immanuel Kant (1724–1804)

"Morality is not properly the doctrine of how we may make ourselves happy, but how we may make ourselves worthy of happiness."

Edmund Burke (1729–1797)
"The only thing necessary for the triumph of evil is for good men to do nothing."

Johann Wolfgang von Goethe (1749–1832)
"Whatever you can do or dream you can, begin it. Boldness has genius, power, and magic in it. Begin it now."

Georg Wilhelm Friedrich Hegel (1770–1831)
"When philosophy paints its gray in gray, then has an age grown old. . . . The Owl of Minerva spreads its wings only with the falling of dusk."

John Stuart Mill (1806–1873)
"The liberty of the individual must be thus far limited; he must not make himself a nuisance to other people."

Søren Kierkegaard (1813–1855)
"Life must be lived forward, but can only be understood backward."

Karl Marx (1818–1883)
"So soon as a table steps forth as a commodity, it is changed into something transcendent. It not only stands with its feet on the ground, but in relation to all other commodities, it stands on its head, and evolves out of its wooden brain grotesque ideas, far more wonderful than 'table-turning' ever was."

William James (1842–1910)
"Great emergencies and crises show us how much greater our vital resources are than we had supposed."

Friedrich Nietzsche (1844–1900)
"The surest way to corrupt a youth is to instruct him to hold in higher regard those who think alike than those who think differently."

John Dewey (1859–1952)
"Every great advance in science has issued from a new audacity of imagination."

Ludwig Wittgenstein (1889–1951)
"A man will be imprisoned in a room with a door that's unlocked and opens inwards, as long as it doesn't occur to him to pull rather than push."

Karl Popper (1902–1994)
"Science must begin with myths, and with the criticism of myths."

Ayn Rand (1905–1982)
"Man is a being with free will; therefore, each man is potentially good or evil, and it's up to him and only him (through his reasoning mind) to decide which he wants to be."

Simone de Beauvoir (1908–1986)
"One is not born, but rather becomes, a woman."

Willard Van Orman Quine (1908–2000)
"I see philosophy and science as in the same boat . . . we can rebuild only at sea while staying afloat in it. There is no external vantage point, no first philosophy."

Albert Camus (1913–1960)
"Virtue cannot separate itself from reality without becoming a principle of evil."

Robert Nozick (1938–2002)
"From each as they choose, to each as they are chosen."

Current Hogwarts Faculty

DAVID BAGGETT is Assistant Professor of Philosophy at King's College, Pennsylvania. He's published articles in ethics, epistemology, and philosophy of religion. Dave travels the train stations of the world looking for fractional platform numbers, and probably needs professional help for his addiction to Fizzing Whizzbees.

GREGORY BASSHAM is Director of the Center for Ethics and Public Life and Chair of the Philosophy Department at King's College, Pennsylvania. He is the co-editor of *The Lord of the Rings and Philosophy: One Book to Rule Them All*, author of *Original Intent and the Constitution: A Philosophical Study*, and co-author of *Critical Thinking: A Student's Introduction*. Like Fred and George Weasley, Greg feels his future lies outside the world of academic achievement.

CATHERINE JACK DEAVEL is assistant professor of philosophy at the University of St. Thomas (St. Paul, Minnesota). She specializes in ancient Greek philosophy. David Paul Deavel, by no means the lesser of two Deavels, is a doctoral candidate in historical theology at Fordham University and consulting editor for *Logos: A Journal of Catholic Thought and Culture*. The Deavels have two children currently transmogrifying their house, which has recently been featured in the "Runes and Ruins" column in the *Daily Prophet*. Recently they have experimented with the use of margarine in butter beer to very mixed results.

JASON T. EBERL is Assistant Professor of Philosophy at Indiana University-Purdue University Indianapolis. He's published in metaphysics, bioethics, and medieval philosophy, and is slated to co-edit (with Kevin Decker) *Star Wars and Philosophy* in this series. Jason spends his off-hours repeatedly watching the special edition DVD of "Quidditch's Most Gruesome Injuries" frame by frame.

MIMI R. GLADSTEIN is Professor of English and Theatre Arts at the University of Texas at El Paso where she functions as an itinerant administrator, having chaired the departments of English, Philosophy, Theatre Arts and Film, Women's Studies, and Western Cultural Heritage. She has published books and numerous articles on Ayn Rand, Faulkner, Hemingway, and Steinbeck. All of Mimi's exams have been bewitched with an Anti-Cheating spell.

BEN LIPSCOMB and CHRIS STEWART are both philosophy professors at Houghton College. Ben specializes in ethical theory, with further research and teaching interests in environmental and political philosophy, and in Kant. Chris is a specialist in the history and philosophy of science. His other research and teaching interests include the history of philosophy, business ethics, Kierkegaard and American pragmatism. Ben is particularly famous for his defeat of the cute, freckly, brown-haired girl in their class spelling bees in 1983 and 1985 (though not in 1984), for the discovery of the twelve uses of rolled oats, and his work on alchemy with his partner, Chris, who although he has abandoned natural magic for philosophy, retains an active interest in potions. They also both speak fluent Troll.

DIANA MERTZ HSIEH is a graduate student in philosophy at the University of Colorado at Boulder. Her interests range from metaphysics to politics, although virtues such as honesty have long held particular interest. Diana opted for a Muggle degree program only after discovering that no American university offers a doctorate in the History of Philosophy of Magic, and she wants everyone to know that there's nothing, *nothing at all* wrong with being in Hufflepuff.

SHAWN E. KLEIN is the Undergraduate Advisor for the Arizona State University Philosophy Department, where he is also working on his doctorate in philosophy. He teaches philosophy both there and at Mesa Community College. His main interests are ethics and social philosophy, and he is still waiting for his favorite Quidditch team from Boston to win the World Cup in his lifetime.

GARETH B. MATTHEWS is Professor of Philosophy at the University of Massachusetts at Amherst. He writes a regular column called "Thinking in Stories" for the journal *Thinking*. He is the author of *Socratic Perplexity and the Nature of Philosophy* and *The Philosophy of Childhood*. While Gareth was on holiday in London recently, he could be seen repeatedly slamming his baggage cart into the barrier between platforms 9 and 10 of King's Cross railway station. He was eventually asked to stop.

TOM MORRIS, unaccustomed to travel by Portkey, touched the bust of Knute Rockne at Notre Dame and suddenly found himself at the beach in North Carolina. Without a Hagrid to bring him back, he paced the sand in search of wisdom and became a public philosopher. Now he brings the best of philosophy to hundreds of thousands of Muggles in talks to Fortune 500 companies. After writing numerous academic books, and serving as national spokesman for Disney's Winnie the Pooh, he's authored such tomes as *If Aristotle Ran General Motors*, *Philosophy for Dummies*, and *The Stoic Art of Living*. You can visit him any time by simply using your computer and clicking on www.MorrisInstitute.com. It's less dangerous than Portkeys.

STEVEN W. PATTERSON is Assistant Professor at Marygrove College in Detroit, Michigan, where he teaches ethics and political philosophy, and he was gracious enough to teach an overload for us this term at Hogwarts for Muggles. While a philosopher, Steve harbors ambitions to become the next Defense Against the Dark Arts teacher at Hogwarts. (We keep trying to tell him there's no such thing.)

MICHAEL SILBERSTEIN is Associate Professor of Philosophy at Elizabethtown College and an adjunct at the University of Maryland, where he is also a faculty member in the Foundations of Physics Program and a Fellow on the Committee for Philosophy and the Sciences. His primary research interests are philosophy of physics and philosophy of cognitive neuroscience. His most recent book is *The Blackwell Guide to Philosophy of Science* (co-edited with Peter Machamer). Michael once had a bad experience when his local fraternity pranksters replaced his Floo powder with Tang.

HARALD THORSRUD is Assistant Professor of Philosophy at New Mexico State University. When not eating chocolate frogs or working with dragons, he studies Greek and Roman philosophy. Harald's been warned repeatedly against padding his vita by insisting he's done some adjuncting at the real Hogwarts, and he's not above using the Agitatio spell to keep students awake in the classroom.

JERRY L. WALLS is Professor of Philosophy of Religion at Asbury Theological Seminary in Wilmore, Kentucky and Senior Speaking Fellow for the Morris Institute for Human Values. His fourth book was *Heaven: The Logic of Eternal Joy*, published by Oxford University Press, and his fifth and most recent book is *Why I Am Not a Calvinist* (with Joe Dongell). Jerry likes to reflect on philosophical issues while driving the back roads of Kentucky in his blue 1973 Triumph TR6. He still hopes to find the button that will make it fly.

JENNIFER HART WEED is Assistant Professor of Philosophy at Tyndale University College in Toronto. She specializes in medieval philosophy, contemporary metaphysics, and philosophy of religion. Jennifer has been trying to transfigure herself into a cat since 1987, and has appeared twice on the cover of *Witch Weekly's* "Most Bewitching Eyebrows" issue.

A Wizard's Index